Perspectives on Development

Electoral politics in an emergent state

Perspectives on Development is organized by and edited from the Centre for Developing-Area Studies, McGill University, Montreal, Canada. The primary focus of the series is on economic, social and political development in third world countries. The series includes works of a broad, comparative and interpretive character as well as specific institutional and empirical studies which stem from research activities of the Centre. However, the series also includes other works judged by the Editors to be valuable contributions to our understanding of the development process.

Series Editors

R. Cranford Pratt, Professor of Political Science, University of Toronto, Chairman
John A. Barnes, Professor of Sociology, University of Cambridge
Irving Brecher, Professor of Economics, McGill University
Peter C. W. Gutkind, Professor of Anthropology, McGill University
Ben Higgins, Professor of Economics, University of Montreal
Kari Levitt, Associate Professor of Economics, McGill University
Richard F. Salisbury, Professor of Anthropology, McGill University

1 I. Brecher and S.A. Abbas, *Foreign Aid and Industrial Development in Pakistan*
2 T. C. Bruneau, *The Political Transformation of the Brazilian Catholic Church*
3 A. Jeyaratnam Wilson, *Electoral Politics in an Emergent State: The Ceylon General Election of May 1970*
4 R. Sandbrook, *Proletarians and African Capitalism: The Kenyan Case, 1960–1972*

ELECTORAL POLITICS IN AN EMERGENT STATE

THE CEYLON GENERAL ELECTION OF MAY 1970

A. Jeyaratnam Wilson

Professor and Chairman, Department of Political Science
University of New Brunswick
formerly Professor of Political Science and Head
Department of Economics and Political Science
University of Ceylon (Sri Lanka)

Cambridge University Press

Published by the Syndics of the Cambridge University Press
Bentley House, 200 Euston Road, London NW1 2DB
American Branch: 32 East 57th Street, New York, N.Y. 10022

© Cambridge University Press 1975

Library of Congress Catalogue Card Number: 74–79136

ISBN: 0 521 20429 1 hard covers

First published 1975

Photoset and printed in Malta by
St Paul's Press Ltd

To the memory of my beloved father

KANAGASABAI RAJARATNAM WILSON

By the same author
POLITICS IN SRI LANKA, 1947–1973 (Macmillan, 1974)

Contents

Note

Ceylon became known as Sri Lanka in May 1972.
For the purposes of this book, however,
the earlier name has been retained.

List of tables and maps

Tables

Maps

Acknowledgements

The project for an election study on the lines undertaken here could not have been executed but for the interest and encouragement given me by Dr Irving Brecher, the Director, at the time, of the Centre for Developing-Area Studies of McGill University. While I was at the Centre, Dr Brecher kept in touch with me and made useful suggestions, rare for a busy Director and a zealous teacher of economics.

I am deeply grateful to the Centre for not only awarding me a Research Associateship but also providing me with the research expenses for initiating this study. Special thanks are due to Dr Theo Hills, the present Director of the Centre, and to Dr Baldev Raj Nayar, Head of the Centre's South Asia Program, at the time, for their continuing interest in this project. Dr Richard F. Salisbury rendered very useful advice on effecting changes in the manuscript and Dr R. Cranford Pratt gave me the extra fillip necessary for a tired investigator to finalise the manuscript for publication.

The staff of the Centre was indeed helpful, particularly Mrs Ellinor Williams and Miss Ann Greengrove, its past and present Secretaries respectively.

To Rosalind E. Boyd, the most exacting and efficient but kindliest of editors, I owe a special debt. She spent long hours reading with enormous patience several drafts of the manuscript, suggested numerous improvements and at every stage kept urging me to complete the task. Jay Bosanquet did a thorough job in the final stages of editing the manuscript at Cambridge.

Deans Cuthbert Amerasinghe and Justin Labrooy of the University of Ceylon helped me to obtain my leave. Dean Thomas J. Condon of the University of New Brunswick gave me a generous subsidy to cover typing and other incidental expenses.

Mrs N.M. Hettiaratchi of the University of Ceylon did an exhausting typing of many drafts. Mrs Rheta MacElwain of the Department of Political Science, University of New Brunswick, did a perfect typescript before it was despatched to the Editor. Miss Inez Whittle of the Centre was responsible for the final version, which she did with care and expedition.

My friends in the University of Ceylon were indeed helpful with their ideas and assistance, in particular, Professors H.A. de S. Gunasekere, Stanley Kalpagé, K.M. de Silva, Mr H.A.I. Goonetilleke, Drs L. Panditharatne, B. Hewavitharana, W. Wiswa Warnapala and Mr N.M. Abdul Cader. Dr Calvin A. Woodward of the University of New Brunswick read through the drafts and offered a number of suggestions.

My students in the University of Ceylon, too many to be mentioned individually, collected election literature for me and obtained responses for my questionnaires. They also attended election meetings to which they were deputed and made detailed notes of important election addresses. I would however like to

xi

make mention of Messrs K. Wijeratne and D. S. Rupasinghe for translating a great deal of Sinhalese election literature for me. Messrs P. Amarasinghe, E. S. Basnayake, U. E. Perera and P. W. Wickremaratne helped me in other ways.

Dr Brendon Gooneratne and Mr Sarath Amunugama (Director of Information at the time) gave me many valuable cartoons and election posters.

A large number of public servants of all grades provided me with much inside information. For obvious reasons they wish to 'suffer' anonymity. Mr E. F. Dias Abeysinghe, Commissioner of Parliamentary Elections, very kindly sent me his *Report* on the election weeks before it was officially released.

My elder brother, S. J. Wilson, and his students collected useful data on the election campaign in the key constituencies of the Eastern province. My brother also provided me with a useful analysis of electioneering in some of these constituencies.

My friend Denzil Peiris, one of Ceylon's ablest journalists, covered all the meetings of Dudley Senanayake and allowed me the use of his diary and notes. He spent long hours with me giving me his own observations of Senanayake's electioneering. My former student, Philip Fernando, now a skilled journalist, did the same for Mrs Bandaranaike and made available to me his extremely useful diary and his impressions of her election campaign. The leading LSSP theoretician and editor of the left-wing weekly *The Nation*, Hector Abhayavardhana, gave me the benefit of his views and experience of the election.

My wife and children were patient with me while I spent the early hours of the morning and late evenings during the better part of 1970–1 on this project.

Fredericton, N.B.   A. JEYARATNAM WILSON
1973

Abbreviations

ATM	Adanga Thamil Munnani (the Tamil Front that cannot be suppressed)
BLPI	Bolshevik Leninist Party of India
BSP	Bolshevik Samasamaja Party (the Bolshevik Equal Society Party)
CP	Communist Party (Moscow)
CWC	(Indian) Ceylon Workers' Congress
DMK	(Ceylon) Dravida Munnethra Kazhagam (Dravidian Progressive Front)
DWC	(Indian) Democratic Workers' Congress
FP	(Tamil) Federal Party
IBRD	International Bank for Reconstruction and Development
IDA	International Development Association
IMF	International Monetary Fund
ISF	Islamic Socialist Front
JVP	Jathika Vimukthi Peramuna (Sinhalese) National Liberation Front
LPP	Lanka Prajathanthrawadi Party (Ceylon Democratic Party)
LSSP	Lanka Sama Samaja Party (Ceylon Equal Society Party)
MEP	Mahajana Eksath Peramuna (People's United Front)
PLF	Popular Liberation Front
SLFP	Sri Lanka Freedom Party
SLFSP	Sri Lanka Freedom Socialist Party
SMP	Sinhala Mahajana Peramuna (Sinhalese People's Front)
SMS	Sinhala Maha Sabha (the Great Council of the Sinhalese)
TC	Tamil Congress
TSRP	Tamil Self Rule Party (Thamil Suya Aadchi Kadchi)
TUF	Tamil United Front
UF	United Front (Samagi Peramuna)
ULF	United Left Front
UNP	United National Party
VLSSP	Viplavakari (Revolutionary) Lanka Sama Samaja Party

Glossary of Sinhalese and Tamil terms

ayurveda	native medicine
balaya	power
bhikku	Buddhist monk
buth	food
dagoba	a huge dome-shaped Buddhist shrine usually storing a relic of the Buddha or one of his important disciples
feec	foreign exchange entitlement certificate
goigama	farmer/cultivator caste (Sinhalese)
govi peramuna	farmers'/cultivators' front
govi rajas	farmer/cultivator kings
hartal	a general stoppage of work
itti haal	sticky rice
jalaya	water
kachcheri	office of government agent
kantha balamandalayas	women's organisations
kantha peramunas	women's fronts
kantha samithiyas	women's associations
karaiyar	lit. 'frequenter of the coast', i.e. fisherman caste (Ceylon Tamil)
karawe	fisherman caste (Sinhalese)
maha nayake thero	Chief High Priest (Buddhist)
mammoty	spade
mukuwar	fisherman caste (Ceylon Tamil)
nindagam	feudal land tenure
Pacha Bahu	'Great Liar'
panpiti yugaya	age of wheat flour
pawul balaya	family power
perakum yugaya	era of prosperity
poya	days of religious significance to the Sinhalese Buddhists, coinciding with the waxing and waning of the moon
prakashanaya	statement
radalaya	feudalist
saiva vellala	Saivaite Hindu cultivator caste (Ceylon Tamil)
salagama	cinnamon peeler caste (Sinhalese)
sama samaja	egalitarian
samadhi	monument
sangha	Buddhist clergy
siam nikaya	Siamese sect (Buddhist)
swabasha	vernacular
vellala	farmer/cultivator caste (Ceylon Tamil)

Map 1.   Ceylon: provincial and district boundaries.

This map has been redrawn from E. F. C. Ludowyk: *The Modern History of Ceylon* (London 1966) and is reproduced by permission of George Weidenfeld & Nicolson Ltd.

1. Introduction

Electoral systems

For the student of elections and party politics, the emergent states of Ceylon, India and Malaysia show an interesting process of democratic evolution.[1] Parties have developed as electoral behaviour has changed, and it is difficult to disentangle the two phenomena. The political groupings that their societies have nurtured and continue to nurture are parts of ongoing movements which can be traced back to the colonial period and the Anglicised elites that gave leadership to them.

The three emergent states in question have wrestled with complex problems– national integration and economic development – and, despite many obstacles, they have to date attempted solutions to these successfully within the democratic framework. Whereas other societies with their Westernised elites following similar steps in constitutional government, such as those of Pakistan and Burma in Asia and others in a number of African states, have opted for one-party systems or dictatorships of various forms.

All three states inherited at independence considerable goodwill and an exploitable votebank because of their (Indian National) congress-style nationalist movements and the charismatic leaders that emerged therefrom. The Indian National Congress (1885) with Gandhi and Nehru, the Ceylon National Congress (1919) which later became the UNP (1946) of Don Stephen Senanayake and the United Malay National Organisation (1948), transformed by 1954 by Tunku Abdul Rahman into the Alliance Party, not only brought independence but made constitutional government viable. Further, for many years they remained the single dominant party while continuing to operate within the parliamentary system of government.

The ability of these parties to survive in office for so long can be attributed to a number of factors. They all had Anglicised elites firmly committed to the belief that Parliament was the safest instrument of legitimacy and consensus. These elites were farsighted enough to accommodate for some time their indigenous counterparts – the vernacular school teachers, native medicine men, priestly sects, small traders and persons engaged in the indigenous arts and crafts. By this ongoing process of extended recruitment to the ruling class, the system was kept in balance.

All of them opted for the first-past-the-post electoral system with a minimum of multi-member constituencies. Such electorates encouraged the emergence and growth of governing and oppositional coalitions rather than a fragmented and fractured party system under proportional representation, the second ballot and other related systems.[2]

Their ruling coalitions were essentially establishment-oriented, tradition-bound, conservative in political attitudes with no defined ideology but tending to be pragmatic. They exercised a hold because the politically backward

1

electors, especially in the rural areas, could be manipulated by paid brokers, wealthy patrons, party bosses, village headmen, as well as landlords and rich peasants. In course of time, however, with political education, radicalisation of politics and growing political awareness, the need to submit to pressures from factions within and outside became urgent and a matter of practical political expediency. At a later stage there occurred a break-up of the coalition and its displacement by another more radical group within, or by a rival group which had earlier departed from the parent organisation. An example of the former is the Congress-Revolutionary (R) of Mrs Gandhi and that of the latter is the SLFP of the late S.W.R.D. Bandaranaike who left the UNP in 1951 and established his own political organisation.

Ruralism and conservatism are entrenched in the electoral systems of these states, ensuring resistance to radical change. In both Ceylon and Malaysia,[3] the rural areas have been given weightage at the expense of the supposedly progressive urban areas on the pretext that the former need weightage for their interests to be articulated adequately in the legislature. The greater part of India is in the rural areas (82 per cent rural population). Besides, the single-member constituency has a voting strength of 500,000 to 750,000 and this makes it impossible for any national party without the backing of wealth and organisational resources, such as Congress has, to make a serious bid for power other than to seek to undermine the strength of the dominant ruling party in those regions where it is markedly weak. The Alliance has been in a similar situation, with the Pan-Malayan Islamic Party making inroads into its position primarily in two states (Kelantan and Trengganu).[4]

Party systems

The test of successful one-party dominance however, is, firstly, not its skill to survive endlessly, but its willingness to spawn a legitimate oppositional group or coalition capable of not only replacing it but also working the system in the established way. In a sense, all three states accomplished this task with reasonable and varying degrees of success. It is true that Malaysia suspended parliamentary government for a period after the inter-ethnic clashes between Malays and Chinese following the general election of May 1969 but the normal processes have now been restored.[5]

Secondly, a transfer of power to the opposing coalition must be effected in a peaceful and constitutional manner. Only Ceylon to date has successfully contrived this, not once but on five different occasions – in 1956, March 1960, July 1960, 1965 and 1970.

Thirdly, the ruling party or coalition, when displaced, must be able to sustain the continuing loyalty of its members and work towards the objective of returning to office. Its conduct in opposition must be responsible. Again, taking all factors into consideration, Ceylon is the only one of the emergent states whose political coalitions have effected this operation successfully. Neither the SLFP in opposition from 1951 to 1956 and again from 1965 to 1970 nor the UNP from 1956 to 1965 resorted to reckless and extra-constitutional tactics to achieve their goals. They maintained their cohesion and waited patiently for the ballot box in order to return to power.

However, it is argued that Congress in India since 1947 and the Alliance in Malaysia from 1955 have continued uninterruptedly in office, providing evidence of their success as umbrella parties and of the ability of their leadership over a long period of time to share power with other social groups striving for recognition and upward mobility. Ceylon, on the other hand, is criticised because the UNP squandered the goodwill and legacy it obtained at independence within the short period of nine years (1947-56).

The UNP and its pre-independence progenitor, the Ceylon National Congress, the latter a loosely knit and fragile political organisation, nevertheless held office continuously in the context of universal suffrage from 1931, under the Donoughmore constitution (with its liberal institutional framework of internal self-government) through to 1956. Looked at in this way, the UNP's term in office – 25 years before it lost to its rival – can be compared with the record of the old Congress – 24 years (1947–71) – and the Alliance's run of 18 years (1955–73) to date. On the average, it seems 25 years is about the limit that congress-style parties can hope to remain in power.

Electoral behaviour

Ceylon's unique experience lies in that its electors have had a process of political education longer than any of the emergent countries, from 1931 onwards. Education has been reinforced by the exercise of the franchise at two general elections before independence and even after. Added to this is the fact that the literacy rate in Ceylon is the highest among the new states – 89 per cent compared with pre-Bangladesh Pakistan's 18.8, India's 23.7, Malaya's 47.0 (the figures for Sabah and Sarawak were 23.5 and 21.5, respectively, in 1960) and Singapore's 49.8, with the African countries way down below.

This situation makes Ceylon the ideal laboratory for the study of electoral behaviour. The conditions prevalent – societal and political – are reproduced in the neighbouring states with varying modifications. The pattern in all three countries, however, is broadly the same, with Ceylon having a richer experience and with the likelihood of this experience being repeated in the other states concerned.

Against this background, a close examination of the 1970 Ceylon general election is of particular interest. It came at an important phase in the development of the party system. The contest was between two rather equally balanced coalitions led by influential rival leaders, each endowed with about as much charismatic power as the other. More importantly, the election marked a stage in the evolution towards the near-complete socialisation of Ceylon's traditional Marxist parties (the LSSP and CP) into the parliamentary process. The measure of Mrs Bandaranaike's success will depend on her skills in continuing to keep these Marxist parties within the framework of parliamentary politics. At the same time, the Marxists for their part have been able to introduce modernising elements into the rural-based, culturally chauvinistic and Sinhalese Buddhist-oriented but radicalised SLFP. Would the other emergent states be as successful in synthesising rural radicalism and urban Marxism? The indications are that Congress-R may very well follow the same path, with Congress-Old(O) and other Indian Right-wing organisations adopting UNP-style politics.

Further, the 1970 general election marked a break from the consensus politics that the two rival coalitions had been committed to up to then. There had been broad agreement between them to differ on details but to be fundamentally at one in regard to the foundations of the political order. But since the 1970 general election, the UF has sought to manipulate Parliament for their immediate purposes. It will only confine Parliament to providing leadership of the social forces that are clamouring for rapid change. Parliament has become more an instrument for ratifying the decisions of the supreme policy-framing body, the Cabinet, than the forum where Government and Opposition would normally seek to accommodate each other. In effect, there is now the possibility that what one Parliament ordains, the other, if it is of a different political complexion, will undo deliberately or alternatively indirectly by the Cabinet refraining from implementing legislation enacted.

For all these reasons, the study of electoral behaviour in Ceylon is profitable and has its lessons for other emerging countries. Further, the study of the *1970* election epitomises Ceylon's political evolution through the years since 1931.

Methodology

This study is basically designed on the lines of the investigations of British general elections so admirably undertaken by Nuffield College, Oxford. It is both a description and an analysis of what we consider was Ceylon's most important general election to date. As well, we have endeavoured to present a record of the events leading to the election, the course it took, the issues that were pertinent to the determination of the result, an assessment of the result and a critical account of the consequences to Ceylon that flowed therefrom. We have further sought to examine the gamut of electoral events in the wider context of Ceylonese politics and the country's election procedures and legislation.

The Nuffield approach is more appropriate, under the circumstances, to a study of Ceylonese electoral behaviour than, say, the methods used by American sociologists or social psychologists. For example, the counting of votes in Ceylon is organised by constituencies not by polling stations. The voting behaviour of important social groups in particular areas could not therefore be quantified.

We hope that our material will benefit psephologists who seek to make comparative studies of elections in emergent states as well as students of politics and recent history in the developing areas.[6]

We depended on two types of evidence for our investigations – written and oral. Newspapers in Ceylon provided a useful coverage of the entire campaign in all its details from start to finish. The data were overwhelming but were very often determined by the political slants of the newspaper combines and therefore loaded in favour of some contenders as against others, sometimes misleading, and at other times heavily embroidered. It was our responsibility to sift the evidence and double-check it before using it for our purposes. Only when we were satisfied that what was said was absolutely correct did we utilise the evidence. In all instances where we were in doubt, we verified the facts from the speakers themselves. We, and those who helped us, were also present at all of the important rallies to record the evidence at first hand. Party literature, which we obtained in an over-abundance through our own efforts, provided a second source of written evidence. We have spent many hours going through the mass of data, the polemics and the propaganda to arrive at our conclusions. A third source was a fair quantity of party records in the form of confidential documents, private memoranda and correspondence made generously available by party functionaries and politicians. This was of added help in enabling us to look at the events in as objective a way as possible and to interpret them in the best possible light.

Our second type of evidence was the spoken word in interviews. Many of the important leaders and officeholders in the different parties spoke to us, or to those whom we directly deputed to speak to them. We prepared our questions in keeping with what we thought should be the relevant information that should be elucidated. We also interviewed many of the candidates or their agents and principal supporters. Our questions were in the 'open-ended' form, not straightforward ones which required a 'yes' or 'no'. In this way, our respondents talked to us at length but at the same time we did not lose track of the immediate information we were seeking. With the best will in the world, the interviewed person could not be as exact as we would have liked him to be. Apart from the fact that in the majority of cases he was directly involved, we were also aware that time always tends to take toll of the memory. Besides, truth is many-sided and facts are sometimes disputable. We took note of all these circumstances when analysing our material.

The wealth of evidence we collected helped us to understand better the course of the campaign as it developed from day to day. We were also able in this way to comprehend what was taking place not merely at the national level but in the constituencies as well. We did not, however, for the reasons already stated, depend entirely on the spoken word. Whenever doubts arose, we had recourse to other sources to verify our findings.

Some of the material collected has been digested into statistical tables. Other material has been worked into the body of this book. Our respondents could feel satisfied that they have contributed in no small way to the completion of this study.

Finally, in our efforts to get a complete picture of the campaign and of the performances of the leading rival politicians in order to reinforce our findings, we were assisted by some of the cleverest and most able journalists in the Ceylon press at the time.

The author is fortunate in that he served a period as a journalist in the leading newspaper combine in Ceylon, Lake House, before entering the academic field. Some of his students and friends now occupy key positions in the important newspapers. Both these factors gave him access to well-placed journalists who kindly made available to him their own impressions of the campaign, some extremely useful documents in the form of the diaries they kept while covering election meetings of the important political leaders, as well as other confidential literature and notes of discussions they had with the men or women at the top in the different parties.

Aims

This study is intended to serve two purposes. It details the way in which a keenly fought election campaign went through its various paces in Asia's oldest and most successful democracy. In another sense, we have undertaken this task in order to provide a record of what really happened. In a country where memories tend to be short, we hope that the written word will, especially after the passage of time, throw light on what actually took place. We trust that it will also help to interpret the sweeping changes that are at the present time taking place in Ceylon's political and economic set-up. From this point of view and for many other reasons as well, the general election of May 1970 is, as we have already stressed, of immense significance in Ceylon's post-independence development.

Our design was restricted from the outset. But within the confines we set ourselves, we have tried as best as we may to produce a dispassionate record of the campaign and its result. We hope our efforts will set the pace for future studies covering a wider framework than the present.

2. Politics and society

The background

Societal divisions in Ceylon are deeply complex.[1] Ethnic rivalries bedevil politics and interfere with economic progress; the principal rivalry is between Sinhalese and Tamils (both Ceylon and Indian). Religious conflicts are just as pervasive; the Sinhalese Buddhists grieve the neglect of centuries of foreign rule and fear for their religion because of the overzealous proselytising activities of Christian missionary organisations. Caste differences exist beneath the political surface but politicians and parties in pursuit of power and/or office know when to do what is expedient on this sensitive issue.

The Sinhalese Buddhist ethos of compassion, tolerance and the middle way, however, operates as a moderating factor. At the same time, a responsible political leadership at the higher levels, deriving its concepts and values from Western democratic thought and/or Marxism, restrains extremism at levels where communal conflict can otherwise become intense. Firmly countering manifestations of Sinhalese majority extremism are strong and powerful minority political organisations. These too serve towards a build-up of a centrist position in the political stances of major political groupings. Out of these dialectics there has emerged a Ceylonese version of parliamentary government which has survived the test of time since the introduction of an adapted form of the Westminster model in 1947.

The Westernised intelligentsia

The process of deracination and Westernisation had started from the time of the Portuguese and Dutch but was accomplished with greater thoroughness during the one and a half centuries of British rule, mainly through secondary schools organised by Christian missionary societies administering instruction largely in the English medium. The alumni of these schools in course of time became a class in themselves, privilege-ridden by virtue of their easy access to white-collar jobs and the success they achieved in the professions, in commerce and to some extent in the planting industry – coconut, rubber and tea, respectively.

In the latter part of the nineteenth century, the elitists among this intelligentsia organised themselves into various associations and societies mainly for the purpose of agitating for further reform of the constitution. They were moderate in their demands and preferred to gain their objectives right up to the grant of independence by using peaceful devices such as memorials, petitions, prayers, negotiations and, on occasion, protests.

There was the element of mild protest against colonial rule among these elitists which savoured of nationalism, but it lacked the fervour and agitational content that characterised the parallel populist Buddhist revivalist movement gathering force at about the same time. In their anxiety to bring all sections of the

7

island's multi-group society under a broad-based Ceylonese leadership, they refrained from emphasising the past history of wars between Sinhalese and Tamils and the achievements of Sinhalese heroes, for this would have stimulated mutual antagonisms.

However, the inevitable split occurred when the Ceylon Tamils among this elite saw the gradual erosion of their political strength with increasing instalments of reform. They pressed the imperial power for safeguards in any proposed constitutional framework, demands which their Sinhalese counterparts construed as being obstructionist.

In the 1920s the Ceylon Tamil leadership asked for communal ratios in representation; in the 1930s and 1940s the more articulate among them demanded a system of 'balanced representation' under which 50 per cent of the seats in the legislature should be reserved for the minority communities; since the 1950s they have been agitating for the preservation of 'the traditional homelands of the Tamil-speaking peoples' either within the framework of a federal constitution or by other guarantees, parity of status between the Sinhalese and Tamil languages, and citizenship and voting rights for the vast majority of the 'stateless' Indian Tamil population mainly resident in the plantation districts. These Indian Tamils had lost their citizenship and had been disfranchised under legislation enacted in 1948 and 1949.

The problem for the Sinhalese leadership was how best to accommodate these claims consistently with the due rights of the majority Sinhalese. There were various groups among the latter – the impoverished Kandyan Sinhalese, along with the Low Country Sinhalese, resentful of the 'Indian presence', the antagonism of the Sinhalese Buddhists to the Christian 'monopoly' over education (the best schools were theirs), the powerful non-*giogama* (cultivator) Sinhalese caste groups striving for upward political and social mobility – but the most pressing question was the Tamil one.

The Sinhalese leadership was willing to accommodate the Ceylon Tamil claims up to a point but, with economic contraction, the rivalries between the two communities, or at any rate their middle classes, grew sharper until Sinhalese Buddhist reaction reached peak levels in the mid-1950s. At this point the Sinhalese political elite itself split, one section, the United National Party (UNP), with little success seeking to placate both Sinhalese and Ceylon Tamils, the other, the Sri Lanka Freedom Party (SLFP), willing to go along, but only to a certain extent, with the militant forces of Sinhalese Buddhist nationalism.

The UNP of D. S. Senanayake (founded in 1946) and his successors endeavoured to maintain the unity of most sections of the English-educated in Ceylon's plural society while being authoritarian and paternal *vis-à-vis* the non-English-educated and the underprivileged. But it did not make any serious attempt to integrate the latter elements into the political processes. The unity it maintained at the higher levels was only surface deep. The party eventually succumbed to the pressures of the Sinhalese Buddhists in the mid-1950s but returned shortly after to its earlier theme of national unity.

The pro-Sinhalese Buddhist forces and the aggrieved Sinhalese rural middle classes received leadership from S. W. R. D. Bandaranaike and his successor, his wife, Sirima Bandaranaike. At first it was the Sinhala Maha Sabha (founded in 1937) of the 1930s and 1940s which politicised these neglected layers of society. Thereafter the SLFP (formed in 1951) in alliance with other political groupings gave them direction while also restraining them from extremes. The Bandaranaikes provided a moderate and responsible leadership, especially at crisis points when Sinhalese Buddhist chauvinism threatened to engulf society.

Certain facts emerge from the way in which the Ceylonese Westernised intelligentsia evolved and established itself.

Firstly, their value orientation – language, clothes, manners, ostentation, etc. – resulted in their cutting themselves off from 95 per cent of the mass of Ceylonese society who, to begin with, looked on them as successful but later saw them as a class gorged with privileges which must be destroyed. The latter feeling became intensified when the 'have-nots' were made aware by political catalysts that their success was no more than the result of preferential treatment deliberately made available to children of Christian parents (Sinhalese and Ceylon Tamils) as well as to those who belonged to the better-off sections in society. Movements directed against Christians, Ceylon Tamils and the English-educated were the inevitable result.

Secondly, Westernisation of the future power elites as a result of English education in local schools and/or a university or professional education in Britain (the 'England returneds') inculcated Western ideals of democracy and parliamentary government in them. Added to this were the invaluable insights into the administrative processes and training in ministerial government afforded them under the Donoughmore constitution from 1931 to 1947. Consequently the future Ceylonese power elites, conservatives, centrists and Marxists, were socialised into a political order which was resolutely committed to constitutional government.

A final aspect of this process was the creation of a yawning gap between the English-educated and the rest of Ceylonese society. The former manned the public and private sectors and the professions and looked down contemptuously at the vernacular or *swabasha* layers in Ceylonese society. This alienation was more evident among the administrators and even among those who occupied the lower rungs of bureaucracy. Government therefore came to be looked on by the masses as a distant object, awesome, and its members as persons to be approached with fear and reverence. It was not 'their Government' but a process turned over by their British 'masters' to the local versions of this masterdom. Only after 1956 with the advent to power of Bandaranaike was the bureaucracy gradually democratised.

The Sinhalese Buddhist-oriented intelligentsia

Within a few years of Britain gaining control over the whole island, Sinhalese Buddhist opposition to the Christianising process began to make itself evident. In 1826 parodies of Christian tracts were published by dissenting Buddhists. In

1839 a *bhikku*, the Venerable Valave Sri Siddhartha, founded the Paramad-hammacetiya Pirivena which became a centre of Buddhist learning and the nursery of Buddhist revivalism.

However, Christian endeavour by the 1850s had been so thorough that in 1852 a Christian, James D'Alwis, a distinguished orientalist and politician of the time and an ancestor of S. W. R. D. Bandaranaike, remarked that 'the day may yet come when the Trio of the one Great God will become a substitute for the Triad of Buddhism'.[2]

But Buddhism was not to be submerged. In the succeeding decades it threw up leaders who sought to revitalise Buddhism by providing it with an intellectual and agitational content.[3] Among the more prominent of them was the Reverend Migettuwatte Gunananda, the skilled debater of Panadura fame, and the zealot Anagarika Dharmapala, the greatest of them all. From 1883 until his death in 1933, he dedicated his life to fighting for the rights of the Sinhalese Buddhists and inspiring a nationalism among them which railed at the Wester-ners, Christians and the non-Sinhalese groups.[4] The journalist and publicist Piyadasa Sirisena (1875–1946) followed the Anagarika in condemning the 'evils' of Westernisation and voicing the ideas of the Sinhalese-educated through the newspaper he edited, the *Sinhala Jatiya* (Sinhalese Nation), which com-menced publication in 1910.

A few Westerners themselves made noteworthy contributions towards the Buddhist revival. The American, Colonel H. S. Olcott, arriving in Ceylon in 1880 with a Russian friend, Helena Petrova Blavatsky, embraced Buddhism at a time when it was in need of prestige and respectability. Olcott pioneered the Buddhist educational movement. In 1886 his British associate, C. W. Leadbeater, founded Ananda College, which soon became the island's leading Buddhist secondary school and helped to produce public servants, professional men and political agitators with a Buddhist background. In the field of Sinhalese arts and crafts, the nationalist movement received encouragement and scientific guidance from the scholarship of Dr Ananda Coomaraswamy, more a Wester-ner despite his Ceylon Tamil–American parentage.[5]

At various points there were links between the Sinhalese Buddhist nationalists and the Westernised intelligentsia. Quite a few among the latter joined in the temperance movement lauched against the excise policy of the colonial Govern-ment from 1904 onwards by the Anagarika and his associates. There was liaison between the two groups during the Sinhalese Buddhist–Muslim riots of 1915.

The Anagarika's nationalistic religio-economic message of the 1920s became the political manifesto of the Buddhist movement in the 1950s and 1960s. He urged the Sinhalese Buddhists to imitate the industrious Muslim traders. He attacked the Ceylon Tamils, Indian Tamils and Muslims, who he said 'are employed in large numbers to the prejudice of the people of the island', meaning the Sinhalese Buddhists.[6] He condemned the 'economic exploitation' of the island by Britishers and Indians.[7] In June 1922 he objected to the use of the word 'Ceylonese' for Sinhalese and in the same month he said he wanted 'the whole of the present government to be a Buddhist government . . . the Governor to be a Buddhist . . . the Colonial Secretary and all other officials to be Buddhists'.[8] The All-Ceylon Buddhist Congress in its dramatic report of 1955, *The Betrayal of Buddhism*, voiced similar demands, within the context, of course, of an independent Ceylon.[9]

However, the gap between the English-educated and the Sinhalese-educated really began to widen only in the 1940s and thereafter. No doubt the granting of universal suffrage in 1931 contributed towards the growing alienation. But the introduction of the free education scheme in 1945 and the Government policy thereafter of switching to the national languages as media of instruction accelerated the process. Growing numbers of the *swabasha*-educated swelled the ranks of the unemployed till in 1956 they constituted a large group in themselves[10] – the Senior School Certificate (SSC) qualified – in search of white-collar jobs. Presently there are about 100,000 school leavers, mainly in the liberal arts, looking for similar employment with the prospects just as bleak. To this number should be added the 13,000-odd *swabasha* graduates of the various universities in the island who between 1965 and 1970 were without suitable employment.

The Bandaranaikes made their appeal to these discontented sections of the intelligentsia, the overwhelming majority from the rural areas, as well as to the other frustrated rural intelligentsia and middle class comprising the Sinhalese school teachers, native physicians, dancers, petty shopkeepers and Buddhist monks. Many opportunities thus opened up for the traditional political parties in view of the fact that the bulk of the island's population is rural-based, some 73.7 per cent, as against an urban distribution of 15.4 per cent, while the large majority of the balance (10.9 per cent) constitute voteless Indian Tamil labourers.[11] Added to this, the rural areas are given an excess of representation by constitutional provision.

The workers

At first the urban workers were led by A. E. Goonesinha, whose militant trade unions were most active in the 1920s. Goonesinha was a British Labour Party-type politician. His socialism proved too mild for the Sinhalese revolutionary Marxist intellectuals and professionals who, returning from their studies abroad in the early 1930s, edged him out by unionising labour on much more radical lines.[12] These Marxists – Trotskyists and communists – also strongly opposed the British colonial administration.

Their main area of concentration, however, is in the city of Colombo and its environs. They have unionised workers in some of the other large towns and have their own organisations among the Indian plantation workers as well.

However, until the 1960s the Marxists failed to make much political headway, chiefly because the Sinhalese peasantry and rural middle classes viewed them as Westernised and secular, more Ceylonese than Sinhalese and unsympathetic to the aims and aspirations of the Buddhist movement. Since then, they have discarded their orthodox textbook Marxism for a Sinhalese Buddhist-oriented

Leftist socialism and have consequently become integrated with the established political order.

The peasantry

More than half the population, approximately 52.3 per cent, is engaged in agriculture and forestry.[13] The largest cultivated area is under paddy, but there is tremendous pressure of population on land. Population per acre of agricultural land rose from 1.56 in 1946 to 2. 24 in 1962.[14]

Owing to the concentration of population in the wet zone areas, the state has since the 1930s undertaken major land settlement and irrigation schemes in the dry zone areas. By 1953 90,000 colonists had been settled in these places from the congested wet zone.[15]

The main problem in paddy cultivation, however, is land fragmentation. About 64 per cent of holdings are below one acre each and about 31 per cent below half an acre each.[16] All in all about 85 per cent of paddy land is below two acres each. Only about 60 per cent of this land is owner-cultivated while 25 to 30 per cent is cultivated by tenants.[17] The inevitable result is heavy indebtedness and low levels of productivity.

The Paddy Lands Act of 1958 sought to remedy this situation by, among other things, giving tenant cultivators a measure of security in the possession of their lands and by providing incentives to increase production. The state further operates a liberal agricultural credit scheme for paddy cultivators and offers fertilisers at subsidised prices.

Political developments, 1947–65

The welfare state

Ceylon of all Asian countries maintains the basis of a welfare state, which she can ill afford, given the fact that she relies largely on three primary products – tea, rubber and coconuts – and these depend for their prices on the vagaries of the international market. Education is free at all levels, inclusive of the university. Free medical attention until recently was available to those who could not afford to pay for it. Since 1971 a nominal levy has been imposed. Further, a minimum ration of a measure of rice (two pounds) is distributed free by the state to the population, and the second measure is provided at subsidised prices. There is also a liberal system of payments by the state to the old and incapacitated. All these absorb between 35 to 40 per cent of the annual budget, leaving very little for economic development.

The burden on welfare is increased by the rapid growth of population and a marked imbalance in the age composition, with 52 per cent of persons below 19 years and 40 per cent under 14. Between the censuses of 1946 and 1971, the population nearly doubled from 6.7 million to 12.8 million. Though the annual rate of increase declined from 2.8 per cent in 1953 to 2.4 per cent in 1968, it is nevertheless anticipated that if present trends persist, Ceylon's population will double itself in 29 years, compared to the three-score years and ten that developed nations take to double theirs.

The high rate of population increase has brought a corresponding increase in the work force. According to a socio-economic survey conducted in 1969–70, there were some 550,000 unemployed, comprising 14 per cent of the country's total labour force in the age group 15 to 59, or approximately 4.3 per cent of the population.[18] This is considered a high rate of unemployment by international standards.[19] Further, this work force is expected to increase to about 7 million in 1981[20] and, unless there is an unlikely 'rapid economic development', this could create grave problems in the field of manpower planning and employment.

Just as serious is the fact that 43.6 per cent of the population have incomes which fall below the poverty line (less than Rs. 200 per month).[21] This partly explains the need for the 'extravagant' welfare services.

The strange aspect of this welfare system is that it is based on a dualised economy, each sector of which works in almost complete isolation from the other. Tea, rubber and coconuts account for some 90 per cent of Ceylon's foreign exchange earnings and nearly one-third of her national income. But about 45 per cent of tea is owned by British companies and 13 per cent by companies registered in Ceylon where ownership is divided between Ceylonese and non-Ceylonese. Thirty-three per cent of rubber is under British control. This comparatively modernised plantation sector provides, to a large extent, the revenue for the welfare services for the rest of the population, which lives and earns in the traditional sectors of the economy, and the much needed foreign exchange for the import of consumer items and capital goods. Stranger still is the fact that the overwhelming majority of the 10.9 per cent of the island's population that works the plantations, mostly Indian Tamil labour, has no citizenship or voting rights. The Indo-Ceylon Agreement of October 1964 eased the situation somewhat.

Leadership patterns

Political leadership at the higher levels comes from a relatively small category of professional men, mostly lawyers and doctors, as well as retired public servants, including school teachers, and some industrialists and businessmen. There is also a minuscule group of full-time professional politicians who generally form the top-rung leadership in all parties. The 52.3 per cent of the population engaged in agricultural pursuits hardly provide a recruiting base, though at the middle and lower levels some farmers take an active interest in local government and constituency politics. However, even at these levels, the big and small shopkeepers and traders, the local legal profession, the Buddhist monks, the native physicians, the *swabasha* school teachers and trade union workers form the major component of local bodies and the constituency organisations of the political parties.

As 67.4 per cent of the population is Buddhist with economic, social and cultural problems which are attributed to the neglect and oppression of centuries of foreign rule and disregard of their problems by the Westernised intelligentsia, political ideology in the island tends to take a Sinhalese Buddhist orientation.

A majority of the Sinhalese population belongs to the *goigama* (cultivator) caste, though this does not mean that the other castes, especially the *karawe* (fishermen) and *salagamas* (cinnamon peelers) are without influence. There are also depressed caste groups in the Kandyan Sinhalese areas which wield considerable electoral influence. But because the *goigama* Sinhalese Buddhists are the majority in the Sinhalese population, the power elite at most levels is primarily from this layer.

Until 1956, that is during the first phase of UNP rule, this *goigama* Sinhalese Buddhist power elite was significantly drawn from the English-educated Westernised intelligentsia, more at the middle- and upper-middle-class levels. The rural intelligentsia provided a grudging allegiance to this elite and recorded its dissent by voting for Left-wing candidates of both the Trotskyist and communist groups. Neither group of Marxists was prepared to provide an alternative to the UNP, nor would the electors have accepted them. But they welcomed them as a vigilant and critical Opposition to the UNP.

The conduct of this power elite tended to be traditional, characterised especially by an outward conformity to the tenets of Buddhism, the veiled observance of caste differences which placed a premium on *goigama* Sinhalese Buddhists, antipathy to the Ceylon Tamil middle class because of competition from them, and to the presence of Indian Tamil traders and labourers in the island. Alongside this was an innate conservatism manifested in strong opposition to Marxism, the trade unions and even to any form of neo-liberalism.

Politics and governmental performance, 1947–56

In the economic sphere, there was a drawing towards Britain and a belief that prosperity lay in trade ties with the West and in the improvement and diversification of agriculture. There was little attempt at economic planning. A six-year plan of development which was a mere collection of the hopes and schemes of the various ministers was drawn up for the period 1947–8 to 1953–4 but no serious steps were taken to set up any machinery to implement the plan.

What was worse, the country's valuable sterling balances, some Rs. 1,260 millions, were frittered away in an orgy of unplanned spending, mostly on imported consumer goods. The situation was saved when rubber prices rocketed with the outbreak of the Korean War, but again it was a repetition of the earlier record of wasteful expenditure. Shortly thereafter, American stockpiling of rubber caused a depression. A calamity was averted when Dudley Senanayake's Government (May 1952–October 1953) entered into a rubber–rice agreement with China, the terms of which were advantageous to Ceylon, in late 1952. But adverse terms of trade continued unabated and in July 1953, when Dudley Senanayake's Government took the extreme step of raising the price of rice which had hitherto been heavily subsidised by the state, from twenty-five to seventy cents a measure, widespread violence broke out in the wake of a protest *hartal* (a general stoppage of work) called by Left-wing parties on 12 August 1953. A number of deaths from police firing affected the health of the sensitive and inexperienced Prime Minister and he tendered his resignation in October of the same year.

Parliament was regarded as the forum for the discussion of the nation's problems where Opposition spokesmen and Government backbenchers had the opportunity of expressing views and ventilating grievances. The Cabinet was a collective leadership representing most of the upper layers of the island's multi-group society – community, religion, caste, as well as economic interests. But the representatives were more in the nature of showpieces than genuine spokesmen. The bureaucracy was colonial-oriented, spiteful of the masses, willing to cooperate with the new political elite but old-fashioned, generalist and geared to the operation of an old-type colonial export–import economy. Government and administration were heavily Colombo-centred.

D. S. Senanayake (1947–52) and his successors Dudley Senanayake (1952–3) and Sir John Kotelawala (1953–6) in a way personified this elite and this kind of thinking. They were conservative, pro-West, anti-Marxist and hoped that everything would be well if the surface of political life was kept unruffled. The defence and external affairs agreements concluded by D. S. Senanayake with Britain in November 1947 prior to the grant of independence, the virtually wholesale imitation of the Westminster model, the decision to remain within the Commonwealth and to accept the British sovereign as Ceylon's when India and Pakistan had decided to go republican, the enactment of such legislation as the Public Security Act of 1947 and the Trade Union (Amendment) Act of 1948 which were directed against Marxist-dominated working-class organisations, and the Citizenship Act of 1948, the Indian and Pakistani Residents (Citizenship) Act of 1949 and the Parliamentary Elections (Amendment) Act of 1949, all of which deprived the vast majority of the Indian Tamil population of its citizenship rights and the franchise, provided evidence of the basic political ideology of this conservative class.

One of the most pressing problems that Ceylon had to deal with shortly after independence was that of the future of the Indians in Ceylon. The UNP and the SLFP have been sensitive to Sinhalese opinion on this question, especially in the Kandyan areas. The intensity of feeling against the Indians was best expressed by a Sinhalese M.P. in the House of Representatives when he referred to the presence of these Indian Tamils in the Kandyan areas as 'a life and death question', 'a menace to their race, with the possibility of the extinction of their race, the disappearance of their religion and their language'.[22] Many Sinhalese look on these Indians as a potential 'fifth column' and the visible evidence of the exploitation of the Kandyan areas.[23]

The position is complicated by the support the Indians receive from the political parties of the Ceylon Tamils, especially the Tamil Federalists, and from Left-wing organisations. The Ceylon Tamils regard the Indians as an additional source of political strength to them, electorally speaking. The Sinhalese, on the other hand, would not like the two groups to combine into what they fear might well be a pan-Tamil movement, while the Kandyan Sinhalese in particular object to the inclusion of Indian Tamil voters in their electorates. Left-wing groups look on the Indian workers as a potentially powerful component of their trade union movement once they are weaned off from the two communal workers' organisations – the Ceylon Workers' Congress (CWC) and the Democratic Workers' Congress (DWC) – which now control a majority of them. At the general election of 1947, in about twenty constituencies, the Indian vote went to Left-wing and anti-UNP candidates.

The situation is further aggravated by the influx to Ceylon of illicit Indian immigrants from the South Indian coast and the recent emergence of a militant Tamil Dravida Munnethra Kazhagam (DMK) organisation in the plantation areas.

The Indians for their part protest, with justification, that the majority of them know no other home than Ceylon. One solution seriously suggested is to assimil-ate the Indian population by making it adopt the Sinhalese language and culture. But this is not feasible. The other is to persuade the Government of India to take back as many of them as possible. In fact this has been the strategy employed by all Ceylonese Governments up to date, with varying degrees of success. Thus the Nehru–Kotelawala Pact of 1954 provided for those Indians who obtained citizenship under the existing law and became qualified to vote to be included in a separate all-island Indian and Pakistani electorate, except where their numbers did not exceed 250 in any electoral district. This all-island electorate was to return four members to the House of Representatives. The pact further provided that Indian Tamils who wished to qualify as citizens should learn 'the language of the area'; in this case, it meant the Sinhalese language. The agreement, however, failed because neither side took any meaningful steps to implement its difficult provisions.

The problem, however, came closest to a solution when Mrs Sirima Bandar-anaike entered into a pact in October 1964 with the Indian Prime Minister of the time, Mr Shastri. Briefly, this pact provided for 525,000 Indians resident in Ceylon with their natural increase to be repatriated to India over a 15-year phased programme, 300,000 to be absorbed as citizens of Ceylon, and the future of the remaining 150,000 Indians to be negotiated later by the two countries. During the general election campaign of December 1964–March 1965, Mrs Bandaranaike and her Left-wing allies took the position that Indians registered as Indian nationals should be compulsorily repatriated, that those admitted to Ceylon citizenship should be placed on a separate electoral register, otherwise they would dilute the electoral strength of the Sinhalese voters in the Kandyan areas, and that Indians awaiting repatriation should have their conditions and terms of employment controlled and regulated by the state. This was in conflict with the stand taken by the CWC and the Tamil Federal Party (FP) and even with the interpretation given to the pact by the Govern-ment of India. As a consequence, the CWC gave its support to the UNP at the general election and the SLFP suffered a number of reverses in the Kandyan Sinhalese areas. The Government of Dudley Senanayake ironed out most of the difficulties in question when it enacted legislation in February 1968 to give effect to the terms of the agreement.

During this phase the attitude of UNP Governments to the religious and cultural questions was advisedly to refrain from controversy. UNP ministers patronised Buddhist occasions but they took the position that Buddhism required no special protection or any specific constitutional guarantees. They held that what was important was freedom of worship, now threatened by Left-wing parties. Not even the criticisms of the unofficial Buddhist Commission of Inquiry set up by various Buddhist organisations in the country in 1954, through the years 1954 to 1956, could make the UNP aware of the magnitude of the Buddhist problem.

Their indifference was no better in regard to the demand that the national languages be given their due place in the administration of the country. The UNP no doubt had to take note of the difficulties of the English-educated public servants, but it did not wish to make even a start until it was too late. It made a faint claim that it stood for a gradual transition and that an overnight switch was impracticable. It had changed the medium of instruction in the schools to the mother tongue, but evidence of its indifference was seen in that, even as late as 1955, English was the primary language of debate and discussion in Parliament.

On the Buddhist demand that all denominational schools should be taken over by the state, the response was a stout refusal. The policy was laid down by D. S. Senanayake in July 1948 when he said that 'the services of all people who are engaged in education should be utilised'.[24] He added that attempts were being made by some people to destroy missionary schools but that his Government 'had no intention of doing any harm to anyone'.

The conflict between the UNP and its Marxist opponents in the House of Representatives – the LSSP and the CP – grew sharper as it increasingly dawned on the UNP that the alternative to it would be a workers' and peasants' dictatorship. In June 1950 Sir John Kotelawala then a minister in D. S. Senanayake's Cabinet, characterised the Opposition as one which did not believe in the democratic system, adding that 'once they got in they would not get out. There is no guarantee you would ever have a chance to go to the ballot again.'[25] These fears were confirmed when, at the general election of 1952, the LSSP put forward a fourteen-point 'anti-imperialist and anti-capitalist programme' with a call for a *sama samaja* (egalitarian) government. How this could have been effected is hard to envisage; the party was contesting only 40 out of the 95 seats.

The UNP has persistently taken the position that the Marxists present a threat to democratic institutions and that any alliance they may enter into with democratic parties can only be for the purpose of infiltrating and ultimately seizing leadership. This was alleged for instance when the United Front of the CP and the Viplavakari Lanka Sama Samaja Party (VLSSP, Philip Gunawardena's breakaway group from the LSSP when the latter coalesced with its splinter, the Bolshevik Sama Samaja Party, in June 1950) campaigned for a 'democratic government' at the general election of 1952 and supported the candidates of Bandaranaike's democratic socialist SLFP as against those of its Trotskyist rivals. The same charge was levelled when the CP and LSSP entered into a no-contest electoral agreement prior to the general election of 1956 with Bandaranaike's broad-based coalition of diverse interests, the Mahajana Eksath Peramuna (MEP).

Conservative middle-class Ceylonese society was ill at ease owing to Bandaranaike's alliance with the Marxists. In particular, the inclusion of Gunawardena's Marxist VLSSP as a constituent of the MEP and the appointment of two of its representatives to the Cabinet increased their disquiet.

The UNP's attitude to the Ceylon Tamil minority during its first phase of political power was one of an attempt at reconciliation. After their relentless battle for 'balanced representation' the Ceylon Tamils under the leadership of G. G. Ponnambalam's Tamil Congress (TC) remained sullenly and uneasily on the Opposition benches with the Marxist parties, having scored notable victories in the Tamil majority areas of north Ceylon at the general election of 1947.

D. S. Senanayake, in his anxiety to indicate to Whitehall that he had secured the cooperation of the Ceylon Tamils, included two uncommitted Tamil M.P.s in the Cabinet he formed in September 1947. He preferred to wait where the TC was concerned, as he knew perhaps too well that it was only a question of time before its leaders would want to enter his Government. And in fact this did happen. Within a year of the formation of his Government, Ponnambalam and a majority of his party decided to cross the floor. Ponnambalam was given a portfolio in the Cabinet.

Some members of the TC did not support this line and they launched their own organisation, the Tamil FP, in December 1949. This new organisation did not make an impact until the general election of 1956, when it won the majority of seats in the Tamil areas. The Ceylon Tamil problem in its contemporary forms was only at its incipient stages during this phase.

The question of a national flag for Ceylon was opposed by the parliamentary representatives of the Ceylon Tamils, who were averse to the adoption of the lion flag of the last king of Kandy. The matter was eventually resolved satisfactorily by a select committee of Parliament recommending three stripes to be added to the lion emblem for the purpose of signifying the presence of the three minority groups in the island – the Ceylon Tamils, the Muslims and the Burghers.

The legislation to deprive the Indian Tamils of their citizenship and voting rights began the process of alienation. It was on this specific issue that dissenting Tamil Congressmen led by S. J. V. Chelvanayakam broke away from the parent body and formed their own organisation.[26] The Ceylon Tamils who supported Chelvanayakam felt that the disfranchisement of the Indian Tamils would weaken Tamil political strength in Parliament. There was no other permanent bond of interest between this largely middle-class group and the community of Indian Tamil plantation workers.

The Federalists further objected to what they alleged was the planned state-sponsored colonisation of 'the traditional homelands' of the Tamils in the northern and eastern parts of the island with Sinhalese settlers. Despite their protests, colonisation went on apace. Owing to the prevailing harmony, there was at that time no significant friction between Sinhalese and Tamils in these frontier areas.

However, over the question of official status for the Tamil language the cleavage between the two communities came out sharply. D. S. Senanayake and his successors preferred to retain English as the language of administration while permitting the use of Sinhalese and Tamil for certain restricted official purposes such as transactions with the public at large. This policy suited the English-educated Sinhalese and Ceylon Tamil intelligentsia. But in the meantime there were growing demands for the introduction of the national languages, demands which the UNP leadership successfully resisted until the mid-1950s. When these demands gained momentum, the Ceylon Tamils insisted that their language should be accorded parity of status with Sinhalese. The Sinhalese language movement reacted strongly with the slogan 'Sinhala as the only official language throughout the length and breadth of the island'. The clamant forces among the Sinhalese-educated intelligentsia hoped that such a step would give them an advantage over the Ceylon Tamils in the competition for jobs in the public service.

In the years 1954 to 1956, the problem was how to allay the fears of the Ceylon Tamils and satisfy the aspirations of the Sinhalese. Sir John Kotelawala's impolitic handling of the situation soon brought it to crisis proportions. While on an official visit to the Ceylon Tamil north, in late 1955, he rashly promised the Ceylon Tamils that he would make constitutional provision for the Sinhalese and Tamil languages to have parity of status. The reaction in the Sinhalese areas was electric, and Kotelawala's immediate political rivals in the SLFP, who had up to this time also stood for Sinhalese and Tamil as the official languages of the country, now capitalised on the situation by changing their stance to Sinhalese as the only official language, with provision, however, for the 'reasonable use' of the Tamil language. It was only a matter of months before Kotelawala and the UNP (in February 1956) effected a *volte-face* by opting for Sinhalese as the one and only official language with no provision for the Tamil language, much to the discomfiture of their Tamil supporters.

During this phase, the UNP's alienation from the rural masses and the underprivileged urban classes was becoming increasingly apparent. Though the party stood not at the extreme Right in politics but to the Right of Centre and had been responsible for establishing firmly the foundations of a welfare state, its leadership, especially at the top and middle levels, had only tenuous links with the ordinary mass of voters. This leadership regarded itself as the natural rulers of the country and since the opposition to it was disorganised and splintered, it tended to have the feeling of a monopoly of power.

The party had the confidence of business interests, large sections of the middle classes, the administrative grades in the public services and the higher rungs of the Buddhist clergy. It had fair support from all the minority groups, but it failed to respond to the lower layers of society.

One of the UNP's principal leaders during the 1940s, S. W. R. D. Bandaranaike, whose indigenous-style nationalism and neo-liberal attitudes to political, economic and social questions made him suspect in the eyes of the UNP top echelons, tried unsuccessfully to make the party aware of the dangers of the developing crisis. He sought to give expression to the needs and aspirations of those sections of the Sinhalese-educated rural and urban classes which were being tolerated only on the fringes of society – the neglected and underprivileged Buddhist monks, the Sinhalese small shopkeepers and petty traders, Sinhalese native physicians, school teachers, novelists, musicians and artists, and the urban workers.

In 1947 Bandaranaike, in winding up the debate on the address for the Government, obviously had these interests in mind when he spoke of living 'between two worlds today, the one dying and the other struggling to be born'.[27] Later in the year, he discoursed upon the dangers emanating from big-business interests.[28] In the 1949 budget debate, he deplored the discrimination practised against the national languages in the Government of the country. He continued to warn them that if no changes were effected in the social and economic policies of the Government, there would be a revolution. In March 1951, in a speech at the Young Men's Buddhist Association hall, he protested against the Government's indifference to the Buddhist religion and to Sinhalese culture.[29]

In the middle of 1951 Bandaranaike resigned his Portfolio of Health and Local Government and crossed the floor of the House. Shortly afterwards he formed the SLFP, a centrist organisation, which became immediately the focal point of all interests dissatisfied with the UNP and at the same time opposed to Marxist solutions.

Bandaranaike had many opportunities. The radicalisation of politics had been undertaken since the 1930s by young intellectuals who had returned from their studies abroad and had organised a Left-wing movement in the urban sectors and plantation areas. These Left-wing elements spoke in a modern idiom to the rural masses, the urban workers and to the lower middle classes generally. Their economic programme sought social welfare benefits for the under-privileged and the improvement of the conditions of the working class.

Much of the work of the State Council and the Board of Ministers under the Donoughmore Constitution (1931–47) as well as of their ideological successors, the UNP, was a fairly successful implementation of the Left's social welfare programme. When this happened, the Left-wing parties concerned became more or less urban-based organisations concentrating on building a powerful trade union movement, on appealing to the youth of the country in general, the young intellectuals in particular, and to the workers in the city of Colombo and its outskirts. They proposed 'extreme' Marxist remedies to the country's economic and social problems but it is unlikely that their message was clearly understood, much less accepted by those to whom it was addressed. The serious ideological disputes that broke out among them with the resultant rifts and splinterings proved incomprehensible to the mass of voters. The electors who supported Left-wing candidates were mainly seeking to record a dissenting vote.

The leadership on the Left failed to make a significant impact on the rural areas. To the people there it seemed politically too sophisticated, preaching alien and materialistic doctrines and unsympathetic to their national aspirations with regard to Buddhism, the Sinhalese language and Sinhalese culture. Bandaranaike responded, and responded in the end with resounding success, to this large area of society with its deep cultural frustrations and perennial social and economic discontent, neglected by both the Left and the UNP.

The general election of May 1952 came too soon after Bandaranaike's departure from the UNP for his SLFP to rouse and organise the passive protest forces in the rural areas. But the economic difficulties that followed, particularly the attempt by Dudley Senanayake's Government in July 1953 to raise the price of subsidised rice and the several cuts on the social services imposed later by the successor Government of Sir John Kotelawala, gave the SLFP an opportunity.

The personality of Prime Minister Kotelawala seemed to epitomise, for the nationalistically inclined Sinhalese Buddhist forces in the urban and rural areas, everything that was antithetical to the development of Buddhism and Sinhalese culture. The Prime Minister's anti-communist performances on the world stage, particularly at the conference of Afro-Asian powers at Bandung in 1955, were stark evidence to many that the UNP wished to identify itself completely with the 'materialistic' West. There was a fear that Ceylon might in the event of war become a target of an atomic attack. At home Kotelawala was much embarrassed because of his contradictory pronouncements on the language question.

By 1955 there had emerged considerable anti-UNP opinion which coalesced behind Bandaranaike and the SLFP. Influential Sinhalese anti-UNP organisations of Buddhist monks, Sinhalese school teachers, unemployed senior school certificated youths and an entire range of disaffected elements placed themselves behind a broad political coalition, the MEP, comprising the SLFP (the major component), the Marxist-oriented VLSSP of Philip Gunawardena, and the Sinhala Bhasa Peramuna (Sinhalese Language Front) of W. Dahanayake. Bandaranaike also successfully negotiated no-contest mutual aid electoral pacts with the LSSP and CP shortly before the general election of 1956.

The MEP programme responded to the cultural and economic aspirations of the dissatisfied Sinhalese urban and rural people. Of necessity its campaign took on anti-Tamil and anti-Christian overtones. But once in power the MEP found it difficult and sometimes impossible to live up to its pledges.

Its promise to make Sinhalese the only official language as soon as it took power gave rise to extravagant expectations. The Sinhalese-educated unemployed youth believed there would be an exodus of the English-educated from the public services, especially those among the Ceylon Tamils, and the way would then be open for vacancies to be filled by them.

Its pledge that it 'generally approves the recommendations of the report of the Buddhist Committee of Inquiry' satisfied the Buddhist pressure groups that had rapidly proliferated throughout the country at the eve of the 1956 general election. Many of these expected the tranformation of state and society on Buddhistic lines. But this did not happen.

On foreign policy, Bandaranaike enunciated his concept of 'dynamic neutralism'. Ceylon would sever its close ties with the West and tread the non-aligned path.

1956 and after

The electoral victory of the MEP in 1956 is the dividing line in Ceylon's post-independence political development. It unleashed new forces hitherto held in check by a colonial-style bureaucracy and a sophisticated and far-removed political process. As a consequence, the Governments in office in the post-1956 period, especially those headed by S. W. R. D. Bandaranaike (1956–9), his widow Sirima Bandaranaike (1960–5) and Dudley Senanayake (1965–70), were obliged to be more responsive to entirely new layers of public opinion from the rural and urban areas. Government policies therefore did not necessarily follow a defined and predictable path. Instead, they were largely formulated on an *ad hoc* basis mainly on pragmatic considerations.

The year 1956 marked a breakaway from the previous near-*laissez-faire* economic doctrine of optimum opportunity for private commercial interests. Henceforth, Ceylon had to move in the direction of a mixed economy with more and more emphasis on state control. In the process, some of the major sources of support for the UNP were eliminated. The nationalisation of the port of Colombo and bus transport in 1958 by Bandaranaike's MEP Government, of petroleum and insurance by Sirima Bandaranaike's SLFP Government and the dispossession of the schools of the Roman Catholic Church and of Protestant missions in 1960–1 endangered the actual foundations of the UNP.

Some economic power was now dispersed among small industrialists and small- and middle-rung Sinhalese traders because of the imposition of severe import controls due to balance-of-payments difficulties. But the important sectors of the economy continued to remain in the hands of British and local big commercial combines.

A wider distribution of rural credit facilities was effected by the creation of the People's Bank in 1961 and the opening of several branches of it in various parts of the island. Peasant cultivators had already gained some security with the enactment of the Paddy Lands Act by Bandaranaike's Minister of Food and Agriculture, Philip Gunawardena, in 1958. The nationalisation of the Ceylonese-owned Bank of Ceylon, the biggest commercial bank in the island, in 1961 was directed at assisting local enterprise in a greater measure than in the past.

More than anything, however, the principle of planned economic development, in which the public and private sectors are defined and progress measured on a timetable of achievement, was now accepted by all Governments. Bandaranaike established a National Planning Council soon after assuming office and by 1958 a ten-year plan of development was worked out by experienced economists from Ceylon, the West, and communist countries. It was released to the public in 1958 and has been used as the basis for economic development by all Governments since then, including the UNP. Under the UNP-led coalition Government of 1965, a Portfolio of Planning under the charge of the Prime Minister was set up in 1966, followed by the establishment of a Department of Plan Implementation in March of the same year and a National Operations Room in 1968. The latter monitors closely the overall progress of the development programmes of the various ministries.

Organised labour experienced a sense of relief under Bandaranaike's MEP Government. The trade union movement exploited the wide tolerance given it to launch a series of mammoth strikes through the years 1956 to 1959. Many of these were politically inspired and were aimed at embarrassing the MEP Government, for the LSSP at this juncture planned to be successors to Bandaranaike. The Prime Minister personally intervened to settle many of these strikes, making many concessions to the trade unions wherever possible. The Bandaranaike Government made May Day a statutory public holiday. This same policy of accommodating labour was continued under Sirima Bandaranaike, though wildcat strikes were stubbornly resisted by her Government.

The most significant outcome of the MEP victory of 1956 was that the rural masses and the nationalistically inclined Sinhalese Buddhist intelligentsia now came to grips with the realities of political power. Bandaranaike, who had reflected as well as articulated their needs and aspirations, found it difficult at times to hold the more militant sections in check. He was, however, ultimately successful in getting these new forces to adapt themselves to the built-in restraints of modern constitutionalism and the parliamentary system.

In the 1947–56 phase, the language of politics had been on two levels. On one level, the language of Sinhalese Buddhist chauvinism was used on most public platforms especially in the villages. But in Parliament, in the committee rooms, in the Cabinet, in the higher rungs of the administration, and in the social centres, it was a sophisticated nationalism that was emphasised – the concept of a Ceylonese nation, the need for Sinhalese and Tamil as official languages, the principle of non-discrimination in the disbursement of public funds and in appointments to the public service – by all political parties. The emphasis was mainly at this level as long as the new forces remained dormant.

But with their upsurge in 1956, the political diction of chauvinism set the tone for all political groupings, including the Left. Bandaranaike thus enacted legislation in June 1956 to make Sinhalese the only official language throughout the island. He set up a Ministry of Cultural Affairs mainly to assist Sinhalese cultural and Buddhist religious activities and a separate Department of Official Language Affairs. The College of Indigenous Medicine was reorganised and a central institute of *ayurveda* (native medicine) was established so that the indigenous systems of medical treatment would obtain their 'rightful' place in the health services of the country. The two main Sinhalese seats of Buddhist learning, the Vidyalankara and Vidyodaya Pirivenas, were granted university status. Finally, in the religious sphere, a Buddha Sasana Commission was appointed in February 1957 to make recommendations for the reform of the *sangha* (the Buddhist clergy) and for 'according Buddhism its rightful place in the country'. There was opposition from the leading influential priestly Buddhist sect, the *siam nikaya*, but the Commission nevertheless proceeded with its work.

Bandaranaike resisted the demand that all schools, a good proportion of which were under the management and ownership of the Roman Catholic Church and Protestant missionary organisations, should be taken over by the state. He was heavily pressured by the Roman Catholic Church. Further, having embroiled himself with the Ceylon Tamils over the language question, he had no desire to add to his troubles.

The Buddhist argument was that education in the schools was paid for by the state but that a majority of students in the schools were Buddhists. Neither the Catholic Church nor the Protestant missionaries were willing to permit any religious instruction in Buddhism or Hinduism to be imparted to Buddhist or Hindu children in their schools, a wholly unjustifiable position. Most of the best schools belonged to the Christians and preference in the matter of admissions and appointments to their staffs was given to Christians. It was alleged, not without reason, that these schools were also used for purposes of proselytisation. How could a country with a majority population of Buddhists finance schools which were antithetical to their interests, argued the militant Buddhist pressure groups. The latter maintained a persistent agitation and achieved their objective when Sirima Bandaranaike's Government nationalised most of the schools by legislation it enacted in late 1960 and early 1961. Some of the schools, particularly the better ones, were permitted under certain conditions to become private institutions, but they have had to labour under severe financial hardships.

The Roman Catholics at first resisted the takeover of their schools by occupying them and refusing to hand them over to the state. The head of the Roman Catholic Church, Archbishop Thomas Cooray, declared that the faithful would continue to resist 'even unto blood'. An ugly situation was averted, however, by the intervention of Cardinal Valerian Gracias of the Roman Catholic hierarchy in India, who it was reported was sent by Mr Nehru to help break the deadlock. In return for certain assurances by the Government, the Catholic Church called off its protest occupation of the schools.

However, the language problem created the greatest difficulties for the post-1956 Governments. Bandaranaike has often been accused of racialism, if not communalism, but, given the context of the times and the fact that the language issue was being exploited by political groupings vying for the favours of the electors, he chose to be no less politically sensitive to Sinhalese opinion than his UNP rivals. If anything, his approach to the language and religious problems was realistic and pragmatic. Given time, he may have found satisfactory solutions to these, but the UNP at the time chose to place the maximum obstacles in his path.

Though in June 1956 Parliament passed the bill to make Sinhalese the only official language throughout the island, Bandaranaike realised the difficulty of effecting an overnight switch and therefore postponed by notification in the *Government Gazette* its full implementation to January 1961.

But trouble was to come from the Ceylon Tamils through their dominant political organisation, the FP. The latter organised a sit-down protest on the Galle Face Green, which is only a short distance from the precincts of the House of Representatives, on the day the bill began its second reading; this set in motion a chain reaction of Sinhalese–Tamil riots in many parts of the island. Shortly thereafter, the FP met in convention at Trincomalee (August 1956) and demanded autonomy under a federal constitution for the Tamil areas, parity of status for the Sinhalese and Tamil languages, and a satisfactory settlement of the problem of the stateless Indian Tamils in Ceylon. Tension mounted in the months that followed and a major crisis was averted when the Prime Minister (Bandaranaike) and the FP entered into a compromise agreement in July 1957.[30]

Under this pact, the Prime Minister agreed to have Tamil declared an additional official language, without prejudice to Sinhalese in the Ceylon Tamil-majority Northern and Eastern provinces, and to a scheme of devolving administrative powers to regional councils. The latter was a concession to the FP's demand for federalism. The FP had since its inception opposed what it alleged was the deliberate state-sponsored colonisation of the Ceylon Tamil areas with Sinhalese from the south. Bandaranaike agreed not to use the instrument of colonisation to disturb the Tamil majority complexion of these areas.

This settlement may have ultimately brought about Sinhalese–Tamil reconciliation. But there was determined opposition from the UNP as well as from Sinhalese extremist forces. Delay in the implementation of its terms made the FP feel that the Prime Minister was cooling off from his declared intentions and drove it to launch a protest campaign against the sending of nationalised buses with Sinhalese-lettered number plates to the Ceylon Tamil areas. This was followed by retaliatory acts in the Sinhalese districts, culminating in a demonstration of Buddhist monks performing satyagraha on the lawn of the Prime Minister's private residence in Rosemead Place, Colombo, and demanding the abrogation of the pact with the Federalists. The Prime Minister gave in to this demand. There then followed the communal holocaust of May 1958.[31] There was an unnecessary delay in declaring a state of emergency and only after much loss to life and property was this done. The FP was proscribed along with the Jathika Vimukthi Peramuna (JVP), a Sinhalese extremist organisation that was a source of continuous embarrassment to Bandaranaike during his premiership. In August of the same year, the Prime Minister had the Tamil Language (Special Provisions) Act passed by Parliament. Though it was an important concession, it failed to satisfy Ceylon Tamil opinion.

Since then, Bandaranaike's settlement with the Federalists has been the basis for negotiations to solve the Sinhalese–Tamil problem. In April 1960, the FP secured such an assurance from Sirima Bandaranaike's SLFP emissaries before it gave its votes to defeat the throne speech of Dudley Senanayake's minority administration. Failure on the part of Mrs Bandaranaike's Government to keep its pledges, the enactment of the Language of the Courts Act in December 1959, under the provisions of which legal decisions would have to be given in Sinhalese even in the Tamil-speaking areas, and her Government's determination to implement Sinhalese as the only language of administration throughout the island as from 1 January 1961, notwithstanding the protests of the Ceylon Tamil representatives in Parliament, led the FP once more to launch a massive civil disobedience campaign in the northern and eastern parts of the island during March and April 1961. On 17 April a state of emergency was again declared to quell the disturbances in the Tamil areas.

The Ceylon Tamil problem is basically middle-class and economic in character. The concentration of well-equipped secondary schools by American and other missionary organisations in the Jaffna Peninsula (where the density of Ceylon Tamils is greatest) during the late nineteenth and early twentieth centuries gave the Tamils an early educational advantage over other groups, especially the Sinhalese Buddhists (the Sinhalese Christians also had similar advantages), in the competition for jobs in the public and private sectors. In a situation where nature is harsh and the terrain is unproductive, the Jaffna Tamils were left with no option but to create a kind of industry from such employment and competence in the professions. Achievement is very high and therefore quite disproportionate to the numbers of the Ceylon Tamil population in the Jaffna Peninsula. This has made the Ceylon Tamil minority readily identifiable and vulnerable *vis-à-vis* the Sinhalese, and the accusation of communalism in the cornering of jobs is often levelled against Ceylon Tamils holding leading positions in the public services. Consequently the dilemma of the Ceylon Tamils has been how best to secure their economic interests and employment advantages in the rest of Ceylon while at the same time preserving for themselves intact the 'Tamil-speaking areas' of north and east Ceylon. The Sinhalese claim is that pressure of population in the 'Sinhalese areas' makes it necessary for these 'Tamil areas' to be opened up for the transfer of population from the densely populated parts, especially of the southwest. The Ceylon Tamils counter by demanding autonomy for 'their areas' or the cessation of these 'state-aided colonisation schemes', as they choose to call them.

The trend after 1956 was to recognise the fears of the Ceylon Tamil minority and to take note of their objections to the settlement of Sinhalese in the 'Tamil areas'. Prior to 1956 the UNP had tried to placate the Ceylon Tamils by including one or two of their representatives in the Cabinet. But this did not provide an adequate solution.

The continuous use of the armed forces and the police to control communal and labour unrest produced the inevitable consequence of some of the army leaders and police officers developing political ambitions themselves. These men, all of them Christians, and a few civil servants of the higher grades, also Christians, planned in January 1962 a *coup d'état* after which they were going to coerce the Governor-General to suspend the Constitution and hand over authority to a 'Government of national safety' comprising leading members of the UNP, some Right-wing ministers in the SLFP and other prominent persons in public life. The attempt was abandoned after some initial planning. In the meantime information leaked out to the Government and the organisers were apprehended and brought to trial. Mrs Bandaranaike's ministers exploited the situation to their political advantage; Christian officers had sought to overthrow a pro-Buddhist Government.

The Left (the LSSP and Philip Gunawardena's MEP) failed dismally in their attempts to gain power through Parliament at the general election of March 1960 and were frustrated (especially the LSSP) in their hope of securing office in Mrs Bandaranaike's Government. In August 1963 they decided to close their ranks and form a united front. Thus emerged the United Left Front (ULF) comprising the LSSP, MEP and CP with its twenty-one demands. The ULF was determined to use its trade unions to achieve its objectives.

Mrs Bandaranaike quickly recognised the dangers of such concerted action. At the same time, political divisions in her Cabinet left the financial situation serious and unsolved. One way out of the impasse was to enter into a coalition with the ULF or its principal component, the LSSP. The latter's leaders were also reputed to possess the required ministerial skills. In June 1964 Mrs Bandaranaike re-formed her Government, allocating three portfolios to the LSSP. Dr N. M. Perera, the LSSP leader, was given the Portfolio of Finance. The CP supported the reconstituted Government but Philip Gunawardena's MEP opposed it. Right-wing elements in the SLFP led by C. P. de Silva had also disapproved of the move.

The opportunity to oust the Government came when the LSSP leaders insisted on going ahead with the proposal to nationalise the Lake House press. The latter published a majority of the newspapers in the island. The UNP under the skilful leadership of Dudley Senanayake mobilised all the diverse forces in the country opposed to the SLFP–LSSP coalition, arguing that democracy was in grave peril. On 3 December 1964, hardly six months after the coalition was formed, Mrs Bandaranaike suffered defeat in Parliament when her government's throne speech, which included the controversial proposal on the nationalisation of the press, was voted out by a combination of all Opposition parties plus a splinter group of thirteen from the SLFP led by C. P. de Silva. Parliament was thereupon dissolved and a general election followed on 22 March 1965.

In the sphere of foreign relations, many changes beneficial to Ceylon were made. Bandaranaike forcefully enunciated his policy of dynamic neutralism, abandoning the pro-West and anti-Marxist policies pursued by all previous Governments. The British were made to give up their naval and air bases in the island by 1957. These changes paid handsome dividends, for Ceylon now obtained various forms of tangible economic aid from both communist and Western countries. For the first time since independence, Ceylon established diplomatic relations with many of the communist states.

Mrs Bandaranaike, however, shifted the emphasis a little in the direction of the communist bloc. In fact, her Government's nationalisation of petroleum antagonised the U.S. Government, especially in regard to the quantum of compensation to be paid and the delay over the actual payment. U.S. aid to Ceylon was thereafter suspended.

The return of the UNP

The UNP fought the general election of March 1965 for the first time as a senior partner in a broad front of 'democratic forces' which was successfully formed under the leadership of Dudley Senanayake. Previously the UNP had stood on its own but it was now felt that only a consolidated electoral front could ensure the defeat of Mrs Bandaranaike's SLFP and her Marxist allies. The front comprised, besides the UNP, five other groupings of varying and sometimes conflicting shades of opinion – the SLFP splinter led by C. P. de Silva which called itself the Sri Lanka Freedom Socialist Party (SLFSP), the JVP and the MEP of Philip Gunawardena (pro-Sinhalese Buddhist), the Indian Tamil CWC and the Ceylon Tamil TC. The Roman Catholic Church supported this front, while the Tamil FP lent indirect support by asking Ceylon Tamils in the Sinhalese areas to vote UNP.

Senanayake, from subsequent statements made in private conversation with political leaders and public servants, believed very fervently in the democratic aspect of his election front which he later transformed into a broad-based coalition Government. He had, besides, shown a flexibility in his political attitudes which was far from evident in his earlier stances, again, presumably because he believed that the urgent need of the hour was to counter the forces of 'Left-wing totalitarianism'. But whatever his beliefs and the reasons for these may have been, six of the seven components of his coalition – the UNP, SLFSP, JVP, CWC, FP and TC – were of the Right wing, while the Left-wing MEP participated only because Mrs Bandaranaike had not invited it when she reconstituted her Government in June 1964.

The issues raised at the general election of 1965 were not much different from those raised in the elections of 1956 and 1960, but the roles were slightly reversed. The spokesmen of Mrs Bandaranaike's coalition (the SLFP, LSSP and CP) said that the Sinhalese race would face destruction as a result of the UNP receiving support from the Tamil Federalists and the Indian workers. LSSP leaders, who had until this time supported the rights of the Indian workers, now, along with their SLFP counterparts, alleged that Mrs Bandaranaike's Pact of October 1964 with the Indian Prime Minister, Mr Shastri, would not be implemented if the UNP and its allies were returned to office. Further, they stated that in view of the Roman Catholic Church rendering assistance to the UNP the very existence of Buddhism was at stake. Mrs Bandaranaike's Marxist partners pointed to the example of Vietnam and stressed that the same fate would overtake the Buddhists in Ceylon if the UNP, which they identified with Western capitalism, obtained control of the Government. In a way, Mrs Bandaranaike and her allies were defending themselves from the attacks of the Buddhist clergy, influential sections of which had been mobilised by the UNP and formed the vanguard of their election campaign against the 'ungodly Marxists'.

The UNP and its Sinhalese allies, the SLFSP, JVP and MEP, for their part stressed the dangers that 'democracy' and 'religion', in particular, Buddhism, would face from the Marxist allies of the SLFP. Their spokesmen alleged that it was a question of time for the Marxists to infiltrate and capture the SLFP. Then not merely Buddhism but the Sinhalese language would be destroyed by 'ungodly' and 'international communism'. The UNP leaders pledged that they would not alter the Official Language Act of 1956, nor would they work to the detriment of the Sinhalese people in trying to find a solution to the problem of the stateless Indians.

Both the SLFP and the UNP in their manifestos indicated that Buddhism would receive special consideration and that they would enact legislation to secure its position. Both parties also guaranteed that, if returned to power, they would provide for *poya* days being declared non-working days.

The question of the 'monopoly press' figured prominently, at times overshadowing other issues. Mrs Bandaranaike and her allies said that the press was a monopoly of privileged families, backed by business interests and controlled by 'Catholic Action'. It was, in their view, unsympathetic to the national aspirations of the Buddhists and the Sinhalese people. They insisted that this monopoly should be broken. This they would do by bringing the press under a broad-based state-supervised corporation. The UNP and its allies alleged that such a step was only the preliminary to the establishment of a 'Marxist dictatorship' and that this in turn would threaten the existence of the Sinhalese race and of Buddhism.

Economic issues were raised by both contenders, but these seemed to play a subsidiary role or were made to do so by the reportings of a press which was openly hostile to the SLFP and its partners. The latter for their part claimed that they wished to 'conserve the people's gains of 1956'. They said they were the poor man's party ranged against 'big business' and 'Anglo-American capital'. The UNP on its side pointed to the dangers of increasing state intervention in the economic life of the people. This, it insisted, would restrict the freedom of the individual. It would result in a Government which was in control of important sectors of the economy being in a position to discriminate against its opponents.

The election proved inconclusive, with no party in command of an overall majority. But the UNP with its allies were in a position to form a Government which would have the confidence of a majority of the members of the new House of Representatives.

Conclusion

The period since 1956 saw evidence of increasing politicisation of the masses, a process which began when universal suffrage was granted in 1931. More and more layers of the population have become interested in the political processes because they see in these a method of finding solutions to the pressing problems of an underdeveloped economy and a multi-group society. Public meetings have large attendances. Newspapers are read by a wide public and they represent all the various points of view. Political leadership is consequently easily identified, which makes the task of apportioning responsibility much simpler.

Parliament has had unexpected success in Ceylon. Its membership has changed considerably from what it was in 1947 when it was first constituted. Recruitment is more from the lower rungs of society, and Members after 1956 tend increasingly to speak in Sinhalese or Tamil because they can be sure of a wider audience. This is confirmed by the sale of large numbers of copies of the published proceedings of Parliament whenever there are important debates in the House of Representatives. Parliament is regarded as a problem-solving mechanism whose views the Cabinet takes into account before arriving at decisions. More and more of the voting population are therefore focusing their attention on Parliament; this is evidenced by the large numbers participating at general elections – 55.9 per cent in 1947, 70.7 in 1952, 69.0 in 1956, 77.6 in March 1960, 75.9 in July 1960, as many as 82.1 per cent in 1965 and 85.2 per cent in 1970. The rural intelligentsia, the trade unions, the student population, the urban elements, including the professional classes and commercial interests, are all interested in the processes of decision-making; the results of these processes involve society as a whole and they have far-reaching consequences.

3. The pre-election setting: The 'National Government', 1965–70

After the 1965 general election

The party position at the end of the general election of March 1965 left no single grouping with an absolute majority, as Table 1 illustrates.

In the circumstances, Mrs Bandaranaike delayed her resignation in the hope that she would be able to secure the support of the FP and a few of the Independents. Two LSSP ministers approached the FP leader with a view to exploring the possibility of assistance from that quarter, but the FP had made up its mind to back Dudley Senanayake in the formation of a Government. The decision was made on the basis of a pact drawn up between Senanayake and Chelvanayakam.

Under this pact, Senanayake agreed to (a) a scheme of district councils under the direct supervision of the central Government, (b) preference being given to the people of the area in any colonisation scheme in the Northern and Eastern provinces, (c) Tamil being made a parallel language of administration with Sinhalese in the two provinces mentioned, (d) amending the Language of the Courts Act by providing for the use of the Tamil language in judicial administration in these two provinces in addition to Sinhalese, and (e) relief for Tamil public servants who had failed to gain proficiency in the official language.[1]

Senanayake also came to an understanding with the CWC.[2] The points of agreement were eventually set out in a draft note which the CWC handed to Senanayake for the record. No signatures were appended to the document as was done in the case of the agreement with the FP. Broadly, it was agreed that no hardships would be created for Indians who were to be repatriated under the Indo-Ceylon Agreement of October 1964, that Indians who opted for Indian citizenship would be able to continue in their occupations, positions, etc., in

Table 1. *Party positions after the 1965 general election*

UNP and allies		SLFP and allies		Uncommitted		Appointed members
UNP	66	SLFP	41	FP	14	6[b]
SLFSP	5	LSSP	10	Independents	6[a]	
TC	3	CP	4			
MEP	1					
JVP	1					
	76		55		20	6

SOURCE: All of the tables, unless otherwise stated, were prepared by the author.
[a]Of the six Independents returned only one had firm SLFP sympathies (the M.P. for Habaraduwa), two had separated from the SLFP (the M.P.s for Dambadeniya and Nikaweratiya) while the other three were 'available' to the group forming the Government.
[b]Whoever is Prime Minister has the right to recommend to the Governor-General the appointment of six members of the House of Representatives. They usually support the Government in office.

Ceylon until they retired, that the element of compulsion in repatriating Indians would not be enforced, and that those Indians obtaining Ceylonese citizenship would not be discriminated against by being placed in separate electoral rolls but would be included in the general electorate.

Some of these points of agreement were against the spirit, if not the letter, of the Indo-Ceylon Agreement of October 1964. They were nevertheless extracted from a party leader (Senanayake) in search of a majority. The CWC had rendered electoral support to the UNP and the FP would not have backed Senanayake had not these concessions been made to that organisation.

The CWC had two of its members, including its leader, S. Thondaman, nominated as Appointed Members to the House of Representatives. Thondaman later boasted in private conversation, quite rightly, that he had been successful in altering the provisions of an agreement arrived at between two sovereign states.

Mrs Bandaranaike recognised her unalterable minority predicament in the new House and accordingly tendered her resignation on 24 March 1965. Senanayake, as leader of the largest single grouping, the UNP, was commissioned by the Governor-General to form a Government. It was a broad-based coalition comprising seven parties – the UNP, FP, SLFSP, TC, CWC, MEP and JVP.

Formation of the 'National Government'

Since the new administration enjoyed the support of the Ceylon Tamils of the FP, the Indian Tamils belonging to the CWC, the Sinhalese nationalists in the JVP, SLFSP, and the MEP, Senanayake called his administration the 'National Government', a description which his opponents refused to accept. They for their part chose to stigmatise it, for obvious political reasons, as the 'UNP–FP Government' and at other times as 'the seven-party coalition'. They accused the new Prime Minister of betraying the Sinhalese to the Tamil Federalists and the Indians and of being a prisoner in their hands.

Senanayake tried to make the best of his uncomfortable coalition of diverse and opposing elements by establishing two objectives. After having secured the electoral defeat of those who he alleged stood for totalitarianism, his Government would dedicate itself to the maintenance of democracy. Secondly, he was pleased that 'circumstances had enabled (him) to form a "National Government"' and he hoped he could be 'the instrument of bringing together the different communities living in the island'.[3]

Economic policies

Maintenance of democracy for the UNP implied a return to a mixed economy where the greater emphasis was on the private sector. The new Government did not try to reverse the nationalisation policies of the Bandaranaike Governments of 1956–64. Senanayake's position was that he could not 'unscramble scrambled eggs'. But hereafter the benefits of development were to be enjoyed more by the private entrepreneur. The broad exposition of this policy was seen in the first budget speech of the Minister of Finance. He said, on 3 August 1965, that 'the "National Government" was committed to the strengthening of democracy in the country; they believed that individual freedom and the democratic tradition could not be ensured without a healthy, controlled private sector functioning according to a national plan as an integral part of a mixed economy.'

In the implementation of this policy, the private sector was invited to participate in the running of a few of the nationalised enterprises while in others, such as the Fisheries Corporation and the Ceylon Transport Board, patronage became rampant and so absurdly excessive that they began to be burdens on the national exchequer. Further, the Government took vigorous measures to attract foreign private capital.[4] There was some inflow of such capital. But it was felt that foreign entrepreneurs repatriated grossly excessive profits in the five-year term of the Government, claiming that these were gains from their investments.

However, certain advantageous results also flowed from these policies. For instance, 1968 was a peak year when Ceylon's GNP rose by an unprecedented 8.3 per cent and the rate of growth, in per capita real terms, was 5.8 per cent. In the last year of the Government's term of office, that is in 1969, the performance was also good. GNP rose in real terms by 5.7 per cent while the rate of growth was, after making allowance for a population growth of 2.2 per cent in that year, 3.5 per cent. Per capita real product rose from Rs. 739 in 1968 to Rs. 764 in 1969.[5]

More significant, there was a phenomenal increase in investment expenditure, the highest on record and evidence of the confidence that the Government had inspired. The rise in private-sector investment was almost double that in the Government sector. Capital formation in the private sector inclusive of public corporations increased from Rs. 1,101 million in 1968 to Rs. 1,678 million in 1969 or by 52 per cent, and Government sector investment in respect of these two years rose from Rs. 466 million to Rs. 564 million or by 21 per cent.[6]

Foreign aid

An obvious corollary to the Government's new economic policies was a softer attitude towards the United States and the West in general. The new Government proceeded to compensate the foreign petroleum companies (mostly owned by U.S. companies) whose businesses had been nationalised by Mrs Bandaranaike's Government during 1962–4 and whose claims for adequate compensation were still outstanding. As a result of this delay, U.S. aid to Ceylon had been stopped under the provisions of the Hickenlooper Amendment.

The payment of this compensation in September 1965 resulted in U.S. aid to Ceylon being resumed. Further, the Government stood to benefit from the international credit agencies – IMF, IBRD and IDA.[7] Between 1965 and 1970, the five-year term of the Government, the IMF gave short-term credit amounting to Rs. 723.4 million, of which Rs. 301.7 million was paid back, leaving a balance of Rs. 421.7 million. IBRD and IDA agreed to finance a number of projects. Foreign commercial banks were also not averse to granting loans. Temporary borrowings from various financial institutions and banks in Europe and America stood at the end of the five-year period at Rs. 350 million, bringing the total of the country's short-term debts to approximately Rs. 772 million. The Opposition however alleged with some substance that the credits were wastefully spent, leaving the country with a large debt.

Further, the consortium of foreign Governments, also referred to as the Aid Ceylon Club, set up under the auspices of the World Bank, held four meetings during the period in question and promised Ceylon assistance totalling Rs. 1,012.4 million to tide over her balance-of-payments difficulties. Of this sum, by mid-1968, Rs. 484.6 million had been made available for the import of industrial raw material, machinery, and fertilisers.[8]

Aid from the sources mentioned resulted in certain changes in Ceylon's foreign policy. After Bandaranaike's victory of 1956, the UNP too had accepted the principle of non-alignment. Under Mrs Bandaranaike, Ceylon came to be more closely involved with the socialist group of Afro-Asian powers, as well as with communist countries.

Under Senanayake there was a change in policy. While his Government protested that Ceylon was still in the neutralist bloc, in actual fact Ceylon came to develop closer ties with the West. That was the inevitable result of the Senanayake Government's dependence on international and other credit agencies and the donor countries of the Aid Ceylon Consortium for assistance of various kinds.

Credit facilities from the IMF carried with them further implications which were more serious for the Senanayake Government's popularity in Ceylon. If loans were to be given for development, Ceylon must show a willingness to restrict her extravagant social services. Four 'Letters of Intent' to the IMF, in July 1965, July 1966, May 1968, and August 1969 indicated that the Government was contemplating significant curtailments in the social services, and that steps were being taken to correct the country's financial position.[9] For obvious political reasons these 'Letters' were withheld from the public.

Implications of foreign aid

The rice subsidy was the first to be affected. In December 1966 the Government reduced the weekly rice ration from two measures per person given at the subsidised price of fifty cents, to a measure free of charge to each person.[10] The other measure, if it was needed, had to be purchased by the consumer in the open market at prices ranging from Rs. 1/- to Rs. 1/60 a measure. Senanayake's reason for this unpopular decision was the scarcity of rice in the world market, bringing with it an unprecedented increase in the price of rice.

Relying on his usual political skills of making virtues out of necessities, the

Prime Minister launched a 'grow more paddy' campaign which yielded good results. As a Senanayake, he had the advantage of charisma which he and his father developed over the years by their efforts in opening up the dry-zone areas of Ceylon for paddy cultivation. The Government's strategy was to patronise the peasant farmer at the expense of other sections of the community. There was a dramatic increase in paddy production, from 46.3 million bushels (approximately 680,380 tons) in 1965 to 65.9 million bushels (990,000 tons) in 1969 – the last year of the Government's term of office.[11] In 1967 the Government increased the guaranteed price on paddy which it had been paying the farmer since 1952. The price of paddy also went up appreciably in the open market, to Rs. 15.86 per bushel as against Rs. 13.61 in 1967. Besides, there was a sharp fall recorded in the import of rice. It was 642,000 tons in 1965; in 1968 it had dropped to 344,000 tons. This meant that locally produced rice constituted, in 1968, 74 per cent of the total rice consumed in the country. It was said as supporting evidence of the success of the 'grow more paddy' campaign that savings deposits in rural banks had increased several-fold and that there were signs of increased purchasing power among the rural people. But, judging from the election results even in the traditional paddy-growing areas, there seemed to have been many errors in the Government's calculations, especially in the statistics collected by its officers in the field.

The Opposition used the rice cut as its principle election strategy. It promised to restore it if returned to office at the next election.

Almost a year after the reduction in the ration of subsidised rice, the Government launched its second unpopular course of action, the devaluation of the Ceylon rupee by 20 per cent, followed shortly after by the introduction of a foreign exchange entitlement scheme in May 1968 which depreciated the exchange rate further for a number of transactions. The effect was a sharp rise in the prices of consumer articles. These measures were intended to diversify exports and to improve export incomes from the traditional export commodities (tea, rubber and coconuts) but the results were not noteworthy.

Unemployment and rising living costs

Although the Government increased the salaries of public servants, and compelled some employers in the private sector to increase wages, these were not adequate to meet the rising cost of living. In the five years of the Government's term of office, the cost-of-living index rose from 112 to 137.

Scarcely any proper steps were taken to tackle the problems of the unemployed, numbering some 700,000. An added factor was the presence of about 13,000 jobless graduates from the four universities in Ceylon. The Government instead adopted a harsh attitude to the universities, bringing them under the rigorous control of an unsympathetic Minister of Education. This was done through the Higher Education Act of 1966, passed despite opposition from the majority of teachers in all four universities in the island.

Communal harmony

The Senanayake Government did record a few successes. In January 1966 Parliament passed the Tamil Regulations under the Tamil Language (Special Provisions) Act, enacted by S.W.R.D. Bandaranaike in 1958. They provided some satisfaction to the Tamil minority. At the same time, the Government did not strictly enforce the implementation of the official language in the administration and this gave Tamil public servants a measure of relief.

The Prime Minister, however, was not able to fulfil his promise to the FP of establishing district councils under the supervision of the central Government.[12] The FP hoped that these councils would be a step in the direction of their objective of obtaining regional autonomy for the Ceylon Tamil areas. But a threatened revolt from the ranks of the Government's parliamentary supporters forced the Prime Minister to abandon his district councils bill in mid-1968. Senanayake himself had no convictions about the utility of these councils. In fact, in the negotiations with the FP leaders on the details of the powers to be devolved on these councils, he had hoped that they would give up their demands once they began working with him.[13] But the FP remained inflexible.

Shortly after, the FP's representative in the Government resigned his portfolio on an unimportant issue,[14] but Senanayake's tact in disposing of the district councils issue left the Federalists, despite all their disappointments, convinced of the Prime Minister's sincerity. The Opposition alleged that the FP's exit from the Government was 'staged', and that it was merely a divorce of convenience.

The departure of the Federalists proved embarrassing to the Prime Minister. He had concentrated on preaching to the Sinhalese the virtues of national unity and the economic development that could result from communal harmony. He claimed to have established national peace by bringing the Ceylon Tamil Federalists into his Government. The economic successes he claimed for his Government on the food front were due to the cooperation he had been able to obtain from all sections of Ceylon's plural society. When the Federalists left, the Prime Minister found himself without an argument. The Opposition thereafter ridiculed his claims of restoring goodwill in the country, with the Federalists sitting in opposition. The Prime Minister nevertheless continued to argue with much substance that whether there were Federalists in his Government or not, he had the goodwill of the Tamils in the country at large.

The Indian issue was settled to the satisfaction of the CWC. The Indo-Ceylon Agreement (Implementation) Act of 1968 removed the fears prevalent regarding the possibilities of compulsory repatriation of Indians who chose to become citizens of India, and of Indians registered as Ceylon citizens being placed on a separate electoral roll.

The Prime Minister was unable to keep his promise to the Roman Catholic Church of providing relief to their schools, which they were compelled to run on their own resources after Mrs Bandaranaike's nationalisation of the schools in 1960. The Government evidently feared repercussions from Buddhist pressure groups.

Opposition strategies

The Opposition exploited the weaknesses of the Senanayake coalition to the maximum, particularly his ties with the two Tamil organisations, the FP and the CWC. The Left-wing parties in particular utilised racial slogans in their street processions to scoff at the Prime Minister. Two Left-wing dailies which developed a wide circulation at this time, the *Aththa* (Truth) of the CP and the *Janadina* (People's Daily) of the LSSP, were very effective in their lampooning of the Government and their exposures of its blunders. The *Janadina*, in fact, reproduced a verbatim report of Senanayake's pact with the FP. In Parliament, this pact was the subject of repeatedly searching questions from the leading Opposition spokesmen until Senanayake was compelled to admit that he had entered into an understanding with the FP leader, S. J. V. Chelvanayakam, *before* he became Prime Minister, and he was therefore not obliged to disclose its contents.

The Opposition maintained a constant vigil within and outside Parliament during the five years of Senanayake's Government. Public meetings were regularly organised throughout this period to expose the Government as occasion demanded, as well as to explain Opposition policies. The Opposition scored a victory when it organised a public protest on the day of the passing by the House of Representatives of the Tamil Regulations under the Tamil Language (Special Provisions) Act of 1958, on 8 January 1966. Police action resulted in the accidental death of a Buddhist monk from a ricocheting bullet.

The consequences of this unfortunate death were damaging to the Government. What is more, the Government was compelled to invoke the Public Security Act and declare a state of national emergency. Emergency rule continued thereafter under various pretexts for an unprecedented length of time – 1,086 of the 1,825 days of the Government's term of office – and was the subject of constant Opposition criticism and condemnation both inside Parliament and on public platforms. Under emergency regulations, the LSSP journal *Janadina* was banned for several months for publishing what the Government considered inflammatory material. The Opposition once again scoffed at the 'saviours of democracy' and 'the guardians of a free press' acting in this manner.

On the district councils issue, the Opposition was successful in rousing sufficient public resentment during mid-1968 to force the Prime Minister, under further pressure from his parliamentary supporters as well, to abandon this project. When he explained his predicament to the FP, Senanayake offered to resign. The Federalists, however, accepted his basic good faith. They were satisfied that he had done all he could to honour his pledge but that circumstances beyond his control had led him into an unfortunate situation.

On the question of the implementation of the official language, the Opposition accused the Government of being excessively generous to Tamil public servants. They further alleged, not without foundation, that English was being quickly reintroduced into the administration. They were successful in creating misgivings and anxiety among large sections of Sinhalese public servants who were eager to maintain Sinhalese as the only official language in the country.

On the Indian problem, the Opposition confined itself to remarking that the

Prime Minister had sold out to the Indians and sacrificed the interests of the Kandyan Sinhalese. They alleged that the Indo-Ceylon Agreement of October 1964 was not being properly implemented. They were able to stir up so much controversy on the Indo-Ceylon (Implementation) Act of 1968 that the Government had difficulty in mobilising a majority in the Senate. The bill passed narrowly, particularly as a number of Government supporters opposed it.

Mrs Bandaranaike and her colleagues were successful in disaffirming the loyalty of sections of Roman Catholics as well. SLFP spokesmen criticised the Government for not including a Roman Catholic in the Cabinet during the first half of its term, deciding to substitute *poya* days for the sabbath, ignoring the problems of the Roman Catholic areas and for its breach of faith in regard to the schools question.

Sections of Muslims were also won over through a growing Muslim organisation, the Islamic Socialist Front (ISF), which emerged at this time under the leadership of the SLFP's veteran Muslim politician, Badiudin Mahmud. SLFP politicians played on Muslim fears of possible Ceylon Tamil encroachment on some of their spheres of interest. They alleged that Senanayake was 'looking after' the Ceylon Tamils at the expense of the Muslims. The dangers immanent in demarcating the island into autonomous areas under the charge of district councils were brought to the attention of the Muslims. ISF leaders as well as other Opposition spokesmen alleged that in such a set-up the Muslims would become a minority within a minority since there were considerable Muslim concentrations in the areas traditionally inhabited by the Ceylon Tamils and they would become victims of 'Tamil rule'.

Further, the Prime Minister was not willing to go as far as the Muslim political elite would have preferred him to in taking a definite stand against Israel in the Israeli-Arab dispute. Mrs Bandaranaike and her allies proclaimed that, if returned to power, their Government would sever diplomatic relations with Israel until the issue was resolved to the satisfaction of the Arabs. The Prime Minister's reluctance was understandable in the context of his Government's foreign policy.

Towards the last years of Parliament, the SLFP and its allies curtailed their attacks on the Tamils. They recognised the possibility of sections of the Tamil vote coming to them. Some of the SLFP leaders paid goodwill visits to the Ceylon Tamil areas with a view to establishing bases in this 'hostile' territory.

Economic issues provided the Opposition with enough critical facts to make it unnecessary for them to emphasise the communal line. The halving of the rice ration, the scarcity of consumer goods, the rise in prices of essential commodities considerably aggravated by the devaluation of the Ceylon rupee, the Government's failure to take steps to increase wages and salaries consonant with price increases in the daily items of food and clothing, and widespread unemployment, all were sufficient to destroy the Government's edifice of a 'you never had it so good' Lanka. At least three 'unemployment marches' to Colombo were organised by the communists.

The whole gamut of Senanayake's policies for promoting development came in for the most scathing criticism. Statistics relating to development were questioned. There were complaints that the IMF was gaining a stranglehold on the economic affairs of the country. Foreign aid and foreign loans were being utilised for conspicuous consumption and wasteful expenditure. The Opposition further alleged that foreign monopolists were being given ever-increasing privileges and at the expense of local entrepreneurs whose interests the Government professed to have at heart. These monopolists were accused of depressing the prices of primary products and increasing the prices of industrial goods sold to Ceylon. The Government's financial policies, the Opposition alleged, had only strengthened the private sector and encouraged monopolistic structures to control the economy.

The Common Programme

In their campaigns, the Opposition met with much success because they had united under the leadership of Mrs Bandaranaike. Both in Parliament and outside they worked in close cooperation. They set the seal to their unity when in March 1968 the SLFP and its two Marxist allies, the LSSP and the CP, agreed to form a Samagi Peramuna (the UF) and to implement a 25-point programme of work if returned to power. They made it clear they would form a 'people's Government' of all three parties under Mrs Bandaranaike and that they were not, as in the past, merely entering into an electoral arrangement to defeat the UNP.

The Common Programme, as it came to be called, was the culmination of efforts that had been made for almost two decades to enable what were called 'the progressive forces' in Ceylon to come to an agreement to work together. The traditional Marxist parties had at least gained their limited objective of being assured of portfolios in a future Government which was pledged to implementing socialist policies. Mrs Bandaranaike for her part had the satisfaction of support from major sections of the working class. The trade unions would not now create problems for a Government she would lead.

The Right-wing of the SLFP viewed the alignment with dismay. Promising politicians in that party disliked the alliance, for it reduced the opportunities of political advancement for them, now that there were two other parties whose claims would have to be duly considered in the allocation of offices. This opposition was however only marginal. Mrs Bandaranaike was in full command of the situation and she had the support of a majority of the SLFP leadership.

The Common Programme firmly established that the SLFP had decided to move further to the Left, from the usual Left of Centre position it had earlier adopted. There was agreement on the need to regulate the economy, to increase Government control of the economy as a necessary corollary to this and to extend the public sector considerably.

During its period in opposition, the Left-wing leadership of the SLFP organised a Fabian Society-style Socialist Study Circle which organised discussions, seminars and study groups on the various aspects of the programme that the UF would implement when it came to power. Outsiders too were invited to participate in its work and much useful ground was covered. In fact, the Circle provided a framework of thinking and research on many subjects which a UF Government could utilise when called upon to implement its programmes.

What gave the Opposition so much strength in Parliament and in the country was the unity of purpose that it succeeded in achieving especially from 1968 onwards. It spoke with such unanimity and confidence on every issue that it was sometimes almost a parallel Government. And the UNP feared to act in blatant disregard of Opposition criticisms on the controversial issues of the day.

Conclusion

By 1965, prior to the advent of the 'National Government', the pressing problems of the Sinhalese Buddhists had been reasonably dealt with. No doubt, the solutions effected had not met with the approval of the Sinhalese militants. Nonetheless there was a wide range of middle opinion among the Sinhalese as a whole who felt a sense of relief and assurance that their basic interests had been reasonably safeguarded.

With the return of the UNP to power in 1965 backed by the Tamil parties, the FP, CWC and TC, and the Roman Catholic Church, there were fears on the part of sections of the Sinhalese Buddhist rural and urban elites of a return to the pre-1956 arrangement of forces under which strong minority ethnic and religious groups had exercised disproportionate power and influence. The Tamil Regulations of January 1966, the reversion to English in some areas of the administration, and the failure of the 'National Government' to implement the Indo-Ceylon Agreement of 1964 in the way in which Mrs Bandaranaike had intended it, confirmed these fears.

In the years 1965–70 the battle lines between the rival social and political forces in the island came to be demarcated in a way that had not happened before. The divergences of opinion that had existed earlier among the social layers which the UNP had failed to cater for and the political differences of those groupings were now reconciled within the broad confines of the UF – the result of the successful endeavours of amalgamators and political brokers. Spanning this spectrum was the personality of Mrs Bandaranaike which had instilled sufficient confidence among these disparate elements to keep them together. However, there had been no polarisation in the political spectrum as some observers at the time emphasised.

The personality of the rival leader, Dudley Senanayake, was just as successful in its ability to penetrate different and sometimes conflicting social and political layers. Senanayake appealed to both rural and urban conservatives as well as to the conservatives among the island's different ethnic and religious groups. He was able to weld together these diverse and sometimes warring interests into a coalition of 'democratic forces'. Thus, the old and the new, the traditional and the progressive had come to co-exist in opposite camps under their respective charismatic leaders on the eve of the general election of May 1970.

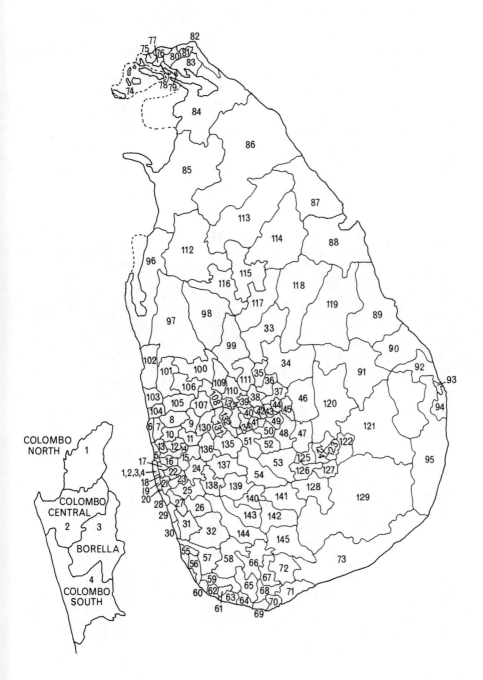

Map 2. Electoral map of Ceylon, 1970.

KEY TO CONSTITUENCIES (IN ALPHABETICAL ORDER)

ELECTORAL DISTRICT NUMBER	NAME OF CONSTITUENCY	ELECTORAL DISTRICT NUMBER	NAME OF CONSTITUENCY
32	Agalawatte	49	Hewaheta
61	Akmeemana	58	Hiniduma
38	Akuruna	99	Hiriyala
65	Akuressa	23	Homagama
56	Ambalangoda	25	Horana
91	Amparai	114	Horowupotana
112	Anuradhapura	13	Jaela
11	Attanagalla	78	Jaffna
24	Avissawella	144	Kalawana
59	Baddegama	116	Kalawewa
123	Badulla	89	Kalkudah
141	Balangoda	93	Kalmunai
55	Balapitiya	29	Kalutara
27	Bandaragama	68	Kamburupitiya
127	Bandarawela	42	Kandy
90 (2 seats)	Batticaloa	76	Kankesanturai
71	Beliatta	7	Katana
57	Bentara-Elpitiya	105	Katugampola
30	Beruwala	74	Kayts
121	Bibile	132	Kegalla
101	Bingiriya	117	Kekirawa
3	Borella	16	Kelaniya
26	Bulathsinhala	21	Kesbewa
83	Chavakachcheri	84	Kilinochchi
102	Chilaw	138	Kiriella
2 (3 seats)	Colombo Central	145	Kolonna
1	Colombo North	17	Kolonnawa
4 (2 seats)	Colombo South	80	Kopay
107	Dambadeniya	52	Kotmale
33	Dambulla	22	Kottawa
130	Dedigama	18	Kotte
137	Dehiowita	106	Kuliyapitiya
19	Dehiwala–Mt Lavinia	44	Kundasale
66	Deniyaya	109	Kurunegala
70	Devinuwara	34	Laggala
8	Divulapitiya	14	Mahara
111	Dodangaslanda	120	Mahiyangana
15	Dompe	85	Mannar
39	Galagedara	54	Maskeliya
131	Galigomuwa	35	Matale
62	Galle	69	Matara
12	Gampaha	31	Matugama
50	Gampola	134	Mawanella
63	Habaraduwa	110	Mawatagama
67	Hakmana	113	Medawachchiya
48	Hanguranketa	115	Mihintale
128	Haputale	46	Minipe

ELECTORAL DISTRICT NUMBER	NAME OF CONSTITUENCY	ELECTORAL DISTRICT NUMBER	NAME OF CONSTITUENCY
118	Minneriya	60	Ratgama
10	Minuwangoda	139	Ratnapura
9	Mirigama	36	Rattota
129	Moneragala	136	Ruwanwella
20	Moratuwa	43	Senkadagala
72	Mulkirigala	124	Soranatota
88 (2 seats)	Mutur	45	Teldeniya
79	Nallur	73	Tissamaharama
103	Nattandiya	87	Trincomalee
51	Nawalapitiya	41	Udunuwara
6	Negombo	81	Udupiddy
97	Nikaweratiya	77	Uduvil
94	Nintavur	125	Uva-Paranagama
143	Nivitigala	75	Vaddukoddai
53	Nuwara Eliya	86	Vavuniya
92	Paddiruppu	47	Walapane
28	Panadura	100	Wariyapola
122	Passara	5	Wattala
140	Pelmadulla	37	Wattegama
82	Point Pedro	64	Weligama
108	Polgahawela	126	Welimada
119	Polonnaruwa	104	Wennappuwa
95	Pottuvil	98	Yapahuwa
96	Puttalam	40	Yatinuwara
142	Rakwana	135	Yatiyantota
133	Rambukkana		

4. The electoral framework

The 1970 election witnessed the highest percentage of voting at any general election held in Ceylon since the introduction of universal franchise in 1931. To comprehend this, it becomes necessary to examine the way in which the franchise evolved from colonial times to independence and the stages through which election procedures came to be democratised.

The period before independence

Prior to the McCallum Reforms of 1912, there were no elections to the legislature whatsoever. The Colebrooke constitutional system which operated from 1833 to 1912 provided for nominated Executive and Legislative Councils which functioned in an advisory capacity to the Governor of the colony. Representatives of recognised local families and/or leading professional men were appointed as Unofficial Members to the Legislative Council to represent the main communal groupings. The Council had an Official majority comprising Britishers. As for the Executive Council, it was wholly Official and British in composition.

With the emergence of an English-educated Ceylonese middle class in the second half of the nineteenth century and growing political awareness among them, there arose an agitation for, among other things, the extension of the elective principle in the matter of legislative representation.[1] It was stimulated to some extent by the fact that municipal councils established in Colombo and Kandy (1866) and in Galle (1867) admitted of the elective principle, though with various restrictive qualifications. The Colombo council had ten elected and nine nominated members and the Kandy and Galle councils had five elected and four nominated members. Further, other local bodies established in 1852 and 1876 and the village communities ordinance of 1889 provided for the franchise to be exercised by certain classes of inhabitants.

Consequent on the agitation for elections, provision was made in the McCallum Reforms of 1912 for an 'Educated Ceylonese Member' to be returned by an all-island electorate comprising Ceylonese (excluding Burghers) possessed of income, educational or professional qualifications.[2] The Burghers and Europeans were granted the right to elect members from specially constituted separate Burgher and European electorates. But the majority of the Unofficial Members of the council continued to be nominated by the Governor.

The first election for the 'Educated Ceylonese seat' had caste undertones. An eminent *karawe* Sinhalese physician, Marcus Fernando, lost to a prominent Ceylon Tamil, Ponnambalam Ramanathan. The latter had the support of sections of the majority *goigama* Sinhalese electors who did not on that occasion wish to vote for a *karawe*.

The reforms of 1921 and 1924 provided for elections to the Legislative Council on a limited franchise comprising only 4 per cent of the island's population.[3] The majority of the electorates concerned were territorial, returning Sinhalese or Ceylon Tamils but there was also a number of seats reserved for the smaller minority groups and for certain commercial interests. The principle of gubernatorial nomination however continued. The whole arrangement (nominations plus elections) was aimed at achieving a kind of communal balance under which no single community could impose its will upon the other communities.[4] Naturally the Sinhalese political leadership chafed at these restraints and demanded territorial representation pure and simple. They obtained this under the Donoughmore reforms of 1931. The Donoughmore Commission held that the communal principle in representation had had a deleterious effect on Ceylonese society.[5]

But the most far-reaching recommendation of the Donoughmore Commission was the decision on universal suffrage. Ceylon became the first colony to exercise universal adult franchise from 1931 and the experience gained by the Ceylonese electors through the years has enabled changes in government to take place in a constitutional manner.

The Donoughmore commissioners had recommended that a delimitation commission should redistribute the territorial electoral areas on the basis of one constituency for every 70,000 to 90,000 units of population. On this basis, the number of territorial electorates should have increased from 23 to 65. In actual fact, however, the delimitation commission of 1930 demarcated 50 territorial electorates.[6] An important term of reference of the delimitation commission was that it should endeavour to establish equality of population for each electoral district. The new demarcation therefore reduced the area of electoral districts from what it had been under the previous set-up. But a further consequence was that the areas of the new electoral districts varied depending on their population composition.

Two general elections were held under the Donoughmore constitution, in 1931 and 1936. There were certain inevitable shortcomings in the way the electors made their preferences. In the absence of an organised party system – and the constitution seemed deliberately to encourage individualistic patterns of behaviour on the part of legislators and those aspiring to be legislators at the expense of group politics – electors when they had no other knowledge of the candidate were influenced by considerations of race, religion or caste. Communal tensions developed, as did political organisations which were frankly communal in their objectives. Many legislative proposals put up for the consideration of the State Council were examined from a communal angle by the representatives of minority groups who were becoming increasingly apprehensive of 'Sinhalese domination'.

Consequently there were demands for all forms of protection against possible discrimination in any new constitutional set-up. Composite cabinets which included representatives of the minority communities, built-in provisions in the constitution against legislative and administrative discrimination, weightage in representation for the minorities, and 'balanced representation' between the Sinhalese majority and all the other minority groups, were some of the safeguards suggested.

Electoral arrangements from 1947

The basis of representation today derives from the scheme drawn up in 1944 by the Ceylonese Board of Ministers.[7] It was designed in part to meet the fears of the minority groups. The Soulbury Commission made certain revisions in their Report of 1945[8] and a further revision was made in 1959 by constitutional amendment. The scheme of representation in existence today therefore combines territorial and communal principles. But the latter factor is reduced to a minimum.

The Ceylonese ministers believed that the minorities should have additional weightage in representation, but they were averse to members being returned to the legislature on purely ethnic, religious or social grounds. 'Every member', they said, 'should be elected as a Ceylonese.'[9] They felt that the distribution of communities in the island provided a solution which would accommodate the communal factor within the territorial principle. 'The great majority of the Sinhalese', they said, 'are to be found in the densely populated areas, especially in the Western and Southern provinces. The great majority of the (Ceylon) Tamils and Muslims are to be found in the less densely populated areas.'[10] It was also desirable that the Kandyan rural population should have special consideration. The ministers therefore decided that adequate representation could be given to the Ceylon Tamils, Muslims and the impoverished, backward Kandyan Sinhalese peasantry, without resorting to the communal principle as such. This they did by providing what they called 'weightage to area as well as population'.[11]

In a legislature therefore of 101 members (95 elected, and 6 appointed by the Governor-General after a general election to represent inadequately represented interests), each province would have one member for every 75,000 inhabitants (on the basis of the last general census) and an additional member for every 1,000 square miles of area. The result would then be as indicated in Table 2.

The delimitation of electoral districts within a province should, the ministers decided, be undertaken by an independent commission of three persons with the chief justice or a judge of the supreme court as chairman. They recommended that the commission in delimiting electoral districts within each province should ensure that electoral districts shall have 'as nearly as may be an equal number of persons, but shall also take into account the transport facilities of the province, its physical features and the community or diversity of interest of its inhabitants'.[12] The 'community or diversity of interest', the ministers felt, could be 'economic or social'. This would then allow the delimitation commission a discretion to carve out constituencies within a province for caste, ethnic or religious groups which they (the commission) thought were sufficiently important.

Table 2.   *Basis of electoral demarcation, 1947–56*

Province	Number for population	Number for area	Total
Western	19	1	20
Central	13	2	15
Southern	10	2	12
Northern	5	4	9
Eastern	3	4	7
North Western	7	3	10
North Central	1	4	5
Uva	4	3	7
Sabaragamuwa	8	2	10
Total	70	25	95

SOURCE: *Report of the First Delimitation Commission, Sessional Paper XIII* (Colombo, 1946).

Each constituency under this scheme would be about one half the size of the constituencies under the Donoughmore delimitation, and in the less thickly populated provinces, much less than one half. The scheme should be revised with every census. The ministers were of the opinion that, under their scheme, 'it would be much easier than it is at present to provide representation for homogeneous economic and social groups.'[13]

In their representations to the Soulbury Commission (not the ministers who were pledged to boycott the Commission) the advocates of this scheme estimated that, of the 95 elected seats, 58 would go to the Sinhalese and 37 to the minority communities (15 Ceylon Tamils, 14 Indian Tamils and 8 Muslims). For instance, the Northern and Eastern provinces which have a majority of Ceylon Tamils and Tamil-speaking Muslims would obtain 16 instead of only 6 seats. The Soulbury commissioners thought that the figure in relation to the Indian Tamils 'should be accepted with caution' but that 'a figure approximating to the estimated result' could nevertheless be achieved.[14]

In order to make doubly sure that minority groups would secure the best representation possible, the Soulbury commissioners suggested amplification of the ministers' scheme in two ways. Firstly, wherever it appears to a delimitation commission that there is 'a substantial concentration in any area of a province of persons united by a community of interest, whether racial, religious or otherwise, but differing in one or more of these respects from the majority of the inhabitants of that area', the (delimitation) commission should be at liberty to modify the factor of numerical equality of persons in that area and make such division of the province into electoral districts as may be necessary to render possible the representation of that interest.[15] Secondly, they recommended the creation of multi-member constituencies in appropriate areas. This would enable minority communities, if they were sufficiently united, to concentrate all their votes on any one candidate seeking to represent their interests and in this way ensure the election of that candidate to Parliament. The proposals of the Board of Ministers and the Soulbury Commission were incorporated in Sections 40–44 and 76 of the Ceylon (Constitution) Order in Council 1946.

Sir Ivor Jennings, who functioned as constitutional adviser in an unofficial capacity to the ministers, and was draftsman of the constitution, helped most to frame the scheme of representation. He stated that this scheme had, among other things, four objectives in view.[16] Firstly, it gave increased representation to minority communities without introducing the purely communal element. The Ceylon Tamils and Muslims occupy the sparsely populated Northern and Eastern provinces, while the Indian Tamils are mostly in the Uva and Sabaragamuwa provinces. These four provinces under the scheme in operation obtained 13 of the 25 additional members. Secondly, it provided weightage to the rural as against the urban population. Jennings argued that the urban population 'are necessarily much more highly organised' and that in the past they had provided most of the members of the State Council even for the rural areas. There was however a deeper significance in this apparently serious concern for the rural element, as will be seen in the third and fourth reasons adduced by Jennings to justify the scheme. The third argument was that it gave weightage to the Kandyan Sinhalese as against the Low Country Sinhalese. Eleven if not 14 (if the North Western Province is taken as a Kandyan area) of the additional seats went to the traditional Kandyan Sinhalese areas. Lastly it gave weightage to the backward areas.

'Rural', 'Kandyan Sinhalese' and 'backward' areas in the Ceylonese context are synonymous with political conservatism, traditional values, political and economic lethargy and a willingness to accept the established order without much fuss or protest. On the other hand, political radicalisation had gone on apace since the early 1930s in the urban areas, the Low Country Sinhalese western coastal belt, and the developed plantation districts to the south of the Kelani river. It is mostly in these areas that the Ceylonese Marxists have made their biggest impact. This scheme of representation, whatever the motives (and the motives are open to question), by constitutional sanction reduced the electoral influence of radical and Left-wing parties to a minimum.

The first delimitation commission comprising three eminent persons was appointed by the Governor on 23 May 1946 and submitted its report on 29 August of the same year.[17] In demarcating constituencies, the commission paid meticulous attention to the provisions contained in the constitution, and the recommendations of the Board of Ministers and the Soulbury Commission. The commission also paid due consideration to the claims of minority ethnic, religious and caste groups in demarcating constituencies so as to give such groups a clear chance, or at least the opportunity of influencing the decision.

The delimitation commission in paragraph 51 of their report drew attention to the disparity in the population strengths of electoral districts between provinces, which resulted from the directives they were obliged to follow as contained in sections 40–44 and 76 of the constitution. These disparities have a bearing on the probable motivations for the basis of representation already referred to. According to the commissioners, the provincial average for each electoral district within each of the nine provinces was as shown in Table 3.

Table 3. *Voting disparities at the 1947
general election*

Province	Average voting strength per constituency ('000)
Western	93.4
Central	75.5
Southern	80.2
Northern	53.3
Eastern	38.8
North Western	66.8
North Central	27.9
Uva	53.1
Sabaragamuwa	74.6

SOURCE: Same as Table 2.

In actual fact, after the preparation of the registers under the new delimitation, 23 constituencies had voting strengths of between 40,000 and 60,000 while as many as 26 had between 5,000 and 25,000 voters. The voting strengths of the remaining constituencies were distributed between these two sets of figures.

The commissioners demarcated 84 single-member constituencies, four double-member constituencies and one three-member constituency. They used the figures of the 1931 census to allocate seats on the basis of population among the nine provinces. Within each province, however, the figures of the 1946 census were utilised to allocate seats.

Under their scheme, the Sinhalese obtained, at the general election of 1947, three seats more than their proportionate due and the Ceylon Tamils one more than was their due. The Muslims were slightly under-represented (by one seat) and the Indians fell short of three seats (see Table 4).

The disparities in constituency voting strengths widened considerably at the general election of 1952, owing to a new factor. By legislation enacted in 1948 and 1949, virtually all the Indian Tamils who had the right to vote in the general election of 1947 were excluded.[18] The Ceylon Citizenship Act of 1948 and the Indian and Pakistani Residents (Citizenship) Act of 1949 prescribed the terms on which Ceylon citizenship could be acquired. They were rigorous and extremely difficult to obtain where the Indian Tamils resident in Ceylon were concerned. A further Act, the Ceylon Parliamentary Elections (Amendment) Act of 1949, restricted the vote only to citizens of Ceylon.

A further consequence of these Acts was that at the general election of 1952 and at every general election thereafter, the Sinhalese, especially the Kandyans, obtained an excess of representation at the expense of the disfranchised Indians (see Table 4).

The Indian Tamils, it was estimated, besides winning 7 seats at the general election of 1947, had influenced the decision in 20 other constituencies in all of which a majority of them had cast their votes for candidates opposing the UNP – mostly Marxist candidates or their sympathisers. Whatever the motivating

Table 4.   *Communal distribution of seats, 1947–70 (House of Representatives)*

	Sinhalese	Ceylon Tamils	Muslims	Indian Tamils	Others	Total
Seats due on basis of population[a]	66	12	6	10	1	95
Seats obtained						
1947	68	13	6	7	1	95
1952	75	13[b]	6	0	1	95
1956	75	12	7	0	1	95
Seats due on basis of population[c]	106	17	10	18	0	151
Seats obtained						
March 1960	123	18	9	0	1	151
July 1960	122	18	11	0	1	151
1965	121	17	11	0	1	151
1970	123	19	8	0	1	151

SOURCE: *The Ceylon Daily News Parliament of Ceylon* for 1947, 1956, 1960, 1965 and 1970 (Colombo, Associated Newspapers of Ceylon Limited).
[a] *Report of the First Delimitation Commission, Sessional Paper XIII* (Colombo, 1946).
[b] S. Natesan, an Indian Tamil, was elected to represent a Ceylon Tamil constituency (Kankesanturai). He identified himself with the Ceylon Tamils and we have therefore counted him as a Ceylon Tamil.
[c] *Report of the Delimitation Commission, Sessional Paper XV* (Colombo, 1959).

factors for the legislation against the Indians referred to may have been, it gave the UNP a considerable accession of strength. They increased their share of seats from 41 in 1947 to 54 in 1952 while the Left-wing strength fell from 20 to 13 (see Table 5).

The disparities in question were even more marked at the general election of 1952. There were 25 constituencies with 40,000 to 60,000 voters and 31 with 5,000 to 25,000 voters. In Table 6, figures of the average voting strength in electoral districts within each province illustrate these glaring disparities.

A census was held in 1953 and, in keeping with the requirement of Section 40 of the constitution, a delimitation commission was appointed to effect a fresh demarcation of electorates. However, it was terminated before it completed its endeavours. In 1954, the Ceylon Parliament by the Ceylon Constitution (Special Provisions) Act suspended the provisions (Sections 41–44) of the Ceylon Constitution relating to the delimitation of electoral districts for a specified term, in addition to increasing for a definite period the number of

Table 5.   *Party composition before and after the 1952 general election (House of Representatives)*

	Parties	Before the election	After the election (1952)
	UNP	41	54
Left-wing	LSSP	14	9
	CP	4	3
	VLSSP	2	1

Table 6.　*Voting disparities at the 1952 general election*

Province	Average voting strength per constituency
Western	45,789
Central	22,282
Southern	41,050
Northern	29,674
Eastern	20,708
North Western	34,143
North Central	15,292
Uva	15,241
Sabaragamuwa	30,149

members of the House of Representatives to 105 from its existing limit of 101. The length of time referred to extended to a date in 1966 to be determined by the Governor-General on Prime-Ministerial advice. If there was no dissolution of Parliament in 1966, these provisions would operate until the date at which Parliament was actually dissolved. Thereafter these provisions would cease to have effect.

The four additional members referred to were to represent an islandwide electorate called the 'Indian and Pakistani electoral district'. To be included in this 'electoral district', a person had to be registered as a citizen of Ceylon under the Indian and Pakistani Residents (Citizenship) Act No. 3 of 1949, have his name entered in any valid register of electors and have his name marked in such a register of electors with the 'disqualification mark'. The 'disqualification mark' was to be an asterisk or a distinguishing mark which a registering officer used when the total number of persons *exceeded* 250. If the total number was *less* than 250 registered citizens, then no 'disqualification mark' needed to be placed.

The purpose of these provisions was to prevent Indians registered as citizens of Ceylon from having a say in any of the other constituencies, especially those in the Kandyan Sinhalese areas. They would however have had to be given representation in Parliament once the provisions of the Nehru–Kotelawala pact of 1954 on the 'stateless' Indians came into operation. This was to be done later by the demarcation of separate electorates for them. The whole scheme was condemned by the Ceylon Indian leaders, as well as others, as being discriminatory to those Indians accepted as citizens of Ceylon. These provisions, though enacted as law, were for various reasons not brought into operation, and the House of Representatives continued as before with 101 members.

The general election of 1956 was, in the absence of changes, conducted on the basis of the delimitation of 1946. The electoral registers used were those of May 1954, in which those Indians who had succeeded in obtaining citizenship under the rigorous legislation of 1948 and 1949 and were of voting age were included. But they were only a few in number. Consequently, disparities in constituency voting strengths remained as they had been, and in some instances, owing to population expansion and growing densities in the Western and Southern provinces, a little more marked. There were nine constituencies with a voting strength of over 60,000, eight with between 20,000 and 25,000, eleven between 15,000 and 20,000, two between 10,000 and 15,000, and three between 5,000 and 10,000. One constituency had a voting strength of below 5,000.

With a new Government in office in 1956 (comprising some of the Opposition groups of the preceding Parliament), it was only to be expected that the whole question of delimitation of constituencies would be looked into afresh. This was in fact done, but there was not much deviation from the well-trod path.

A joint select committee of Parliament which had examined the existing law, among other matters, recommended certain changes which were accordingly incorporated in the Ceylon Constitution (Amendment) Act No. 4 of 1959. In particular, the latter amended sub-sections 1, 3, 4 and 5 of Section 41 of the Constitution. Further Section 76(1) of the Constitution which fixed the number of electoral areas for each of the island's nine provinces (95 in all) was revoked, so that the new delimitation commission was free to determine the number of members to be returned to the House. The fact of weightage in relation to area was left unchanged.

According to Section 40(1) of the constitution, a fresh delimitation of constituencies must follow within one year after the completion of a general census of the island. On these grounds, a delimitation commission was appointed in 1953 (after the general census of that year) but, as has already been stated, its work was suspended by constitutional amendment. In 1959, when a new delimitation was being envisaged, there had not been a general census. The relevant provision of the constitution [Section 40(1)] had to be amended. Under the terms of the amendment, the Director of Census and Statistics was required to prepare an estimate of the population up to the end of June 1958. An estimate was accordingly published in *Gazette Extraordinary* No. 11669 of 19 February 1959. The total population estimated was 9,361,000, as against a citizen population of 8,213,800. The bulk of the non-citizen population of 1,147,500 comprised Indian Tamil estate workers in the plantation districts.

Important amendments were also made to sub-sections 3, 4 and 5 of Section 41. Sub-section 3, which requires that each electoral district of a province must have as nearly as may be an equal number of *persons*, had *citizens* substituted for *persons*, and sub-section 4, which empowers a delimitation commission subject to certain conditions to render possible the representation of 'a substantial concentration of *persons*' in any area of a province 'united by a community of interest, whether racial, religious or otherwise, but differing in one or more of these respects from the majority of inhabitants of that area', had again *citizens* substituted for *persons*.

As significant was the amendment to sub-section 5 of Section 41. Under the earlier rule, the delimitation commission could, at their discretion, create multi-member electoral districts in a province to provide for the representation of racial, religious or other interests. This could include *caste* interests as well. The amendment excluded the commission from creating multi-member districts for the representation of caste interests. It was felt that such a provision would encourage thinking on caste lines to persist for longer than was necessary. The amendment permitted hereafter a delimitation commission to create multi-member districts only for strong concentrations of racial interests which differ from the majority of citizens in that province.

Under this amendment, therefore, the double-member constituency of Ambalangoda–Balapitiya, which was carved out by the first delimitation commission of 1946 to give two important Sinhalese caste groups in that area, the *goigama* and the *karawe*, the opportunity of securing a seat each for themselves, was abolished. Further, under the amendments to sub-sections 3 and 4 of Section 41, the two-member electoral districts of Badulla and Balangoda, which were created in 1946 to enable an Indian and a Sinhalese to be elected in each of the constituencies, also went, because the majority of Indians were no longer reckoned as citizens, or as persons with voting rights, unless they qualified under the legislation of 1948 and 1949.

There was one unamended provision (Section 41, sub-section 2) which nullified any beneficial results that these amendments may have effected. This provision required a delimitation commission to award seats to a province on the basis of one seat for every 75,000 units of population (together with one seat for every 1,000 square miles of area). This meant that the disfranchised Indian population, especially in the Kandyan Sinhalese areas, had to be counted (in each province) for the purpose of determining the quantum of seats that each province was entitled to. In short, it maintained the existing over-weightage in representation for the Sinhalese areas in general, and the Kandyan Sinhalese areas specifically.

Table 7 gives the number of electoral districts in each province on the basis of population, area and citizenship since the 1959 delimitation. It indicates the even wider disparities in the citizenship population in electoral districts between the Kandyan Sinhalese provinces and the rest of the island's provinces. In this respect, the new delimitation law intensified the existing discrepancies.

The Ceylon Tamil-speaking areas of the Northern and Eastern Provinces where the Ceylon Tamils and Muslims are the major segment of the population received no advantage from the point of view of population, though they continue to enjoy the weightage allowed them in respect of area (8 additional seats for area). On the basis of citizenship, the two Tamil-speaking provinces got 16 seats (inclusive of 1 Sinhalese seat in a Sinhalese majority constituency – Amparai – in the Eastern province). They obtained the same number of seats in respect of population as well (that is, citizens and non-citizens).

The Sinhalese provinces on the other hand should have obtained 95 seats (inclusive of 1 seat in the majority Tamil-speaking Eastern province) if citizenship was the only factor considered (exclusive of the 17 extra seats in respect of area). But they received 16 more seats in respect of the non-citizenship population.

Out of the total of 128 seats (95 + 17 + 16) in the Sinhalese provinces (this includes the Amparai seat in the Tamil-speaking Eastern province), 3 or 4

Table 7. *Electoral districts on the basis of citizens, persons and area*

Province	Total population	Total number of citizens	Number of electoral districts on the basis of 75,000 persons, i.e. citizens plus non-citizens	Area weightage	Average number of citizens to be obtained per electoral district	Total number of electoral districts	Total number of electoral districts on the basis of citizenship only and area
Western[a]	2,547,500	2,392,200	34	1	68,348	35	32 + 1 = 33
Central[b]	1,552,600	1,000,700	21	2	43,508	23	13 + 2 = 15
Southern[a]	1,258,700	1,237,100	17	2	65,110	19	16 + 2 = 18
Northern[c]	664,300	638,600	9	4	49,123	13	9 + 4 = 13
Eastern[c]	496,200	487,300	7	4	44,300	11	7 + 4 = 11
North Western[a/d]	1,000,900	977,700	13	3	61,106	16	13 + 3 = 16
North Central[b]	275,100	270,600	4	4	33,825	8	4 + 4 = 8
Uva[b]	549,900	359,300	7	3	35,930	10	5 + 3 = 8
Sabaragamuwa[b]	1,016,100	850,300	14	2	56,686	16	11 + 2 = 13
Total	9,361,300	8,213,800	126	25	457,936	151	135

SOURCE: Prepared by the author from census data and the *Report of the Delimitation Commission, Sessional Paper XV–1959.*
[a]Low Country Sinhalese.
[b]Kandyan Sinhalese.
[c]Tamil-speaking (Ceylon Tamil and Muslim).
[d]There are 12 Kandyan Sinhalese, 3 Low Country Sinhalese seats and 1 Muslim seat in this province.

are Muslim seats (Akurana, Puttalam and Colombo Central which has on certain occasions returned 2 Muslims, on others 1).

In the final demarcation, out of a total of 151 seats (i.e. on population and area) the Sinhalese (Kandyan and Low Country) obtained 124 or 125 seats, the Ceylon Tamils 18, and the Muslims between 8 and 9. The Ceylon Tamils obtained all their seats in the Northern and Eastern provinces. The Muslims, who have a large concentration of population in the Eastern province, obtained 5 seats there, and 3 to 4 seats in the Sinhalese areas – in Puttalam, in the three-member constituency of Colombo Central and the two member constituency of Akurana. In the Eastern province too, it was not possible to separate the Muslims and Ceylon Tamils in two constituencies – Batticaloa and Mutur – and these were therefore made into double-member constituencies each returning a Ceylon Tamil and a Muslim. In a number of other constituencies in both the Sinhalese and Ceylon Tamil areas, many Ceylon Moor villages were brought into the electorates carved out, so as to give the Muslims a strong voice, if not to enable them to return members of their choice to Parliament on a possible split of votes in the opposing camp. This scheme of delimitation was the operative one at the general elections of March and July 1960, 1965 and 1970.

Representations were made by the underprivileged castes among both the Sinhalese and the Ceylon Tamils to have electorates carved out specially for them. The commissioners rejected these, stating that it would be 'a pernicious policy' to do this, because it would perpetuate 'their alleged underprivileged status, when it is everyone's desire that class distinctions should disappear'.[19] The commissioners added that they had adequately ensured representation for these interests in Parliament, especially in areas where 'economic community of interest . . . coincided with their religious or caste community of interest'.[20] In other cases, they had given 'concentrations of the various so-called underprivileged classes, a strong voice in the choice of their representatives'.

The organisation of elections

Voting abuses

The Soulbury Commissioners in their report had noted certain abuses that had developed in the exercise of the franchise during the Donoughmore period. Some of the witnesses who went before them had blamed these on 'the widespread illiteracy and ignorance' of the electorate. These witnesses stated that the grant of universal suffrage in 1931 had been 'a grave error' and had led to 'wholesale corruption, intimidation, sale of ballot papers and the election of unworthy representatives'. Their view was that literacy or educational tests should be imposed.[21] The commissioners were not disposed to agree, stating that despite the abuses, the grant of universal suffrage has been 'amply justified by the considerable progress made since 1931 in the sphere of social reform'.[22]

The sale of ballot papers, impersonation, and the use of violence and intimidation at elections were some of the abuses brought to the attention of the Soulbury Commission. An election judge, the Commission noted, had said in his judgement on a petition filed in connection with a by-election held in October 1943 that 'unmitigated hooliganism had taken full control of affairs'.[23] However, the commissioners remarked that the question of electoral abuses is a matter 'of internal civil administration' and, as such, a matter for the local legislature to determine.[24]

During the Donoughmore period, the arrangement for voting gave rise to two abuses – sale of ballot papers and violation of the secrecy of the ballot. This was possible as a result of the illiteracy of a large majority of the voters who could not even read the names of the candidates on the ballot paper, candidates consequently being allotted colours, and ballot boxes being provided at polling booths corresponding to the colours assigned. The voter obtained his ballot paper from the presiding officer and retired into a screened cubicle where he either deposited his ballot paper in the box with the appropriate colour, or concealed the ballot paper in his clothing, and on leaving the booth sold it to an agent of one of the candidates, who would arrange for such papers to be deposited by another voter, particularly reliable. Secrecy was not altogether secured because the presiding officer had the right to enter the cubicle from time to time to ensure that the ballot boxes were not being tampered with.

Corrective measures

A new system of voting by symbols was introduced at the general election of 1947 to replace the colour system. Provision for this had been made under the Ceylon (Parliamentary Elections) Order in Council gazetted in September 1946. A symbol was printed on the ballot paper opposite the candidate's name. The determining of which symbol should go to a candidate was decided by lot by the returning officer on nomination day. Twenty-four symbols were approved for the election: elephant, hand, bicycle, house, butterfly, key, pair of spectacles, bird, cart wheel, star, pair of scales, umbrella, omnibus, cup, clock, lamp, chair, tree, pineapple, table, flower, aeroplane, eye and spoon. All that the voter was expected to do was to take the ballot paper to a private cubicle and put an 'X' mark on the square adjacent to the symbol of the candidate of his choice. The procedure was facilitated by the symbol being printed alongside the candidate's name. He would then fold the ballot paper and deposit it in the ballot box placed before the presiding officer. There was thus no possibility of his taking away the ballot paper and selling it to any bidders.

Despite this simple procedure, there were nearly 45,000 spoilt ballot papers. Two multi-member constituencies, Balangoda (3,899 spoilt) and Colombo Central (3,489 spoilt) had the largest number of rejected papers. The practice of assigning symbols to each of the candidates was continued in the 1952 general election.

In the 1956 general election and at every general election thereafter an advance was made on the existing practice when it was decided to assign one symbol to one party – which helped in effect to strengthen party alignments and discourage fragmentation and independent candidates.

The need for a one-day general election

The major defect in the arrangement of the general election was the successive dates fixed for polling in the various constituencies. In other words, the election was not held on a single day. Altogether there were 19 days of polling for the first general election in 1947. Polling commenced on 23 August and ended on 20 September. Fridays, the weekly day of prayer for the Muslims, some of the other days for religious festivals, and the days on which the Kandy Perahera were held, were avoided.

There could not be any serious objection to the different dates fixed, except that these could be manipulated to provide an advantage to the ruling party. For instance, the poll for the constituency of the future Prime Minister (D. S. Senanayake) was fixed for the first day. This left him free for the remaining 18 days to visit the other constituencies, while the constituencies of three of the most important Left-wing leaders, N. M. Perera (LSSP leader), Colvin R. de Silva (BLP leader) and P. G. B. Keuneman (an important leader in the CP) polled on the last day, 20 September. As a result, they were not as free to tour the constituencies in which their candidates were contesting.

At the general election of 1952, the polling was spread through four days in the month of May. There were two factors which provided significance to an otherwise innocuous four days of polling. Firstly, there was a pro-Government press, acknowledged also as national independent dailies, giving headlines to the governing party's electoral successes while minimising the Opposition's performance. I. D. S. Weerawardena, for example, remarked that despite the UNP's loss of 10 seats on the first day of polling, the daily press had headlines that the party was gaining an early lead (they made only two gains).[25] The second was that the polling dates were fixed to help the Government leaders. Their constituencies polled on the first two days or so while the constituencies of the Opposition leaders polled on the last days. Sir Ivor Jennings remarked that all the cabinet ministers' elections were fixed for the first two days, and all the Opposition leaders for the last day. Jennings added:

The effect of this arrangement was that during the election week most of the Opposition leaders were tied to their own constituencies while the ministers, having won or lost in the first two days, were free to devote their attention to their opponents. What is more, the UNP workers and vehicles which were numerous could be used to elect the ministers on the first two days and to defeat the Opposition leaders on the last two days.[26]

A similar pattern repeated itself at the general election of 1956. The dates fixed appeared to suit the leaders of the governing UNP of Sir John Kotelawala. On this occasion the polling dates were reduced to three – 5, 7 and 10 April. Of the 37 electorates which polled on the first day to return 42 members (33 single-member constituencies, 3 two-member constituencies and 1 three-member constituency), there were 36 sitting UNP members contesting, of whom 15 were ministers or parliamentary secretaries. On the other hand, the constituencies of three important Opposition leaders, including that of the future Prime Minister, S. W. R. D. Bandaranaike, polled on the last day. The inference is obvious, especially when the pattern kept repeating.

The Leader of the Opposition at the time, S. W. R. D. Bandaranaike, in fact anticipated such a possibility and wrote on 9 March 1956 to the Commissioner of Elections requesting that polling dates be arranged so as not to allow any political party an undue advantage.[27] The Commissioner replied brusquely that the dates would be fixed so as to fit in with the available resources of men and machinery for the holding of elections. As it happened, the dates suited the ruling party, but the psychological benefits accrued to the winning opposition party, the MEP of Bandaranaike. On the first day, the MEP and its Left-wing allies (the LSSP and CP) obtained 33 seats, the UNP 8 and Independents 1. On the second day, all 23 seats were won by the MEP and its allies, and on the third day 15 MEP, LSSP and CP members, 10 FP members, 4 Independents and 1 Tamil Congressman were returned.

The elections of 1947, 1952 and 1956 established clearly that an Opposition challenging the ruling party such as the UNP, which enjoyed the overwhelming support of the upper stratum of Ceylonese society, which possessed resources in men, finances, organisation and transport, and ability to command senior public servants to do its bidding in regard to the actual administration of the election, will find it an extremely difficult task to push its way to the seats of power. Bandaranaike's MEP accomplished this feat, but afterwards did not attempt to exploit the position it held to its advantage, as the UNP had done.

Changes in election arrangements since 1956

One of Bandaranaike's immediate acts was to set up a select committee of Parliament to look into, among other things, the reform of the existing law of elections. The recommendations of this committee were far-reaching in that the entire basis of elections and electioneering was democratised. Hereafter it was made possible for any Opposition party, provided it had the confidence of the public, to challenge the ruling party in a meaningful manner.

Legislation introducing these changes was enacted in May 1959 – the Ceylon Parliamentary Elections (Amendment) Act No. 11. The significant features of the amending Act were that the general election be held on one day and not spread out over two or three days as in the past; and that provision be made for the recognition of political parties by the Commissioner of Elections. Candidates of such political parties paid only a deposit of Rs. 500 at nomination whereas others paid the usual sum of Rs. 1,000. Recognition was granted by the Commissioner if he was satisfied that a party had been in existence for at least five years prior to the date of application for recognition, or if at least two members of the political party applying were or had been Members of Parliament.

Approved parties had special election symbols assigned to them. Even those parties that failed to obtain recognition were assigned symbols. Under this provision, 23 political parties were recognised by the Commissioner for the general election of March 1960 and, of these, one party, the All Ceylon Dravidian Progressive Federation, did not put forward any candidate.

Due to the increase in the number of constituencies, from 89 electorates returning 95 members in all previous general elections (1947, 1952 and 1956) to 145 electorates returning 151 members, and the democratisation of the basis of electioneering by the amending act, the March 1960 general election saw a large number of candidates and political parties making their bid – 899 candidates from the 23 recognised political parties, other parties, including 167 Independents.

At the succeeding general election in July 1960, 393 candidates contested, inclusive of 39 Independents. Eleven parties granted recognition by the Commissioner did not contest any seats. The drop in the number of candidates contesting was due to the election being mainly a contest between the UNP and the SLFP and their respective allies.

Other provisions introduced under the 1959 Act with a view to reducing the election expenses of candidates and political parties included the right given to all candidates duly nominated to despatch free of charge through the post one postal packet containing election material to each elector in his constituency; and the ban on the display of bunting, banners, posters, handbills or any such material intended to promote the candidature of any person in public places, across roads or in crown property or on vehicles, except in or on any vehicle used for the candidate or his election agent, from the day of nomination to the day following the day on which the poll is taken. Postal voting under the amending Act was permitted for those members of the armed forces and the public services who were on duty on election day and could not cast their votes on that day.

These changes in election procedure ensured that no established political party would be placed at a disadvantage in the future, and no party by virtue of its superior material resources would be in a position to outmanoeuvre its poorer rivals. The obvious target here was the UNP, which is always in a more advantageous position in these matters than any other party. Further amendments were introduced in 1964 and 1969, but the foundation for all these had been laid by the amending Act of 1959.

An all-party select committee of the House of Representatives was appointed in September 1962 to recommend changes in the existing law and practice relating to elections in the light of the experience gained at the two general elections of March and July 1960. The committee submitted a unanimous report in May 1963 and as a result of its recommendations, two amending Acts were adopted by Parliament.

The first was an amendment to the constitution itself – the Ceylon Constitution and Parliamentary Elections (Amendment) Act No. 8 of 1964 – and it sought to strengthen the position of the Commissioner of Parliamentary Elections. The previous amendment of 1959 had granted the Commissioner the same legal status as the Auditor-General – appointment by the Governor-General on Prime-Ministerial advice, and removable only on an address from both Houses of Parliament. This was effected by amending the Ceylon (Parliamentary Elections) Order in Council. Now it was felt that the Commissioner should derive his status from the constitution itself. It would make his position more secure by requiring that the law could only be changed by a two-thirds majority. In the earlier amendment of 1959, a simple majority would have sufficed to change the provision.

The new amendment also made provision for the release of funds from the consolidated fund on the authority of the Governor-General for the conduct of a general election, in the event of Parliament being dissolved without funds having been made available for the conduct of the election.

The other recommendations of the select committee were embodied in the Ceylon Parliamentary Elections (Amendment) Act No. 10 of 1964. These provided for a simpler and more accurate procedure for the registration of voters and for making claims and filing objections with regard to the registers. There were also new criteria for the recognition of political parties, inclusive of those already mentioned in the 1959 amendment. Under these, those parties which contested the July 1960 general election and had at least two candidates elected to Parliament remained recognised political parties for future elections. In all, there were eight such parties. They retained the symbols assigned to them in July 1960 *unless* they themselves desired a change. The LPP made use of this provision to change its symbol from the 'umbrella' to the 'sun'. Except for this alteration, the other criteria under the 1959 amendment were retained. Eighteen new parties applied for recognition under its terms in the allotted time for the general election of March 1965, but of these only the TC qualified, so that in all nine parties were recognised for the March 1965 general election. Deposits from candidates of recognised political parties were reduced further from Rs. 500 to Rs. 250. Independent candidates had to pay the usual sum of Rs. 1,000.

Impersonation was almost completely eliminated by requiring that voters be marked with indelible ink on one of their fingers before being issued ballot papers at polling stations, and by the imposition of rigorous imprisonment, up to a minimum of one year without the option of a fine. Elections were made more peaceful and less expensive. Under this, further bans were imposed on (*a*) the display and exhibition of flags, banners, posters, etc., (*b*) processions from nomination day to the day after the polls, (*c*) erection of booths by candidates near polling stations and (*d*) the transport of voters to and from the polling station except by public transport. Certain exemptions were made for the transport of the sick and the disabled.

Employees in all sectors were able to vote. They were entitled to take time off with pay for the purpose. Further, the earlier provision in the 1959 amendment for certain categories of employees in the public sector to vote by post was extended to include employees of the Ceylon Transport Board and of the Local Government Service who may be called upon to work on election day.

As a result, 34,000 persons voted by post at the March 1965 election as against 18,246 in March 1960 and 26,665 in July 1960.[28]

Corrupt and illegal practices were reduced by making (a) religious sanctions on voters and their families by members of a religious order or by organisations, (b) economic sanctions on employees by employers, and (c) the publication of false reports in newspapers of the activities and utterances of candidates and recognised political parties, offences within the scope of undue influence.

In keeping with the practice of having a select committee of Parliament examine the working of the law relating to, and the administration of, a general election, the 1965–70 Parliament had two select committees investigate these matters. Their reports were considered by the Cabinet and most of their recommendations incorporated in a bill which became law on 1 March 1970. Its details related mostly to procedures regarding the conduct of the general election, and the filing of election petitions.

The administration of the general election of 27 May 1970

Electoral registers

The responsibility for organising the election rested with the Commissioner of Parliamentary Elections whose position is, with the amending legislation of 1964, entrenched under the constitution.[29]

When the date of dissolution was made official, the first task of the Commissioner was to prepare the 145 certified election registers (for the 145 electoral districts) in time, in at least two languages, and sometimes three (Sinhalese, Tamil and/or English as the case may be).

These registers were intended for exhibiting in 43 centres outside Colombo for almost a month from well before nomination day (23 April) for the benefit of those making applications for postal voting facilities, such applicants being members of the Public and Local Government Services and Central Bank employees who would be on duty on election day, members of certain essential services who would have duties connected with the election such as the Railway, Ceylon Transport Board, Postal and Telecommunications Department and the Defence Services. There were 83,471 applications for postal voting and of these 81,754 were allowed. The registers were also intended for scrutiny and sale to candidates and their agents, again well before the date fixed for nominations, and for use at polling stations on election day. Well over 16,000 of these registers were prepared by the Department of Elections and made available for inspection from 3 April onwards.

The law relating to electoral registers states that the register to be used for a general election is the one which is in operation 'on the date of the publication in the *Gazette* of a Proclamation or Notice by the Governor-General ordering the holding of a general election'. The register in operation was that of 1968 which had been duly certified on 27 April 1969. Work on the annual revision of the 1969 electoral register had not been completed at the time of the dissolution of Parliament. Accordingly, the 1968 electoral register was used for the 1970 general election. There were 5,505,028 persons[30] registered as voters for this election, an increase of 794,141 voters (believed to be mostly in the teenage group) when compared with the 4,710,887 voters[31] in the May 1964 electoral register which had been used for the general election, immediately preceding, in March 1965.

Polling stations

To ensure maximum voter participation at the polls, the Commissioner had to arrange for as many polling booths as possible in 144 electoral districts (Welimada electoral district was excluded as it had returned its member uncontested) within walking distance of the voter (see Tables 8 and 9). Polling stations had to be within walking distance in view of the existing ban on the use of private transport for the conveyance of voters to and from the polls. The law permits only the use of *public* transport, but allows exemptions to the physically disabled who are given special permits for the use of vehicular transport on production of a certificate from an authorised medical practitioner.

At the general election of 27 May 1970, provision was made for 5,613 polling stations, inclusive of 154 polling stations specially for females but exclusive of any polling stations for the uncontested Welimada electoral district, with an average of 977 electors to a polling station. These were approximately within two miles walking distance of a voter. At the general election of March 1965, there were 4,771 polling stations (exclusive of any for the uncontested two-member electoral district of Colombo South), inclusive of 147 for female voters, with an average of 975 voters per polling station.

Under the law, each of the electoral districts has to be divided into convenient polling districts of not more than 1,500 electors, unless the Commissioner of Parliamentary Elections directs otherwise. Further, under the law, there cannot be more than one polling station for a polling district unless the Returning Officer of the district considers that special circumstances require a separate polling station for the female voters of a polling district.

It was the view of the Commissioner of Parliamentary Elections that 'the increase in the number of polling stations and the attempt to make voting areas small and more convenient to the voters had its effect on the resultant poll'.[32] Account must however also be taken of the effect that the various issues had on the electors and the impact of party leaders and party propaganda on the electorate as factors influencing voting. Nevertheless the reason advanced by the Commissioner was an important factor. In May 1970, 4,672,656 voters went to the polls, representing an 85.2 per cent turn-out. In March 1965, 3,821,918 voters went to the polls, an 82.1 per cent turn-out.

Poll cards

The preparation of official poll cards was a third major pre-election responsibility of the Department of Elections. The practice started with the general

Table 8. *Electorate, voter participation, and candidates at the general elections of March and July 1960, 1965 and 1970*

General election	Electorate	Turn-out of voters at polls	Number of postal voters	Turn-out as a percentage	Number of party candidates	Number of Independent candidates
March 1960	3,724,507	2,889,282	18,246	77.6	732	167
July 1960	3,724,507	2,827,075	26,665	75.9	344	49
1965	4,710,887[a]	3,821,918	34,000	82.1	389	106
1970	5,505,028[b]	4,672,656	81,754	85.2	305	136

SOURCE: The statistics provided in Tables 8 and 9 have been computed from the Reports of the Commissioner of Elections for the Parliamentary General Elections of 19 March and 20 July 1960, the Sixth Parliamentary General Election and the Seventh Parliamentary General Election.
[a]Inclusive of the two-member electoral district of Colombo South which returned both its members uncontested.
[b]Inclusive of Welimada electoral district which returned its member uncontested.

Table 9. *Polling districts, polling stations and state expenditure at the general elections of March and July 1960, 1965 and 1970*

General election	Number of polling districts	Number of polling stations[c]	Average number of voters per polling station[f]	Total cost of general election (Rs.)	Cost to the state as per voter[h] (Rs.)
March 1960	3,532	3,659	1,018	3,994,148.30	1.07
July 1960	3,532	3,664	1,017	—[g]	—[g]
1965	4,647[a]	4,771[d]	975	5,436,140.30	1.21
1970	5,485[b]	5,613[e]	977	8,444,541.00	1.53

SOURCE: See Table 8.
[a]Including the two-member electoral district of Colombo South which returned both its members uncontested.
[b]Including the electoral district of Welimada which returned its member uncontested.
[c]The figures are inclusive of polling stations especially assigned for females.
[d]Excluding the two-member electoral district of Colombo South.
[e]Excluding the electoral district of Welimada.
[f]The average number of voters per polling station given here is a general average. In densely populated areas like Colombo City where it would have been possible to accommodate a larger number of voters per polling station without inconvenience to the voting public, a higher number per polling station was arranged.
[g]No breakdown for the July 1960 general election is possible as the Commissioner has stated that the expenditure for this election was met from each Department's votes – in view of the fact that the election came so soon after the previous general election held some four months earlier, on 19 March 1960.
[h]The increase in cost per voter to the state is not only due to the increase in size of the voting population and general increase in costs over the years, but also because other items of expenditure which used to be borne by the candidates, such as the issue of poll cards, became the responsibility of the state from the general election of March 1960. Further, the ban on the use of private transport necessitated an increase in polling stations, which meant the use of more personnel to conduct the polls, with its attendant increase of expenditure to the state.

election of March 1960 in accordance with an amendment effected in the law relating to parliamentary elections in 1959.[33] Such cards, it was felt, would provide the voter with most of the information he would require to cast his vote, viz. the name and number of his electorate, how his name, qualifying address and registration number appear in the register, his polling district, the polling station allotted to him and the date and hours of the poll – which are from 8 a.m. to 5 p.m.

By 4 May 1970, 5,399,770 poll cards were written and checked and made ready for dispatch; of these 5,186,403 were delivered by the postal authorities during the period 4 to 9 May 1970. All undelivered poll cards were kept at the relevant post offices till the day of the poll for any voter who had not received his card to call in and claim it.

Other tasks

The Department had to ensure the printing (which was done by the Government Printer), dispatch, and security of over $5\frac{1}{2}$ million ballot papers. The Department had further to have indelible ink ready for marking each voter's little finger of the left hand on polling day before the issue of the ballot paper to him. In addition to all this, the Department had to organise and issue instructions to 56,690 officers whose services it enlisted for polling station duties, and for the count.

Nomination formalities

The formalities connected with nomination day were just as onerous. There was the important task of the Commissioner having to grant recognition to political parties so that they might avail themselves of the concessionary deposit of Rs. 250 for each of their official candidates, instead of a deposit of Rs. 1,000.

The Commissioner was also charged with the responsibility of assigning symbols to the various parties and to Independent candidates. The law had been formulated in such a way as to minimise his burden, but he had still to exercise a margin of discretion judiciously and with caution.

The law relating to recognition of parties was simplified by the amending legislation of 1970. It said that those parties recognised at the general election immediately preceding stood automatically recognised for the succeeding general election. They could also claim the symbol assigned previously to them. They were required to inform the Commissioner within seven days of the dissolution of Parliament of their intention to contest at the general election. Seven of the nine political parties which had contested the previous general election of March 1965 informed the Commissioner of their intention to contest, and were granted recognition accordingly.

In regard to new parties applying for recognition, the Commissioner was required by law to apply two criteria (referred to earlier), in the first of which –

recognition of a political party – he had discretionary authority. The law did not, as the Commissioner remarked, define what constituted 'political activity for a continuous period of five years' or the tests that should be applied to determine whether a party had in fact been engaged continuously in political activity for the five-year period. Fifteen applications for recognition on this count were received by the Commissioner and they were all rejected.

The grounds on which these parties made their claim were an application simply on headed notepaper, evidence of a paid advertisement in a newspaper (which may have appeared any time during the five-year period) about the party or its constitution, press accounts of the activities of the party, and other such insubstantial assertions. On the other hand, the Commissioner's own criteria were, first, availability of proper books of membership showing the size and support that a party had in the five years preceding in various parts of the country, secondly, proper books of accounts and evidence of financial support, or, thirdly, proof of contesting elections to local bodies in the preceding five years.[34] No application for recognition was made in terms of the second criterion.

The procedure in regard to submission of nomination papers was also altered slightly by the amending legislation of 1970. The hour of nomination was changed. Instead of from 12 noon to 1 p.m., it was now to be from 10 a.m. to 11 a.m., with time for objections being allowed up to 11:30 a.m. The number of nomination papers a candidate was required to submit was reduced from six to three.

In addition to the existing four grounds for filing objections, a fifth ground was also introduced, viz. conviction for a corrupt or illegal practice, or by reason of the report of an election judge made in accordance with the law for the time being in force relating to the election of Members of Parliament.

The decision in regard to an objection on this new ground was not left for determination by a Returning Officer. He was required to refer the matter to the Supreme Court which, in order not to hold up election proceedings, was obliged to give its decision within ten days of such reference. No objections, however, were made to the nomination of any candidate on this ground on nomination day.

Of the 441 candidates who submitted nomination papers on 23 April 1970, 305 were from political parties and 136 from Independent candidates. In the case of the Welimada seat, the SLFP candidate filed an objection that his UNP rival had not consented to his nomination papers either by an annex or by an endorsement on any of the sets of nomination submitted by him. The Returning Officer upheld the objection and the SLFP candidate, R. M. Bandara, was accordingly returned uncontested on nomination day.

Election day – 27 May

Despite the rumours of subversion and threats of sabotage, election day itself passed off without incident. Unlike in the previous general election (March

1965), the armed forces (excluding officers) were not called upon to assist the police to maintain law and order. The police themselves maintained order. An important reason for the orderly election was the ban imposed by the law on the display of flags, banners and posters. In addition, the curbs on the use of transport except for legitimate purposes, and the ban on processions till the day immediately following the announcement of results, helped to control, if not inhibit, the enthusiasm of boisterous elements on election day and the day after. But supporters of the winning coalition were involved in sporadic outbursts of violence immediately prior to and a few days after the new Government took office.

Polling commenced at 8 a.m. and ended at 5 p.m. in accordance with the law. Though election day was not declared a public holiday, most employers in the private sector closed their offices early, if not for the whole day. The law in addition requires an employer to grant leave of not less than four hours' duration with full pay to an employee who makes a written application to him for such leave for the purpose of casting his vote.

The procedure for counting is rather elaborate and takes some 10 to 12 hours from the time the actual count begins. This excludes any recounts that a Returning Officer or a candidate might call for.

Conclusion

The changes in election procedures and laws had their greatest impact at the general election of May 1970. These had been effected in instalments from the advent of the MEP government of 1956. Their main purpose was to ensure opportunities for parties which were not as well financed as the UNP to mobilise their vote. At the same time, they sought to eliminate capricious parties and Independent candidates. Both objectives were achieved at the general election of May 1970. The number of parties contesting was considerably reduced and the contest mainly confined to two rival coalitions in the Sinhalese areas, and similarly to two opposing parties in the Tamil areas. The large poll was made possible because of the increase in polling stations, the excellent arrangements with regard to public transport, but above all because of the importance or seriousness of the issues involved.

5. The candidates

The background

Candidates for the May 1970 election were chosen by the rival parties with their eyes on the issues involved. The question of financial resources was not a seriously inhibiting factor in view of the democratisation of election procedures referred to in the previous chapter. What mattered was that candidates contesting for the first time had to be selected not on the basis of wealth or feudal influence but on the extent to which they could identify themselves with the ordinary mass of voters. The UNP seemed more sensitive to this need than the SLFP and its allies. Nonetheless, the nominees of both groupings tended to be drawn from the lower rather than the middle and upper layers of society. However, those of the Ceylon Tamil political groupings came from the established sectors.

The parties in their social and economic composition are a mixed lot. None of them is essentially of a monolithic class composition despite the fact that the two chief rival contenders uphold defined and opposing programmes and policies. There is mobility between the parties, but more from the SLFP to the UNP than the other way.

The UNP has come to be associated with the privileged and possessing classes who by circumstance feel obliged to make concessions of varying measure to placate the poorer sections of the community. The SLFP on the other hand claims to be the party of the 'have-nots', and though its top leadership economically and socially speaking may be no different from that of the UNP, it is nevertheless argued that that leadership believes in a fair deal for the common man. These opposing viewpoints have become veritable axioms in political debate today, so much so that UNP policy-makers have endeavoured, especially since 1956, to erase the image that they are a party of the vested interests. The impression nevertheless remains.

The social and economic backgrounds of the candidates of the minor parties – the LSSP, CP, FP, TC – are percentage-wise more elitist than those of the UNP or SLFP. The Left-wing leadership has generally come from among middle-class intellectuals and seldom percolated to the lower social strata, except at the managerial levels in the trade union movement. The Ceylon Tamil parties have always had their leadership concentrated among the professionally and commercially successful Tamils in Colombo, though those at the top now tend to foster a more localised leadership at urban if not provincial levels (in the Northern and Eastern provinces), obviously to avoid the charge that politics and decision-making are Colombo-oriented.

Selection procedures

Parliamentary candidates were selected by nomination boards comprising senior leaders set up by the various parties. In the case of the UF, the additional question of how many seats should be allocated to the two Left-wing parties was decided by Mrs Bandaranaike in consultation with the LSSP and CP leaders.[1] At a press conference of Opposition newspapers and journals, Mrs Bandaranaike said that the deciding factor in the selection of candidates was which party could, in the circumstances, win a seat. There was also opposition from some quarters in the SLFP to 'too many seats' being conceded to the Left. But this was in the end amicably resolved. The claims of the ISF, the Muslim wing of the SLFP, were also given the greatest consideration. The ISF secured 12 nominations for its members on the SLFP ticket, but there was some resistance from the CP to the nomination of an ISF candidate for the three-member constituency of Colombo Central. The CP feared that its own candidate's position might be jeopardised by the UF vote being split between the CP and ISF nominees. The SLFP could not on the other hand refrain from nominating a Muslim for Colombo Central, for this constituency had always returned one if not two Muslim representatives to Parliament. Colombo Central has a sizeable Muslim population. The obvious charge that the SLFP had sacrificed the Muslim interest for a communist would have been levelled by the UNP, especially by the UNP's Muslim stalwarts.

Officially the UF explained its decision on the ground that it saw no reason why it could not win two of the three seats 'going on the present political trend'.[2] Further, it was argued that if the UNP was putting forward two candidates for Colombo Central, why should not the UF.[3]

The UNP, MEP, TC and FP nomination boards had fewer problems to resolve. The UNP leader, Dudley Senanayake, had an important say in the nomination of candidates. Senanayake persuaded a university professor and a number of public servants (the latter had to retire to contest) to contest seats. The UNP's deputy leader, J. R. Jayawardene, was in charge of the selection of candidates in the Southern province. This province was the UNP's weakest outpost, and selections therefore had to be made with a great deal of care and circumspection.

Factors in the selection of candidates

All the parties preferred, with few exceptions, to re-nominate their sitting members unless of course the latter did not, of their own accord, wish to re-contest. One party leader told us that he was fairly certain that a senior man (sitting member) in his party would lose, but that his party's nomination board would continue to nominate him 'for as long as he would wish to contest a seat'. Some sitting members switched constituencies with party approval; outstanding examples were that of a UNP minister not secure in the seat he held and therefore transferred to a Kandyan Sinhalese constituency (where he lost) and an FP sitting member who left a safe seat to ensure the defeat of the party's rebel leader in another constituency. He succeeded in the operation. In the process, however, the party lost the safe seat, as the seat proved 'safe' only to the sitting member who forsook it.

All parties also showed a preference to re-nominate candidates who had contested and lost in the previous general election, or in an earlier election.

Again, it depended on whether the candidate himself wished to re-contest. A number of such candidates did not want to go through the expense – physical, mental, and financial – of fighting another election.

Sitting members and former candidates were preferred to newcomers because, our investigations indicate, it is they who build up the constituency organisations and develop contacts during the intervening period between elections. They were 'the bosses' of the local party machine in the area concerned. Our inquiries revealed that local party organisations, unless they had strong reasons, preferred those whom they already knew. Where an outsider was imposed by the party central office, a great deal of persuasion had to be done before the choice was accepted. Such outsiders were derogatorily referred to as 'parachutists'.

An instance of a party's slowness and reluctance to adopt a new candidate in preference to even an intractable sitting member who had actually rebelled was that of the SLFP in regard to the Gampaha seat. The sitting member, S. D. Bandaranayake, had been flirting with the Peking-wing CP whose nomination for this seat he eventually accepted. Mrs Bandaranaike stated that even her party's 'usual electoral arrangements were temporarily stopped' to enable S. D. Bandaranayake to decide, but she added that he preferred to contest on his own policies.[4]

In the case of the SMP, a new party making its electoral debut, its leader, R. G. Senanayake, made the decisions on the selection of candidates. In a number of instances he relied on the telephone to persuade persons to contest on his party's ticket. Not much forethought went into the selection of candidates. The party was a hastily organised one-man operation. The majority of its 48 candidates were financed by its leader who even paid their election deposits of Rs. 1,000 per candidate. The party's application for the concessionary deposit of Rs. 250 for its candidates was turned down by the Commissioner of Parliamentary Elections.

Table 10 provides evidence of the preference of political parties for 'old stagers' to newcomers.

Table 10. *Party candidates – old stagers and newcomers, May 1970*

Candidates	UNP	SLFP	SMP	LSSP	FP	TC	CP	MEP	Indepen-dents[a]	Total
Contested previously	96	80	4	17	14	10	6	2	22	251
Newcomers	34	28	44	6	5	2	3	2	66	190
Total	130	108	48	23	19	12	9	4	88	441

NOTE: The UNP contested 116 seats at the general election of 1965 and won 66; the SLFP contested 101 and won 41; the LSSP contested 25 and won 10; the FP contested 20 and won 14; the TC contested 15 and won 3; the CP contested 9 and won 4; and the MEP contested 61 and won 1. The SMP was a new party making its first appearance at the general election. It contested 49 seats, one of its candidates contesting 2 seats.

[a]Among the 88 Independent candidates are included the 7 candidates of the newly formed Tamil Self-Rule Party and the lone candidates of the Peking-wing CP and the Tamil Resistance Front. One Independent candidate contested 2 seats.

In their selection of new candidates, the UNP, SLFP and FP followed similar patterns. A delegation comprising representatives from the central headquarters of the party and the local organisation toured the constituencies concerned, talked to the leaders in the area, discussed with them and the branch organisations the claims of prospective candidates, and reported back to the nominations board. The latter usually accepted their recommendations. In the case of the UNP, the party's zonal leaders had an important voice in the deliberations of the delegations engaged in the search for candidates.

The SLFP's two Left-wing collaborators, the LSSP and CP, did not have to go through such elaborate procedures owing to the limited number of seats made available to them within the broader UF. Besides, the developed nature of their organisational network made it obvious who the candidate should be, once the seat was awarded to them. The MEP had to decide only in respect of two seats, and its leader, Philip Gunawardena, made the selections. As the TC nominations board had only to make decisions on two new candidates, it did not go through the detailed investigation of claims that bigger parties were burdened with.

It is sometimes tempting to try and establish that religion and caste are decisive factors in selection of candidates. But these were marginal to selection and came into play only when a difficult decision had to be made. The ethnic, social and religious composition of the majority of the 145 electoral districts had already been determined at the time of demarcation. Our investigations indicate that seldom did a man who is in a minority caste or a minority religious faith in his electorate apply for party nomination, because the obstacles to surmount are simply too numerous. Party nomination boards did not therefore as a rule have to arbitrate on these matters. But nomination boards certainly had in mind the voter concentrations of minority or depressed castes, or of minority groups within an electoral district which were in a position to influence the electorate's decision. In selecting a candidate, they made sure in most cases that he was acceptable to such groups. There were instances where Roman Catholics and Protestants were nominated to contest overwhelmingly Buddhist electorates and vice versa, and where a Roman Catholic and a Protestant were nominated to overwhelmingly Hindu electorates, but the factors influencing such decisions had nothing to do with the religious beliefs of the persons involved. They were preferred for their national standing or because of their acceptance by their parties as senior leaders.

With constituencies contracting in size, the trend was for parties to prefer local men who had local standing and could command local influence. Table 11 shows that, by and large, with the exception of the two Marxist parties, the LSSP and CP, the other parties depended very much on members of local bodies for parliamentary candidates, the UNP to a greater extent than the SLFP. The LSSP and CP had the greater number of candidates among trade unionists, but many of the latter were part-time trade unionists engaged in other occupations and professions. Social workers and office holders in various societies and associations were next in importance in providing candidates for the parties.

Table 11. *Involvement of candidates in public life, May 1970*

	UNP	SLFP	SMP	LSSP	FP	TC	CP	MEP	Independents
Mayors and Deputy Mayors	13	2	—	2	1	—	—	—	—
Chairmen and Vice-Chairmen of other local bodies	31	34	2	5	4	3	1	—	5
Members of local bodies	17	13	9	3	1	1	3	1	3
Members and office holders in:									
Rural development societies	16	11	1	—	—	—	—	—	17
Cooperative societies	14	14	14	—	—	2	—	—	19
Other associations	8	6	10	7	12	6	1	—	15
Trade unionists	4	3	—	6	1	—	4	1	3
Social workers	27	25	12	—	—	—	—	2	26
Total	130	108	48	23	19	12	9	4	88

SOURCE: Prepared by the author from questionnaires submitted to candidates and from biographies of candidates published in the national dailies.

Most of these organisations were, again with few exceptions, intensely local in nature, rarely exceeding the boundaries of constituencies. Party nomination boards seldom went outside of a constituency to look for a candidate.

Professional, educational and social background

The professional and occupational background of candidates as shown in Table 12 indicate that the majority of the UNP's nominees, at least three out of four, belonged to the possessing class and the successful in society. Only sixteen of the UNP candidates could be described as poor, indigent or of moderate means. The UNP leadership was aware of how exposed it was on this count. Oft-times therefore in their campaign, they invited attention to their candidates being sons of masons, or school teachers, farmers or peons (office boys).[5] They insisted that the Prime Minister did not have to go into 'the family trees' of candidates and that in their ranks were young graduates who were 'village boys' and 'central school products'.[6] J. R. Jayawardene waxed eloquent on this theme in a number of his election meetings. He emphasised that the UNP was built on 'democratic ideals' and committed to 'the democratic way of life' and that is why 'we have put forward educated youngsters, even though they are from poor families, to contest the forthcoming general election.'[7]

It was the same with the Prime Minister. His attachment to his minister, R. Premadasa and I. M. R. A. Iriyagolle, and his personal interest in sponsoring the candidature of the university professor, W. S. Karunaratne, can be attributed

Table 12.   *Occupations of candidates, May 1970*

	UNP	SLFP	SMP	LSSP	FP	TC	CP	MEP	Independents
Landed proprietors and businessmen	74	43	22	6	3	2	1	2	41
Legal profession	13	15	3	8	9	8	2	—	15
Doctors	3	—	—	—	1	—	1	—	—
Native medical practitioners (*ayurvedic* practitioners)	2	2	6	—	1	—	—	—	2
Public servants of the middle and higher grades	10	7	5	1	4	—	—	—	—
Public servants of the lower grades	7	12	6	—	—	—	—	—	15
Private-sector employees of the higher grades	3	3	1	—	—	—	—	—	—
Private-sector employees of the lower grades	1	1	—	1	—	—	—	—	4
Full-time political workers	—	—	—	5	—	—	3	1	7
Teachers	15	22	4	2	1	2	2	—	4
Journalists	2	3	1	—	—	—	—	—	—
Wife	—	—	—	—	—	—	—	1	—
Total	130	108	48	23	19	12	9	4	88

SOURCE: Prepared by the author from questionnaires addressed to candidates, interviews with candidates and party leaders and from biographies of candidates published in the national dailies.

among other things (such as that they were excellent platform speakers) to their social origins being similar to those which were so characteristic of the SLFP's political cadres at the middle and lower levels.

Oddly enough what was true of the UNP's parliamentary milieu was also true of the UF's, though not to the same extent. Twelve of the 108 SLFP candidates belonged to the feudal establishment and were inter-connected by marriage or closer ties. Approximately two out of every three of the SLFP candidates either had interests similar to, or successfully practised the professions of, the better-off UNP candidates referred to. But the presence of those who had humble beginnings and were of moderate or less than moderate means, such as retired Sinhalese school teachers, lower-grade public servants and peasants was more conspicuous in the SLFP. A fair number were unsophisticated villagers who had never used a cheque book in their lives or even knew what a bank account was. But they found themselves at home in the SLFP because that was the ethos that prevailed in the social and political world of that party. Even the 'feudal lords' of the SLFP were mostly country squires who had seldom hobnobbed with the urbane and sophisticated of Colombo City. They still had to go the round of the cocktail circuits. It was more or less the same with the *swabasha*-type rich men and successful professional men in that party. The SLFP leadership had no need to tell the public how humble their party was or the number of sons of poor men whom they had put forward as candidates. In the world of politics, the SLFP had come to stand apart from both the UNP and the Left as the party of the un- sophisticated and underprivileged and of those sections of the rural intel- ligentsia striving for recognition.

Table 12 indicates that more than half the candidates of the two Left-wing partners of the SLFP belonged to the same social and economic upper layers to be found in the UNP and the SLFP, but again there was a difference. The Left wing had been stamped with the image of being of the working class. Thus though there were affluence and bourgeois professional skills in their parties, to the committed public they were no more than the advocates of workers' rights and Marxist ideologies.

The legal profession was strongly represented in both the Ceylon Tamil parties, 9 out of the 23 FP candidates and 8 out of the 12 TC candidates. Since the 1940s, it has been the legal profession, with the exception of a doctor, that has provided leadership to the Ceylon Tamils. This explains the belief in con- stitutional devices on the part of the Ceylon Tamils as a panacea to all their political and economic ills. The sober staid middle classes among the Ceylon Tamils value success in the professions and the public service as the hallmark of achievement more than any wealth amassed through sallies into the world of commerce, agriculture or industry.

As Tables 13 and 14 confirm, political leadership in Ceylon still emerges from the elitist layers of Ceylonese society. This is true of all the parties. With the exception of the SLFP, between one-third and two-thirds of the candidates of all the other parties had a university education or some professional training. This is especially so in the case of the LSSP and CP and the two Tamil parties. The balance is redressed, however, lower down the scale (trained teachers, secondary education) in the case of the SLFP (Table 13).

A glance at Table 14 re-confirms and reinforces our conclusion that political

Table 13.   *Educational background of candidates, May 1970*

	UNP	SLFP	SMP	LSSP	FP	TC	CP	MEP	Independents
University and professional[a]	46	28	19	15	15	10	5	1	23
Persons trained as school teachers	15	22	4	2	1	2	2	—	4
Secondary education	69	57	25	6	3	—	2	3	61
Primary education	—	—	—	—	—	—	—	—	—
No education	—	1	—	—	—	—	—	—	—
Total	130	108	48	23	19	12	9	4	88

[a]Diploma holders in special subjects obtained in a university or a professional school and qualified native physicians (*ayurvedic* practitioners) have been included in the category of 'professional'.

Table 14.   *Candidates from the better schools and other schools, May 1970*

	UNP	SLFP	SMP	LSSP	FP	TC	CP	MEP	Independents
Top-grade collegiate	62	48	12	14	9	3	3	3	33
Other collegiate	68	59	36	9	10	9	6	1	55
No education	—	1	—	—	—	—	—	—	—
Total	130	108	48	23	19	12	9	4	88

leadership in Ceylon is still confined to the well educated – those who have had a good education in the better or exclusive secondary schools. A little less than half the UNP candidates and more than half the number of LSSP candidates had their secondary schooling in the more exclusive institutions, but the SLFP is not far behind with 48 of their 106 candidates having enjoyed the same privilege.

Age

The age composition of candidates in 1970 (Table 15) indicates that the majority of candidates from all parties came from the 40–59 age category. In fact, in the age group 40–49 and 50–59, there is hardly any difference between candidates in the two major parties. The 21–29 group did not provide as many candidates as would have been expected, especially when one bears in mind the fact of the 18-year-olds being included in the electoral registers.

Independent candidates

Every election as Table 16 shows has produced its quota of Independent candidates, but, judging from the numbers returned, they are increasingly being disfavoured by the electors. Besides, Independent candidates do not always come forward with a view to winning an election. Some are deliberately put forward to divide an opponent's vote or to confuse the electorate. Others come forward to make themselves known and referred to in the press and on platforms. While still others have been known to be not quite normal.

Table 15.   *Age composition of candidates, May 1970*

Age	UNP	SLFP	SMP	LSSP	FP	TC	CP	MEP	Independents	Total
20–29 years	3	2	4	—	—	—	—	—	7	16
30–39	21	8	14	6	3	1	2	1	16	72
40–49	46	47	26	9	5	5	2	1	21	162
50–59	40	37	4	4	7	5	3	1	30	131
Over 60	15	8	—	4	3	1	2	1	3	37
Information not available	5	6	—	—	1	—	—	—	11	23
Total	130	108	48	23	19	12	9	4	88	441

Table 16.   *Independent candidates at general elections, 1947–70*

General election	Total number of candidates	Independent candidates[a]	Percentage of Independents to the total to the nearest unit	Seats won
1947	360	181	50	21
1952	303	85	28	11
1956	249	64	25	8
March 1960	899	167	19	7
July 1960	393	49	12	7
March 1965	495	96	19	6
1970	441	88	20	2

[a]The figures for the number of Independent candidates given in the Reports of the Commissioner of Parliamentary Elections can be misleading. We have arrived at the figures after checking the individual candidates who stood for election at the various elections. For instance, the *Report on the Sixth Parliamentary General Election of Ceylon* (p. 30) states 106 Independents stood for election, whereas our figure is 96. The *Report* has included in the figure 106, the candidates of the LSSP (Revolutionary) 4, the United Left Front 2, the Ceylon Tamil United Front 2, and the CP-Peking 2. The *Report* for the Seventh General Election lists the number of Independent candidates at 136 (p. 57), including in it the 48 SMP candidates. Our figure is 88 as we have excluded the 48 SMP candidates.

Our investigations regarding the Independent candidates reveal that their economic and educational background is not very different from the candidates of the political parties. But there is a gap in the political and social experience of candidates of political parties and Independent candidates (see Table 11). The latter have been more active as social workers and members of rural development or cooperative societies, but have not had much experience of membership or office in local bodies. The parties, however, by and large, prefer to draw their nominees from members of local bodies. Some of the candidates who were rejected by the parties for lack of this qualification, among other things, came forward as Independents. This is one more reason for the continued presence of Independent candidates at elections.

Key contests

Public attention was focused on a number of key electorates in both the Sinhalese and Ceylon Tamil areas. In the former, the spotlight was on the Prime Minister's constituency (Dedigama), Mrs Bandaranaike's (Attanagalla), and N. M. Perera's (Yatiyantota). However, contests were also sharp in almost all the constituencies where UNP ministers were involved. The exceptions to the latter were J. R. Jayawardene who was secure in the very middle-class two-member constituency of Colombo South and R. Premadasa who had established firm roots in the three-member Colombo Central seat as its second representative. Premadasa was eager to get close to the top in the UNP's power structure and therefore devoted much of his time to ensuring that he became his constituency's first representative, an exercise in which he eventually succeeded. He had however also to discharge the onerous task of zonal leader of the province of Sabaragamuwa.

The issue in Dedigama was in doubt. The Prime Minister in the previous two general elections had had a rough time. His rival on this occasion was Dharmasiri Senanayake, a younger brother of the person who had contested against him on the previous two occasions. Sections of the Buddhist clergy supported the Prime Minister's rival who also claimed that he had the goodwill of the youth voters. Hema Basnayake visited the Dedigama electorate once. He had his particular brand of anti-UNP literature (dangers facing the Sinhalese Buddhists and the woes of the peasantry) distributed there and he wrote to the leading Buddhist monks of Dedigama constituency concerning the need for them to work hard to oust the Prime Minister.

The importance of the contest in Dedigama was evidenced by the fact that the Prime Minister's brother, Robert Senanayake, took a direct and personal interest in the organisation of the campaign there, and in the Prime Minister's presence in the constituency time and again. In his addresses to his constituents, he dwelt sentimentally on such trivial matters as his supporters having nurtured him from the time he was 'a mere youth of 24' when he was returned as its member, and the presence of friends at his meetings who had grown old with him through the years. Also, he spoke of the roads, bridges, schools and factories he had been responsible for putting up in the constituency. These were trifling matters for a man with a national standing and charisma to harp about but they were indicative of the weakness of Senanayake's position in this particular constituency.

Mrs Bandaranaike faced a very energetic and persistent rival in J. R. P. Suriyapperuma, whose speeches against her stewardship of her constituency made frequent headlines in the pro-UNP national press. Suriyapperuma claimed that he was fighting a campaign against 'a 28,000 acre coconut empire owned by five related feudal families led by Mrs Bandaranaike' in the Attanagalla constituency. He made trenchant attacks against the 'neglect' of the constituency – the absence of proper educational facilities and landlessness among the peasantry. Suriyapperuma had as his principal election lieutenants two former clerks who had been employed in Mrs Bandaranaike's estates. He preferred to lead a one-man operation himself, rejecting offers of help from UNP stalwarts. This was deliberately done with a view to gaining sympathy for a David battling against a veritable Goliath.

The issue was never in doubt in Mrs Bandaranaike's constituency, but Suriyapperuma proved to be of nuisance value, compelling her to organise her forces in Attanagalla. Her son, Anura, played a leading role in the campaign and addressed several meetings there. Though Suriyapperuma tried to heap ridicule on him, Anura Bandaranaike was taken more seriously by the electors of Attanagalla.

N. M. Perera fought a hard battle in Yatiyantota against an experienced campaigner, George Kotelawala. N. M. Perera had in previous elections followed the practice of addressing small intimate meetings in the villages of his constituency instead of involving himself in a house-to-house campaign of canvassing for votes. On this occasion, however, there were a number of areas in this constituency where such canvassing had to be done. His rival alleged that he had done nothing for his electors. They had not been provided with proper schools, roads, dispensaries, etc. To this Dr Perera replied that the people of Yatiyantota elected him to Parliament 'to fight for the liberation of the oppressed masses', not to build culverts. The pro-UNP national press unduly exaggerated Dr Perera's difficulties in Yatiyantota.

In the Tamil-speaking areas, the most keenly fought contests were in Jaffna and Kankesanturai in the Northern province and Trincomalee and Paddiruppu in the Eastern province.

In Jaffna, G. G. Ponnambalam, the TC leader, had to defend his seat (unsuccessfully) against the FP contender, C. X. Martyn (the winner) who in addition to the party vote also had the support of sections of the Roman Catholics (Martyn is a Roman Catholic) and against a former victor, Alfred Durayappah, who had SLFP backing, a fair measure of Muslim support, and local influence especially as he had been mayor of the municipality of Jaffna on a number of occasions. An important reason for Ponnambalam's defeat was that he had not visited his constituency as often as was expected of him. Durayappah's standing among the Muslims prevented Ponnambalam from obtaining much support from among them despite the good offices of his Muslim friends in the UNP. His other rival, Martyn, made inroads into the Catholic vote, a sizeable section of which he used to obtain through his powerful friends in the Roman Catholic Church in Jaffna. Leading members of the UNP also failed to show up on TC platforms in the Jaffna constituency. They could have helped him gather more votes, especially if the Prime Minister had recommended him to the electors and said that he would definitely include him in his next Cabinet. Apparently, the UNP was not too anxious to get embroiled in the FP-TC tussle in the Tamil areas, because the UNP hoped to negotiate for FP support in the event of the party not gaining an absolute majority of the seats in Parliament.

In Kankesanturai constituency, the FP leader, S. J. V. Chelvanayakam, had a section of the caste Hindus against him led by a former pro-UNP minister, C. Suntheralingam, who now headed a social extremist high caste *Saiva vellala* (Saivaite Hindu cultivator) faction, and strong opposition from the CP candidate, V. Ponnambalam, who had established himself in the electorate and had a hold over sections of radical youth and of the depressed castes there. Suntheralingam was splitting Chelvanayakam's Hindu vote. The FP had campaigned for temple entry for the depressed castes, and orthodox Hindu opinion which disapproved of temple entry ranged itself on the side of Suntheralingam. There was also a TC candidate, but he did not make any impression. Chelvanayakam won in the end, though with a reduced majority.

Trincomalee, because of its international reputation for its naval and harbour facilities and its position as a central city for the Tamil areas of the northern and eastern parts of Ceylon, is of 'strategic' importance to the FP. Further, the Tamils of Trincomalee regard the constituency as a Tamil constituency (it is

50.1 per cent Ceylon Tamil) but it has in the past ten years attracted many Sinhalese from the Kandyan areas and from the south (21.7 per cent Sinhalese). There is also a strong Muslim concentration (13.7 per cent) in Trincomalee. The seat can therefore be 'lost' to the Sinhalese or Muslims at any time, if the Tamils do not unite in supporting a strong Tamil candidate. So ran the Tamil argument. The FP since the general election of 1952 always provided the constituency with such a candidate. On this occasion the contest was in sharper focus because the SMP leader, R. G. Senanayake, was also making a bid for the seat, though it was widely known that he did not have a chance. But his presence helped to coalesce Tamil support for the FP candidate. The UNP candidate, who was also a Ceylon Tamil, as a result suffered some loss of Tamil support, while the Muslim and Sinhalese vote was split between the UNP, SLFP and SMP candidates. The FP candidate had therefore no difficulty in winning the seat.

Paddiruppu constituency attracted attention because it was the seat of the FP president, S. M. Rasamanickam, and Prime Minister Senanayake had boldly declared that his UNP candidate would win against the FP president. In the initial stages of the campaign, Senanayake had toured the constituency and urged support for S. U. Thambirasa, the UNP nominee. But in the latter stages, UNP secondliners feared that their party's majority in Parliament would not be absolute, that they would have to coalesce with the FP, and wished therefore to relax their efforts on behalf of their nominee. However, it was too late because, by then, Thambirasa's campaign had gained sufficient momentum to move on its own.

Rival caste groups in the Paddiruppu electorate are evenly balanced, the *mukuwars* and *karaiyars* (both fishermen) having a slight edge over the *vellalas*. Rasamanickam belonged to the *vellala* group while his rival was a *mukuwar* and a brother of a former M.P. (now deceased) who had defeated him in two earlier contests.

Some of the reasons for Rasamanickam's defeat were alleged neglect of his constituency, charges levelled against him by the *mukuwars* and *karaiyars* of discrimination against them in the distribution of benefits, and more importantly, from the party point of view, the defection of relatives and supporters to the UNP. They felt they stood a better chance of gaining preferment through a UNP M.P. than through a FP M.P. who would, if at all, be in a possible UNP government, in only an accessory capacity.

Constituency organisation and expenditure

The organisation of the campaign in each constituency was left very much in the hands of the local candidate who had to depend on his immediate circle of relatives, on friends and personal supporters as well as party sympathisers. These people helped in the house-to-house canvassing which is a vital component of the local campaign. Voters expect either the candidate, members of his immediate family circle, relatives, friends, or party supporters, in that order, to visit them and solicit their support. They would otherwise be offended. The electoral organisation comprised mainly local committees and party offices which were responsible for groups of voters or for a number of residences in the immediate locality.

Public meetings were the usual media of propaganda, great stress being laid on the visit of the party leader to the constituency. Pamphlets about the candidate and the record of his party as well as cartoons, posters and other related literature provided propaganda material. Except for the personal pamphlets about the candidate himself, most of the other literature was supplied by the party. Our investigations indicated that the SLFP's central supply channels were better organised and there was a regular flow of literature to branch offices. The UNP had an over-abundance of literature, but this did not reach their branch offices in as efficient a manner. A fair proportion of UNP election literature was left unused in their central headquarters.

Despite the many amendments to the election law introduced since 1959 which reduced considerably the expenses of a candidate, our investigations revealed that the candidate required a minimum of Rs. 15,000 to Rs. 25,000 to fight an election. There were a few exceptions where candidates had spent many times this amount. There were also many instances where wealthy supporters provided liquor and other kinds of inducements to attract support for the party candidate they preferred, and from whom they hoped to obtain rewards in some form or another, if he was successful. We do not suggest, however, that these forms of bribery determined the result. It was also a fairly common practice for party sympathisers in a village to construct the platform for the local election meeting and meet incidental expenses connected with it. For the rest, the candidate himself circulated lists to supporters in his constituency and to friends and relatives for contributions, and made up the balance from his own resources and a grant from his party's central headquarters. This grant was minimal or substantial, depending on the candidate's financial standing.

Under the law, a candidate is not permitted to exceed a sum of Rs. 8,000 or thereabouts for his election expenses. It must be classified under three separate items of expenditure each of which must not exceed a certain limit. Candidates are required by law to furnish the Commissioner of Parliamentary Elections with a statement of the expenses they incurred within a definite time limit after the election.

The returns to the Commissioner do not reflect the true picture, for the simple reason that, if this was done, the candidate would be guilty of an election offence. Nevertheless the returns furnished after the general election provided clues about the extent of expenditure incurred by the candidates of the leading parties. As can be seen in Table 17, the UNP candidates, excluding the MEP, headed the list, followed by the LSSP and the CP, with the SLFP coming fourth. We have not taken into consideration the MEP, whose candidates had incurred the highest expenditure, because there were only four of them, two of whom were husband and wife. The average expenditure incurred by the LSSP and CP candidates was also comparatively high. But this was because both parties had fewer candidates to devote their resources to.

Table 17.   *Election expenditure per candidate by parties, May 1970*

Party	No. of candidates	Expenditure per candidate (Rs.)
MEP	4	4,370
UNP	130	4,228
LSSP	23	4,118
CP	9	3,907
SLFP	108	3,802
TC	12	3,580
FP	20	3,357

SOURCE: *Report on the Seventh Parliamentary General Election in Ceylon, 27 May 1970 – Sessional Paper VII – 1971.*

Conclusion

Clearly from the selection procedures adopted, the party was more important than the candidate. This was indicated by the few candidates who contested as Independents. The number of Independents returned was the lowest in any general election. Candidates rejected by one party preferred to seek nomination from a rival party. The strength of the parties was increased by the charismatic personalities of the two main rival leaders, Senanayake and Mrs Bandaranaike. Candidates much preferred to have these leaders visit their constituencies and address meetings in the belief that this would have the necessary impact. The 1970 election thus provided proof of a two-party system entrenching itself, with candidates dependent more on the efficiency of the party label than on their own financial resources and local standing.

6. The course of the campaign

On the eve

Parliament was dissolved at midnight on 25 March 1970, but about five to six weeks before the dissolution all political parties were in the field putting across their points of view and in various ways endeavouring to discredit each other.

The probable time of dissolution was well known beforehand, because the Prime Minister was determined to continue through till the end of Parliament's term in order to claim for himself and his Government the credit of being the only administration since independence to have lasted its full term. 25 March was the fifth anniversary of Senanayake's assumption of office as Prime Minister.

Every Government previously had had to dissolve Parliament, in a way unexpectedly, before its term ended, for reasons beyond its control. The politically superstitious said that there was a hoodoo on Ceylon's independence, that the date which the Government of the time selected for the declaration of independence, 4 February 1948, had been inauspicious, and that this explained the reasons for Governments not having been able to complete their terms – a view reinforced by the unexpected deaths of two prime ministers, D. S. Senanayake (1947–52) and S. W. R. D. Bandaranaike (1956–9).

The Sinhalese areas

The principal contestants were the UNP and its two allies, the MEP (Gunawardena) and the TC, and Mrs Sirima Bandaranaike's UF. The pro-Sinhalese SMP led by R. G. Senanayake made very little impression.

Both rivals were eager to choose issues of immediate consequence long before the campaign actually began. The UNP was placed very much on the defensive. To many ordinary voters, its record was not very impressive. The party fared unsatisfactorily at the local government elections of December 1969. It lost its majorities in 10 of 36 local bodies and had its majorities reduced in 3 others. On the other hand, the number of local bodies with pro-UF majorities increased from 13 to 24, while in 3 others the pro-UF position improved markedly. A noteworthy feature of the local elections was the SLFP's (the chief constituent partner of the UF) gains, despite its rural orientations, in the urban areas, mostly at the expense of the UNP, and some Independents. Whether these gains and losses were successes or failures became controversial, each side interpreting the results to suit itself. But the odds were in favour of the UF. The UNP also believed that it had done well; as the Government it had incurred a certain degree of unpopularity and, despite the unemployment situation and soaring living costs, it had nevertheless maintained its position in some of the key towns.

Secondly, in the fifteen by-elections held in the course of the Government's five-year term, the UF had won in a majority of them. Once more, the Government had not fared as badly as expected. On the contrary it had improved its voting strength in some Opposition-held constituencies, and wrested one seat from the LSSP. It had been defeated in most of the by-elections, and UF spokesmen did not hesitate to exploit to the maximum these victories as growing evidence of the public's lack of confidence in the policies of the Senanayake Government. A sixteenth by-election was scheduled for 31 March in a seat held previously by the UNP (Ratnapura). The Government was reluctant to fight this by-election, for it was expected that the SLFP would win convincingly. Mrs Bandaranaike and her colleagues in the UF challenged the Prime Minister to hold the by-election before dissolving Parliament. Senanayake had no proper answer to give.

The third important issue was the agitation over the multi-purpose Mahaveli River Diversion Scheme. This was a grandiose plan envisaged by the Minister of Irrigation, Lands and Power, C. P. de Silva, the former SLFP rebel leader whose defection with thirteen others in December 1964 had brought about the parliamentary defeat of Mrs Bandaranaike's SLFP–LSSP government. The scheme was to cost Rs. 6,700 million, and provide for the cultivation of an additional 900,000 acres of land, an increase of about 75 per cent on the existing acreage of paddy land in the country. Not merely paddy but a number of other crops would be cultivated under the scheme. About 200,000 to 300,000 people were to be re-settled in the new areas which it was anticipated would provide employment for about one million persons. Power supply from the reservoirs and canal drops contemplated under the scheme were to be augmented to the extent of a generating capacity of 50.7 MW, representing an average annual output of power to the extent of 2,611 million kWh. The biggest power station in Ceylon (Laxapana) has an installed capacity of 50 MW but generates only 192 million kWh. The scheme would take thirty years to complete, the work being organised in three phases.

The Government's conduct in the timing of the Mahaveli Bill, the way in which it conducted the debate in Parliament, and the terms and conditions under which it obtained the loan from the IBRD and its sister organisation, the IDA, for the project exposed it to a many-sided attack from the Opposition. Mrs Bandaranaike alleged that the presentation of the bill at the end of Parliament's term, in February 1970, was nothing but an election gimmick intended to deceive the voters. In fact, at an election meeting in Akurana, Mrs Bandaranaike declared that she would filibuster the bill in the House, characterising it as a treacherous sell-out to the World Bank.[1] Her Trotskyist spokesman, Colvin R. de Silva, described the whole operation as 'one of the slickest pieces of drafting ever'.[2] N. M. Perera, the Trotskyist leader, urged that the project be placed before the people. 'It was unfair,' he said, 'to have it debated in the House in that manner on the eve of a general election.' Even the pro-Government national daily, the *Ceylon Daily News*, asked what need was there for the Government to hold up this debate 'until the very fag end of this Parliament's life'.[3]

The way in which the debate was conducted exposed the Government to more criticism. The Government showed unnecessary anxiety to have the bill rushed through Parliament in order to exploit the benefits during the election campaign. The Opposition waited for an opportunity to expose the Government's lack of parliamentary scruples and, when the debate was forcibly brought to a close, their leaders complained that not even their principal spokesman, Mrs Bandaranaike, had been allowed the opportunity to speak.[4] They dramatised their protest by walking out of the chamber at the time of voting. Minister C. P. de Silva, in a statement to the press, said that the time taken to debate the bill was equal to a month and a half of debating time under the standing orders of the House of Representatives.[5] Mrs Bandaranaike, he added, was present in the House on every day the bill was debated and could have spoken at any time if she expressed a desire to do so.

The terms and conditions agreed on by the Senanayake Government came under the severest criticism. The clause in the agreement with the World Bank providing for the levying of a water tax of Rs. 40 per acre on cultivators in the areas developed, instead of the existing nominal water rate of Rs. 2 per acre, gave the Opposition a great opportunity. The farmers of the North Central province, where the Mahaveli river was to be diverted under the scheme, would have been most affected. Maithripala Senanayake, as the SLFP leader in this province, launched a successful campaign against the UNP ministers from that province, C. P. de Silva and E. L. B. Hurulle, and against the UNP in general there.[6] Some of the replies from the Government side were adequate, but not effectively brought out.

The Prime Minister's credibility was further undermined when he denied at first in Parliament that any agreements with the credit agencies concerned had been concluded before the debate commenced. Later, when the necessary proof was provided by the Opposition, he had to admit that it was a lapse of memory on his part. The Opposition dubbed him the 'great liar' (*Pacha Bahu*), making it rhyme with the name of one of the greatest Sinhalese kings, Parakrama Bahu, who was also famous for constructing huge irrigation works. Parakrama Bahu was the name which admiring members of the UNP had conferred on the Prime Minister for his successes in his 'grow more food' campaign.

Economic issues such as the rice subsidy, unemployment, scarcity of consumer articles, problems of development, dominated throughout the campaign. The Prime Minister and his colleagues strove hard to avoid being put on the defensive. They boasted about the success of the food drive, the benefits that had accrued to the farmer, the availability of consumer goods and the absence of queues for essential commodities during their rule.

The most relevant question, however, concerned the rice subsidy. It was raised before the dissolution, but it gathered momentum in the weeks after dissolution, reaching its climax in the four-odd weeks after nomination day (23 April). Neither the Prime Minister nor his colleagues could provide convincing answers to the Opposition's claim that it could provide the second measure of rice at a subsidised price.

As early as 14 March, the Prime Minister raised the question of the rice cut at an election rally.[7] He said that, because of the forthcoming elections, the Opposition was trying to win over the electors by promising to restore the rice ration. He admitted that the cost of living had gone up, but then he said,

people had more money in their pockets than before to cope with a higher cost of living. Five or six years ago, you were not dressed as you are dressed now. You buy your clothes at higher prices than before. You have also bought yourself radios. You have bought many things you were not able to afford before. How was this possible? It was possible because you have more money in your pockets than ever before.

On 21 March, the Prime Minister asked the embarrassing question whether a UF Government headed by Mrs Bandaranaike intended giving both measures of rice free. If both measures were to be given on a subsidy, it was his contention that the farmer would be 'finished'.[8] On the same day, at a meeting in Anuradhapura in the North Central province, the Prime Minister outlined his fundamental political beliefs coupling Buddhism and its religious edifice, the *dagoba*, and the irrigation tank catering to man's material needs as the basis for progress and prosperity.[9]

Mrs Bandaranaike was rather terse in her reply to the Prime Minister's question as to how the UF proposed to restore the rice cut. At a propaganda rally in Colombo she stated that the UF had promised to give two measures of rice to the people 'because Lord Buddha himself had sympathy for the hungry'.[10] She added that they were not prepared to tell the Prime Minister how they would give these two measures of rice.

Other than Mrs Bandaranaike and her deputy, Maithripala Senanayake, the principal spokesmen for the SLFP on economic questions were T. B. Ilangaratne, one of the senior vice-presidents, and T. B. Subasinghe, the general-secretary. Ilangaratne deplored the ruin of the cooperative movement, and the system of people's and rural banks, at the hands of the UNP. These banks were helping the rich, not the local agriculturalists.[11] 'The UF was preparing a scheme to help the small trader, the small industrialist and the agricultural small holder, for it was', he stressed, 'in effect their front'.[12] Subasinghe for his part condemned the existing 'capitalist and imperialist framework' which he said should be replaced by a socialist set-up.[13]

P. B. G. Kalugalle, another senior vice-president of the SLFP, and Felix Dias Bandaranaike expatiated on the unemployment problem, particularly of the educated. Both claimed that the UF had plans ready to provide employment for all concerned.[14] Government spokesmen could not provide satisfactory explanations why they had failed to pay adequate attention to the unemployment question.

Sermons on democracy and constitutional government characterised the speeches of senior UNP politicians. The speeches of the Prime Minister and his deputy, J. R. Jayawardene, were replete with examples of the fate that had overtaken the democratic freedoms in communist countries. There were virulent attacks on the Marxists, who were accused of being saboteurs of the democratic processes. The Marxists were said to be enemies of religion and it was therefore the UNP's contention that both democracy and religion needed to be safeguarded.

Mrs Bandaranaike, on the other hand, protested that the Opposition had always conducted themselves correctly. They had not plotted against the Government nor indulged in unfair methods to capture power. They had never pressured members to cross the floor, as the UNP, she alleged, had done. They were truly democratic and depended on the vote of the people.[15]

Allied to the question of the survival of democracy was that of the national-isation of the press. The pro-Government *Ceylon Daily News* for its own safety sought to make an issue of it, but failed to get any unequivocal statement from the UF spokesmen as to what they proposed to do.

The UNP also tried to cite the prevailing atmosphere of communal harmony as a point in their favour. They claimed that they had achieved a measure of national unity. The Tamils had been reconciled. This was quite different from the inter-ethnic tensions and disturbances that were the feature in the period of the Bandaranaike Governments, from 1956 to 1965. Communal peace, they stressed, was indispensable for economic development.

The UF scoffed at the Prime Minister's claim that he had forged a measure of national unity. Mrs Bandaranaike asserted that 'secret pacts' could not achieve this objective. The UF's propaganda had alienated the Tamils, and they (the UF) were anxious to win the support of other minorities such as the Muslims and the Roman Catholics.

The Prime Minister himself came in for a great deal of personal attack because the UNP was placing too great an emphasis on his record and his personality to win the election for them. This was especially so because large numbers of electors were favourably impressed by the charismatic qualities of his leadership.

The Tamil-speaking areas

The main contest in the Ceylon Tamil areas was between the pro-UNP TC and the FP. Even the latter, it might be argued, would have had no alternative but to support the UNP, subject to certain conditions it would have laid down, had there been an inconclusive result in the Sinhalese south. The SLFP leaders had made it clear that they would not form a Government with the assistance of the FP. The UNP on the other hand was not averse to maintaining its contact with the FP. It believed that the FP could influence the Ceylon Tamil votes in the Sinhalese constituencies.

As the date of dissolution drew near, the issues were clarified by the rivals. There was no serious economic question that bothered either the TC or the FP. The main points of difference were concentrated on the attitude that should be adopted to the Sinhalese parties (as these rivals chose to call the SLFP and the UNP) and the steps that should be taken to preserve 'the Tamil race' and Tamil culture.

At a propaganda meeting in the constituency of the FP president, S. M.

Rasamanickam, Chelvanayakam warned the Tamil-speaking people of what he thought were two major dangers that faced them – colonisation of the traditional Tamil areas with Sinhalese people and Sinhalese being made the medium of instruction for Tamil-speaking children.[16] Chelvanayakam's view was that the Tamil-speaking people should be allowed to exist as a separate entity. At this same meeting Rasamanickam expressed the hopes of his own party when he said that the FP would be called upon to play an important role in the formation of the next Government and the Tamil people should therefore ensure that all of the nineteen candidates of the FP be elected at the forthcoming election. Rasamanickam hoped that his party would hold the balance and be in a position to extract the most favourable terms.

Rasamanickam endeavoured at this meeting also to draw the distinction between his party and the TC. They (the FP) would stand as 'one solid unit preserving their individuality even if they choose to support any political party to form the Government'.[17] The TC's campaign was directed towards the achievement of a united front of Tamil representatives but the FP was unresponsive.

Both the UNP and the SLFP also put forward candidates against the FP. Dudley Senanayake presented this as proof that there was no secret understanding between him and the FP.[18] The two Marxist partners of the SLFP also had their candidates contesting the FP and TC.

Dissolution and after

On dissolution day, both rival leaders issued statements about the Government's record in the five-year period.

The UF speaks

Mrs Bandaranaike issued a statement to the press on 25 March in which she made a scathing denunciation of the 'National Government's' record during the five years of its rule under Senanayake's leadership.[19] She characterised this 'National Government' as an 'odd collection of heterogeneous elements', comprising opportunists who had broken away from the previous Government (hers) for purely selfish reasons and Tamil Federalists with whom she accused Senanayake of entering into 'a secret agreement' thereby acting in 'flat contradiction' to the undertaking he had given the electors that he did not intend to form a coalition with anybody. The '21 promises' the UNP had made at the general election of 1965 will stand as a monument to its 'cynicism and opportunism'. The FP, sections of leading Buddhist clergy and laity who helped Senanayake, the Catholics as well as other minorities, had felt let down.

Mrs Bandaranaike characterised the Government's economic policies as ones which had resulted in its becoming dependent on international finance capital, imperialist economic agencies and international trade cartels. She condemned the food drive as providing opportunities for rich landowners, middlemen and agents of foreign companies dealing in agricultural equipment, not the peasant and the consumer. The 'free-for-all economic policies' of the Senanayake Government, she added, had led to inflation, high prices, and indebtedness. The Government further had failed to solve the problem of mass unemployment.

Mrs Bandaranaike warned that there were signs of Parliament and Cabinet being superseded by 'a small coterie of senior public servants who surrounded the Prime Minister'. This she interpreted as a threat to democratic institutions. 'The day is not far off', she added, 'when the top bureaucracy will nurture ambitions of playing an independent role, relieved of democratic checks and controls.' Encouraging them, she alleged, were foreign organisations with world-wide ramifications.

The Prime Minister replies

The Prime Minister summoned a press conference at his residence in Colombo on the morning of 27 March at which he reviewed the achievements of his administration over the past five years.[20] He stressed that he had been the instrument through which national unity had been forged; this had in turn generated economic development. The country had become 75 per cent self-sufficient and even industry had grown. Economic progress and internal stability had resulted in assistance from the World Bank and from the Aid Ceylon Consortium of friendly countries which had moved into action on the initiative of the World Bank. The Mahaveli scheme would solve many of Ceylon's economic problems.

Defending his economic policies, Senanayake said that a world shortage of rice and the consequent increase in the world price of rice led him to halve the ration. But the other half was given free and this happened nowhere else in the world. He claimed that devaluation and the *feec* scheme[21] had helped to diversify the economy, and minor crops were now paying. At the same time, devaluation had helped to save the tea industry in 1969 when there was a fall in prices.

The Prime Minister explained that the rise in the cost of living must be considered in terms of the people's capacity to pay. Farmers were now prosperous. Public servants had received pay increases amounting to Rs. 225 million. His Government had been the only one which had used the powers under the Public Security Act to compel employers in the private sector to pay wage increases to their employees.

The campaign proper: the contest in the Sinhalese areas

The election campaign can best be examined in its two phases: the period from dissolution to nomination day, which was fixed for 23 April, and thereafter from 23 April to election day, 27 May.

The first phase

On 29 March, the UNP inaugurated its election campaign at a mass rally in the location of a well-known Buddhist temple, the Abeysingharamaya, in Colombo City in the constituency of one of the Prime Minister's favourite colleagues, R. Premadasa.[22] Senanayake in his speech covered very much the same material that had been the theme of his speeches in the weeks before dissolution. R. Premadasa (Minister of Local Government), I. M. R. A. Iryagolle (Minister of Education) and W. S. Karunaratne (Professor of Buddhist Philosophy in the University of Ceylon), all favourites of the Prime Minister and often held up as 'men of the people' in the ranks of the UNP, were among those who addressed the rally, besides J. R. Jayawardene and Philip Gunawardena. The UNP followed this with a number of other meetings throughout the country in which they emphasised the main themes brought out in their inaugural rally.

A constant attack was exerted on the Marxists, whom the UNP leadership realised were 'the evil genius' behind Mrs Bandaranaike. It is doubtful whether these tirades had any effect on the electors.

The UF did not inaugurate its campaign in any formal manner. It concentrated on holding mass rallies in the provincial capitals and particularly in some key constituencies held by UNP ministers. Mrs Bandaranaike was the principal attraction in all these meetings.

A number of front organisations as well as leading personalities emerged to support the UNP or campaign against it. For the UF, the most prominent personalities were Hema Basnayake, former Chief Justice and an influential lay Buddhist who had supported the UNP at the general election of 1965 against the Marxists. Basnayake controlled an organisation of Buddhist monks, the Tri Nikaya Sangha Sabha (the Council of Buddhist Monks of the Three Sects) and a growing small farmers' front, the *govi peramuna*. While the Sabha questioned the Prime Minister's Sinhalese Buddhistic credentials and issued a communication clarifying its 15-point Sinhalese Buddhist-oriented programme for religious harmony, the *peramuna* sought to negate the claim that the food drive was a success.

A university professor, F. R. Jayasuriya, published two vitriolic longwinded denunciations of the Prime Minister's five-year term in the anti-UNP national daily the *Sun*.[23] In both, Jayasuriya dwelt on his usual theme – the danger posed to the Sinhalese language and Sinhalese race as a result of the Prime Minister's *rapprochement* with the Ceylon and Indian Tamil leaders, among other things.

The decision of the eldest son of Philip Gunawardena to identify himself with the CP was a surprise to the general public. Indika Gunawardena in a press release denounced the UNP's economic and foreign policies and declared he would devote his full time 'to the anti-imperialist and socialist movement as a member of the Ceylon Communist Party'.[24]

In the North Central province, P. L. Bauddhasara, one of the UNP's most influential stalwarts, defected to the Opposition, expressing disapproval of his party's policies. In the Southern province, W. D. S. Abeygunawardena, a former Mayor of Galle with some influence in the area, did the same thing after he had failed to get the UNP to resolve his differences with W. Dahanayake, usually a maverick in politics but now caught in the UNP net, and regarded as their southern leader. Then followed R. S. S. Gunawardena, a veteran UNP politician and a leading public figure for many years. In a statement to the *Sun*, he said that the UNP had failed to fulfil the promises it had given to the people and was incapable of setting up a socialist government.[25] Gunawardena campaigned for the UF in a number of electorates where he had influence arising from his caste origins.

For the UNP, much was made of the defections of Jack Kotelawala, the LSSP leader in the province of Uva who accepted the Prime Minister's offer of an ambassadorship in Moscow, of P. B. Wijesundera and Mrs Soma Wickremanayake, both former LSSP M.P.s, Percy Wickremasinghe and Stanley Mendis of the CP, and M. S. Themis of the SLFP. All of them, except Jack Kotelawala, appeared on UNP platforms and roundly condemned the Marxist parties as being anti-democratic and prone to totalitarianism.

Front organisations proliferated overnight, and electorally speaking they did a great deal for both contenders. Organisations of Buddhist monks were once again in the forefront. The powerful Sri Lanka Bhikku Bala Mandalaya (United Organisation of Buddhist Monks), led by three well-known Buddhist monks – the Venerable Henpitagedera Gnanasiha, the Venerable Medagoda Sumanatissa and Venerable Hewanpola Ratnasara – campaigned in almost all the Sinhalese areas on behalf of UF candidates. Their campaign was mostly to do with communal and religious questions. They made charges against the Prime Minister on the subject of religious harmony in a *prakashanaya* (statement) they issued. A Sri Lanka Bhikku Front also campaigned against the Government. One of its leaders, the Venerable Yatideriye Wajirabuddhi, an effective and popular speaker, appeared frequently on UF platforms. These monks confined their activities to addressing public meetings. They did not as a rule canvass from house to house as in 1956, when large numbers of Buddhist monks assisted S.W.R.D. Bandaranaike in toppling the UNP government of the Right Honourable Sir John Kotelawala.

The UNP too was assisted by organisations of monks of which the Maha Sangha Peramuna (the Front of Buddhist clergy) was the most noteworthy. The chief monks here were the wealthy *ayurvedic* physician, the Venerable Malewana Gnanissara, and the powerful orators, the Venerable Metiyagoda Gunaratne and the Venerable Devamottawe. The Venerable Rambukwelle Sri Sobhita, an influential and prominent monk of the Malwatte Chapter, spoke on UNP platforms in and around the city of Kandy.

Lay organisations were just as plentiful. The Sinhala Bauddha Sanvidhanaya (Sinhalese Buddhist Association) was formed 'to fight for the rights of the Sinhalese Buddhists' and campaign against the UNP.

University students and unemployed graduates played a very crucial role in canvassing support for UF candidates in many constituencies. All three parties of the UF had their own graduates' unions – the Graduates' Union (CP), Ceylon

Graduates' Union (LSSP) and the Sri Lanka Graduates' Union (SLFP), besides other independent unions. The leaders of these organisations addressed meetings at which they listed their grievances – mainly unemployment and lack of financial support in the form of bursaries and loans from the state-sponsored people's banks. Undergraduates from the universities also joined these graduates' unions for the purpose of the campaign. They played a key role in a number of important constituencies, especially Dedigama (against the Prime Minister), Kegalla (for P. B. G. Kalugalla who was the SLFP candidate here and was expected to be Minister of Education in a UF Government), Colombo Central (for Pieter Keuneman, general secretary of the CP), Minneriya (against C. P. de Silva) and Mirigama (against the UNP's Professor W. S. Karunaratne). These graduates and undergraduates also organised the election campaign in other constituencies as well, particularly in Yatinuwara, Udunuwara, Matale, Kandy, Senkadagala, Galagedara, Yatiyantota, Borella, Matara, Akuressa, Deniyaya, Mulkirigala, and Batticaloa.

Unemployed youths who had passed the General Certificate of Education also played a part, but they were not as organised as the graduates. A number of UF Members of Parliament reported that most of their propaganda apparatus was run for them by university students and unemployed graduates.

A group of well-known film personalities in the world of the Sinhalese cinema organising themselves as the Film Artists Guild (the Hela Nalu Nili Hawula) began to appear on coalition platforms from early April and denounce the Government's policies, especially in relation to the local film industry. At an election rally on 15 April, their leader, Dommie Jayawardene, accused the Prime Minister of meting out 'stepmotherly treatment' to them when they placed before him their 'reasonable demands'.[26] These film artists campaigned throughout the island. They demanded the banning of South Indian films, the implementation of the recommendations of the Film Commission appointed by the Senanayake Government, and the setting up of a Cinema Corporation. Mrs Bandaranaike promised to implement the report of the Film Commission. Another of the popular film stars in this guild, L. M. Perera, raised issues in a communal form. He accused the UNP Government of assisting the South Indian film industry, of giving jobs to the Ceylon Tamils and South Indians, and of being in league with the Tamil FP. The film artists drew large crowds, especially among young people who it was expected would be the deciding factor in the election.

The UNP film stars entered the campaign rather too late in the day to counter in any effective manner the propaganda of the UF film artists.

The three UF parties also had their *kantha peramunas* (women's fronts). Women from these organisations, mainly middle-class, both English- and Sinhalese-educated, spoke about the rising cost of living, the future of their children, absence of milk foods and difficulties in the admission of children to schools. They seldom raised communal slogans. The most effective *peramuna* was that of the CP, which provided instruction classes to the members of its *peramuna*, as well as to members of its graduates' union. Large numbers of women attended the *kantha peramuna* meetings; they made an especial impact in the Colombo constituencies.

The UNP too had a string of *kantha samithiyas* and *kantha balamandalayas* (women's organisations) working for it. It had the support of the powerful Lanka Mahila Samitiya, a middle-class women's organisation with branches throughout the country. Although this organisation did not officially canvass against the UF, most of its office bearers were well known for their UNP sympathies. Its president in fact actively campaigned for the UNP.[27]

Organisations of public servants also played an important role. The CP-sponsored Samastha Lanka Raja Lipikara Seva Sangamaya (All Island Government Clerical Workers' Union), led by Gunadasa Warnasuriya, alleged that the Official Language Act had been tampered with. It claimed that this was the finding of a team of investigators it had appointed to look into the working of the Act. The Rajya Bhasa Arakshaka Peramuna (the Front for the Protection of the State Language) said the same thing, besides attacking the circulars sent out by the Treasury on the implementation of the official language and the Tamil Regulations. The Sri Lanka National Teachers' Union with a membership of some 5,000 declared on 8 April that it would canvass support for the UF. A spokesman on its behalf said that they had no fears of post-election victimisation because they were certain of a UF victory.[28]

However, it was the Left-wing trade unions which went about their campaigning in a highly organised and efficient manner. This took the form of door-to-door canvassing and leaders addressing political meetings. The LSSP and CP candidates benefited most, but wherever possible the nominees of the SLFP were assisted as well.

The Marxist unions involved most were the General Clerical Service Union, the Public Services Trade Union Federation, the United Port Workers' Union and the Ceylon Federation of Labour. About 15,000 dockers from the port of Colombo were deployed by the Leftist parties on a programmed schedule to undertake canvassing. Further, each of the unions assigned a body of workers to as many electorates as possible in and around Colombo to address political meetings and canvass for votes. Directives on how the campaigning was to be conducted emanated from the executive committees and branch committees of each union. The powerful Public Services Trade Union Federation concentrated its efforts on behalf of the CP candidate for Colombo Central, Pieter Keuneman. It was the opinion of the leader of this federation, Piyadasa Adipola, that Keuneman's victory was necessary if the working class was to have proper representation in Parliament.

Neither the UNP trade unions nor those of its ally, the MEP, were activated in the way that the UF unions were. Their contribution to the election effort was therefore minimal. The UNP had a powerful trade union, the Jathika Sevaka Sangamaya (the National Services Union), which claimed a membership of 60,000 in the principal state corporations and the local government services. They also had the Rajya Seva (Government Services) trade union. Members of these unions expected the UNP Government to use its influence to settle labour disputes and other outstanding questions in their favour. They lacked the militancy or Marxist-or socialist-oriented motivations of members of the UF unions. The same was true of the MEP dock workers' union. The latter hoped for benefits from its leader, Philip Gunawardena, in his capacity as a member of the Cabinet.

Nomination of the candidates

The next stage in the campaign was the nomination of candidates by both groups. On 9 April, the Prime Minister handed over nomination papers to 125 candidates contesting seats on the UNP ticket. Four seats were not being contested as these were assigned to the MEP of Philip Gunawardena. In the Ceylon Tamil areas, the UNP did not put up candidates in constituencies where its ally, the TC, had entered the fray. It clashed with the FP in one constituency in the Northern province and in all the constituencies in the Eastern province.

In outlining electioneering strategy to the candidates, the Prime Minister said that he was not concerned with majorities in the individual constituencies but that his objective would be to win as many seats as possible.[29] He agreed to campaign in those constituencies where a seat held was thought no longer to be secure, and in others where an extra effort would win a seat from the Opposition. The Prime Minister warned candidates to adhere strictly to the new election laws. All candidates were issued with a Roneoed copy of the legislation as it stood at the time.

The Prime Minister explained to his candidates the issues that had already been raised by the Opposition in their campaign, and the replies that should be made to these. In particular, he touched on the conflicting statements of Mrs Bandaranaike and N. M. Perera on the rice issue and urged the candidates to explain to the electors, especially the peasants, the danger of the price level of rice being undermined if the UF decided to import the extra quantity of rice needed to meet the requirements to implement their pledge. On the question of the cost of living, he stressed that what was important was not that it had gone up, which he said was a feature of developing economies, but that there was no longer a scarcity of essential commodities. He also dealt with the facts and details of the Mahaveli river diversion project.

For the purpose of the campaign, the UNP as well as the UF divided the island into a number of zones, each in charge of a zonal leader. The UNP's zonal leaders were almost entirely their ministers, a majority of whom were older men lacking the necessary drive and energy for a sustained campaign, and they had to attend to their duties as caretaker ministers. Mrs Bandaranaike had a number of freer and comparatively younger men as zonal leaders, full of enthusiasm and dedication to prosecute the campaign to a successful conclusion. She did not burden her former ministers excessively with onerous tasks, preferring to keep them as the key speakers at the election rallies.

The United Front candidates were given their letters of nomination on 15 April, by Mrs Bandaranaike, at her country residence in Horagolla. There were 145 candidates of whom 112 were to run on the SLFP ticket, 22 on the LSSP and 9 on the CP. In addition, the UF decided to support 3 Independent candidates, one of whom was contesting the important Ceylon Tamil constituency of Jaffna. The SLFP for the first time also put forward 3 candidates to contest seats under its label in the Tamil majority Northern province, while in addition its two Marxist partners ran 8 candidates there. In the Eastern province, the SLFP had 8 candidates contesting – 7 Muslims and 1 Sinhalese. Mrs Bandaranaike herself went through each of the numerous applications for nomination and, reportedly, gave the nomination to the best person.[30]

Mrs Bandaranaike in addressing the UF candidates stressed that never before were the policies of her late husband more welcomed than at this juncture, as the people 'were fed up with five years of UNP rule'.[31] She emphasised the need for the SLFP to extend its fullest cooperation to its other two partners. She told candidates that they should not offend each other's ideological susceptibilities. She added that since there would be roughly only 30 days available for campaigning after nomination day, she would have to cover at least 4 electorates a day to be able to campaign for every candidate.

Every UF candidate signed a letter individually to the Governor-General stating that in the event of his election to Parliament, he would support Mrs Bandaranaike as Prime Minister, adding that he was conducting his campaign on this assumption, and on the basis of the Common Programme and the common election manifesto agreed to by the three constituent parties of the the UF.[32] Should the results of the election prove inconclusive, this letter it was hoped would serve to remind the Governor-General that when making his decision he should regard the three parties as one. The UF feared that if the UNP emerged as the largest single group, it would refuse to recognise the UF as a single group and would insist that the SLFP should be taken separately for the purposes of determining which party should have the first call from the Governor-General to form a Government.

As with the UNP, all UF candidates were provided with printed digests of the law of elections. A well-known lawyer, K. Shinya, with the assistance of Colvin R. de Silva and Stanley Tillekeratne, addressed the candidates on the implications of the law.

After the formalities of nominations were completed, the UF leaders inclusive of the Marxists went in procession to the *samadhi* of S. W. R. D. Bandaranaike which is situated in the grounds of Horagolla and paid homage at the late leader's tomb with bowls of flowers.

On 17 April Mrs Bandaranaike advertised an appeal in the *Sun* and later in some of the other newspapers 'beseeching' the public to 'save Ceylon' by contributing 'a rupee' to the SLFP election fund. It was a dramatic appeal couched in emotional terms. Immediately after the appeal went forth, the UNP leadership tried to make the rupee fund an election issue and accusations and counter-accusations followed.

Two days later Mrs Bandaranaike warned the electors at various meetings to be on their guard as she was in receipt of information of moves 'to disrupt fair elections and bring about chaos in the country'. She added that there might be moves 'to get the army out in such a set-up.'[33] These warnings of pre-polls subversion became a continuing theme in UF speeches as the campaign drew to its close. UF leaders in fact raised the matter later with the Governor-General.

The second phase

Nomination day on 23 April passed with the usual fanfare and publicity. In a number of instances, party faithfuls had collected the deposits of candidates, but this was not the general rule. After nominations were handed in at the respective centres, candidates were taken in many instances in procession to their constituencies and accorded receptions; some were even given receptions on their way to the nomination centre. The UF gained a psychological victory when its candidate for the Welimada seat was declared elected by the returning officer after his objection against defects in his rival's nomination paper was upheld.

Both parties picked on Kandy[34] as the venue for their mammoth rallies during the week of nomination. The UF had its rally on 21 April, the UNP on 26 April. The candidates of both groups followed the ritual of offering flowers at the Temple of the Sacred Tooth of the Buddha and of invoking the blessings of the Triple Gem before proceeding to their election rallies.

The main manifestos

Both parties published their manifestos during this phase, the UF on 20 April and the UNP on 27 April. The UF manifesto was based on the 25-point programme (the Common Programme as it came to be called) that its three constituent partners had agreed on, in February 1968. The manifesto had been carefully prepared and examined by various committees set up by the three parties before it was finalised. It began with a firm indictment of the UNP's five-year record – alleging failure in the 'grow more paddy' campaign and inviting attention to the rise in the cost of living, which 'has soared like a moon rocket' and the growing grievances of (1) the peasantry who, despite the Government's increase of the guaranteed price of paddy from Rs. 12 per bushel to Rs. 14, found that the purchasing power of Rs. 14 only amounted to Rs. 11/80 because of the devaluation of the rupee; (2) workers by 'hand and brain' who are 'everywhere demanding higher pay'; (3) students in both the schools and the universities, the former because of, among other things, the downgrading of schools and 'curtailments and restrictions' imposed on the free education scheme on the instructions of the World Bank, the latter because of the iniquities of the Higher Education Act which it pledged would be repealed; and (4) Ceylonese small industrialists, handicraftsmen and retail traders because of 'endless discrimination' against them in favour of 'foreign capitalists' and distinguished citizens who are mostly Indian business tycoons. The manifesto also drew attention to 'the unsatisfactory state' of the nationalised services, especially the state-operated omnibus transport system. It added that the UNP's propaganda slogans of 1965 have 'flopped': 'preservation of democratic rights', yet 1,086 of the 1,825 days of UNP rule were under emergency regulations; 'no vengeance, no revenge', yet victimisation of teachers and other public servants; 'freedom of the press', yet official persecution of Opposition newspapers; 'clean up bribery and corruption at all levels', yet illegal foreign exchange transactions by Lake House were not adequately inquired into and the bill for the declaration of assets by M.P.s and senators withdrawn; restoring Buddhism to its former position when Lanka was free, yet 'baton charging, tear gassing and shooting' of Buddhist monks on 8 January 1966 – when Parliament passed the Tamil Regulations under the Tamil Language (Special Provisions) Act of 1958; and 'national unity', yet the Tamil FP is no longer with the UNP. It ended with the condemnation of the terms imposed by the World Bank and the IDA for their loan of 29 million dollars for the Mahaveli river diversion project.

The UF manifesto further accused the UNP Government of frittering away the country's foreign exchange resources by utilising foreign loans to finance over 20 per cent of Ceylon's annual imports, and by trebling Ceylon's foreign debt in the past five years to bridge 'the ever growing trade gap', by paying the nationalised foreign oil companies almost twice the compensation which was legally due to them, by removing restrictions placed on the repatriation of dividends, profits and interest by foreign banks and foreign companies, and by permitting during the five years of its rule the loss of nearly Rs. 5,000 million in foreign exchange through fraudulent foreign exchange manipulations and smuggling activities. The UNP Government had further sought 'to freeze and reverse public sector development' and had encouraged the growth of capitalist monopolies owned mostly by non-Ceylonese.

The manifesto put forward specific proposals for restructuring the economy. These implied a state-controlled economy in which the private sector would have a subsidiary role. The banking system and the import trade in all essential commodities would be nationalised. The Agency houses, mostly British-owned, would be controlled and the plantation industries would be guided and directed by state agencies established for the purpose. Legal provision would be made for the state to acquire shares in both foreign and local companies and the state would follow a policy of Ceylonisation of ownership in the private sector. Heavy, capital goods, and suitable basic industries would be state-owned while other industries would be assigned to cooperative societies and private enterprise.

An extravagant scheme of social benefits was promised. The controversial rice cut would be restored. Infant milk foods would be distributed at cheap rates and the mid-day meal for school children would be improved. Textiles and drugs would be reduced in price and goods in everyday use distributed at cheap rates. Social insurance, including old age benefits and a national pension scheme, would be introduced. Agricultural reforms, including easy loans and other facilities for hiring agricultural equipment at low rates, would be made available to the peasant. They pledged to find employment for the 750,000 unemployed and the 15,000 graduates by a radical restructuring of the economy and by filling the 50,000 vacant positions in the public service left unfilled by the UNP.

All these measures, the UF manifesto stated, could be financed by mobilising domestic savings, with the profits from efficiently run state enterprises, by heavy taxation of the rich, and by putting an end to fraudulent foreign exchange manipulation and smuggling activities which lose for the country Rs. 1,000 million annually.

The UF also offered a wide range of democratising measures to enlist popular interest in the governmental process. The elected representatives of the people would meet in a constituent assembly to draw up a new constitution pledged 'to realise the objective of a socialist democracy' and 'secure fundamental rights and freedoms to all citizens'. Political rights for the large majority of public servants, a comprehensive charter of workers' rights, repeal of all laws and regulations restricting the democratic rights of the people, and trade union rights for public employees were promised. In addition, elected employees' councils, advisory committees in Government offices, and people's committees on a territorial basis to link the administration closely with the people, were to be set up. Further, a thorough-going reform of the colonial-oriented bureaucratic machinery of the administration was to be undertaken.

The UF tended to be favourably disposed towards the socialist and communist states. Its manifesto pledged that a UF Government would break off diplomatic relations with Israel until a satisfactory settlement of the dispute with the Arab states was effected. This offer was designed to attract the important Muslim vote which could be vital to both parties in the event of a close contest. Further, diplomatic relations would be established with the German Democratic Republic, the Democratic Republic of Vietnam, the Democratic People's Republic of Korea and the Provisional Revolutionary Government of the Republic of South Vietnam. The UF declared its acceptance of the principles laid down at the Bandung (1955), Belgrade (1961) and Cairo (1964) conferences.

The manifesto stated that the national unity claimed by the UNP was superficial – 'a temporary alliance of the big capitalists and exploiters of the various communities'. The UF had reason to believe that discontented sections of the ethnic and religious minorities could be won over to its side and therefore preferred not to assume the defiant Sinhalese Buddhist posture that the SLFP had adopted in the past. It agreed to implement the Official Language Act and the Tamil Language (Special Provisions) Act 'fully and fairly' where formerly, in the Common Programme of February 1968, it had pledged to replace the Tamil Regulations framed by the 'National Government' in 1966 with another set of Regulations acceptable to both the Sinhalese and Tamils. On the Indian question, whereas UF spokesmen had condemned the UNP for betraying the Sinhalese interests in the legislation it enacted in 1968 to implement the Indo-Ceylon Agreement of 1965, the manifesto rather vaguely stated that the agreement would 'be implemented fully both in letter and spirit'. To go into further detail would have meant antagonising the Indian vote in the Kandyan Sinhalese constituencies, some of which the UF hoped to collect for itself through the good offices of their ally, the DWC of Abdul Aziz.

The UNP manifesto recounted the achievements of the five-year term of the 'National Government' and took pride in the success of the 'green revolution' effected by Dudley Senanayake's 'grow more paddy' campaign, and the building of national unity. The party claimed that 74 per cent today compared with 44 per cent in 1964 of the rice consumed by the population was locally grown. Self-sufficiency in rice and subsidiary food crops, it said, would be a reality in 1972. The proposed Mahaveli scheme would bring many benefits to the country. It went on to state confidently that 'our next breakthrough will be in the field of industry' and, by 1975, at the end of the second term of UNP rule, Ceylon would produce three-quarters of her own consumer goods.[35] Since there has been a noticeable absence of uniformity in Ceylon's development the party proposed setting up regional development commissions to deal with all aspects of development in their respective areas.

The manifesto claimed that the 'National Government' had cleared 'the mess in education' left by the two Bandaranaike Governments. A national system of education which aimed at diversifying the educational curriculum, reducing the excessive admissions into the humanities and arts, and diverting students to the science and technical fields of study had been introduced. The study of English was being encouraged.

Everything was being done to alleviate the unemployment problem *vis-à-vis* graduates and the youth – for the former, a bureau of graduate unemployment and a steering committee of permanent secretaries were making investigations; for the latter, a national youth council was set up to give those between 17 and 25 years an opportunity to learn a trade to prepare them for future employment.

Where the workers and public servants were concerned, profit sharing and salary increases were, the manifesto stated, significant aspects of UNP policy. The party claimed that farmers, teachers, bus conductors, drivers and other workers owned shares in a number of state-controlled ventures. This practice was being followed by the private sector as well. They (the UNP Government) had cooperated with the private sector to create further employment opportunities. For this purpose, controls had been lifted and trade Ceylonised.

The UNP philosophy was based on respect for the private sector, but a private sector where ownership was not concentrated in a few hands but rather widely dispersed. If power and ownership is concentrated in the hands of the state, individual freedom, the manifesto insisted, would be stifled. The accent was on democratic socialism, not socialism alone.

Such a philosophy 'where rightful ambition is encouraged, initiative applauded and enterprise rewarded' (from the manifesto) cannot in any way result in sympathy for the communist or socialist states. The UNP's manifesto, therefore, while professing to adhere to the principles of nonalignment and pledging support to the aspirations of all Afro-Asian and developing countries, was singularly devoid of the forthright pronouncements contained in the UF manifesto.

Both manifestos had in mind the teenage voters who would make the difference to the final outcome. It was generally agreed (by the UF as well) that at the general election of March 1965, the UNP and its allies had obtained the bulk of this vote. The UF's objective was now to exploit to its own advantage the disillusionment of these voters with the UNP. In 1965, the full complement of teenage voters had not been registered. At this election, the Department of Elections estimated that there were 8 lakhs more voters on the list, the large majority of whom belonged to the teenage group.

UNP criticisms of the UF manifesto

Some of the important proposals in the UF manifesto, especially those concerning people's committees and the Tamil language, gave the UNP and its allies the opportunity of putting the UF leadership on the defensive. The Prime Minister himself in a lengthy statement to the press on 26 April, while drawing attention to these two matters, also sought to contradict what he called 'the monstrous distortions of fact and the gross inaccuracies and lies' detailed in the manifesto. With his own facts and figures, he refuted their charges.

May Day rallies

May Day in Ceylon, which was declared a national holiday by S. W. R. D. Bandaranaike, was on this occasion a test of strength between the two parties. Each side for obvious reasons of propaganda organised the celebrations on the grandest possible scale. This would not only influence their own supporters but the turn-out at the respective rallies would provide evidence of the support that each party commanded in the country. Neither the UNP nor the SLFP are workers' parties as such, though both control and run a number of trade unions. The SLFP, however, had an advantage because of the support of the two leading Marxist parties. The UNP and MEP were closely associated on this particular May Day.

The UNP organised a three-mile-long procession with several feeder processions. It was headed by a cultivator carrying a *mammoty* to draw attention to the success of the food drive and the place of importance given to the peasant farmer in the UNP. There was also a huge portrait of D. S. Senanayake, the 'father of the nation,' carried at the head of the procession. The processionists shouted slogans applauding the Senanayake Government's successes. They carried posters depicting its achievements in the spheres of agriculture, education and industry. Since the Left-wing MEP had joined the UNP, red flags were interspersed with green ones along with the official flag of the country.

The UF procession was the longer one, eight miles, taking four hours to pass any particular point on the route. It was at most points massed eight, ten and twelve abreast. It comprised the SLFP, LSSP, CP, the ISF, members of the unions of state corporations and of mercantile unions, teachers and students. The procession was led by Mrs Bandaranaike's son Anura, in order to remind people of S. W. R. D. Bandaranaike's services to the nation. It carried humorous cartoons ridiculing the Government's successes. Many demonstrators also carried slices and loaves of bread to symbolise the fact that they were forced to eat bread instead of the staple food, rice. The slogans of the UF procession concentrated on the rice subsidy and the readiness of 'our mother' Mrs Bandaranaike to provide the two measures of rice. This slogan was used at meetings all over the island both before and after nomination day. Its effect was electric. To these slogans were sometimes added others which had blatant communal overtones. They were intended to convey disapproval of the UNP's alliance with the two Tamil parties, the FP and CWC.

UNP slogans were confined mostly to references to Mrs Sirima Bandaranaike and her son, Anura, with the demand that she give replies to the questions asked of her, especially on how she proposed to make the second measure of rice available to the consumer.

Both sides in their speeches emphasised the main themes already referred to. For the UNP, its performance was a success. They were comparative newcomers to May Day rallies and had carried it off in grand style. But the UF was just as satisfied. The enthusiasm of the crowds that participated in its processions and rally must have given its leaders all the assurance they needed. Both sides claimed victory, and they were probably both right as far as the occasion went.

Attack and counter-attack on communal questions

In the days that followed, the UNP made every effort to draw the UF into making statements on the Tamil language question, but without much success. Prime Minister Senanayake repeatedly stated at election meetings that the UF had now accepted his stand on the Tamil language, but other than occasional outbursts by Felix Dias Bandaranaike attacking the Tamil language settlement, none of the others in the UF leadership made any definite pronouncement.

On the other hand, Mrs Bandaranaike claimed that there was growing support for her from the minority groups. She alleged that the Muslims had been cheated by the UNP.[36] The Islamic Socialist Front, the SLFP's Muslim political organisation, in an appeal to Muslim voters published in the *Sun* of 22 May, warned that Muslims, especially the younger voters 'were in no mood to be misguided, misdirected or be made a political joke'. The Front complained bitterly that the UNP leadership had tended to take the Muslims for granted. After enumerating the various services rendered to the Muslims by both Bandaranaike Governments, the ISF urged Muslim voters to do the obvious thing on election day. This was its answer to an appeal of the respected Muslim leader, Dr M. C. M. Kaleel, when he asked Muslims to vote for the UNP because among other things the UNP was a democratic party – the Muslims could not support Marxist–Leninist principles and methods, and the UNP had in various ways helped the Muslim community.[37]

In addition to this kind of Muslim support, the UF received the backing of the second largest Indian Tamil workers' organisation, the Democratic Workers'

Congress (DWC). Its general council at its meeting on 9 May endorsed the contents of the UF manifesto and pledged its support to the UF 'to form the next Government of the country'.[38] There was of course no doubt that the Leftist-organised trade unions among the Indian Tamil plantation workers were backing the UF.

Two days after the DWC general council met, the executive council of the Ceylon Workers' Congress (CWC), the leading Indian plantation workers' organisation in Ceylon, called upon its membership and others with common interests 'while pledging to continue to fight for their rights' to 'exercise their franchise effectively at the forthcoming general election by supporting the candidates of the UNP under the leadership of Premier Dudley Senanayake'.[39]

Indian workers in some twenty constituencies in the Kandyan Sinhalese areas could in the event of a sharp division of votes tilt the balance in favour of one side or the other. And it was widely believed that the CWC more than the DWC had the power and influence to effect the shift of votes. When the CWC, therefore, announced its decision to support the UNP, it only gave credence to the UF charge that the UNP was in league with Tamil groups and was therefore 'a danger' to the Sinhalese interests. In fact, the UF press seized the opportunity to drive home the point.

This propaganda was followed by a whispering campaign about threats of violence by UF activists against members of the Tamil minority with a view to scaring them away from the polls. The campaign presumably had some effect, for in Colombo alone numbers of middle-class Ceylon Tamil 'breadwinners' had their families sent to Jaffna during the last week preceding the general election for fear of racial violence breaking out.

When the other main Indian workers' organisation, the DWC, decided to support the UF, some of the Indian Tamil voters in the Kandyan Sinhalese constituencies thought that the UF after all was not as communal as its enemies alleged.

Mrs Bandaranaike made skilful use of the district councils issue which had roused fears among the Sinhalese and the Muslims (the latter feared they would be a minority in the district councils in Tamil majority areas) to embarrass the UNP.

The Prime Minister was forced to reply. In his address to the UNP's May Day rally, he said that in deference to the wishes of the majority of the people, he had abandoned the bill and had no intention of reviving it.[40] He repeated this assurance on a number of other occasions as well.

Towards the end of the campaign, the *Daily Mirror* of 19 May 1970 published in large front-page headlines a report that exploratory talks had commenced between the UF and the Tamil FP with a view to both parties entering into a parliamentary pact. The news item was damaging to both parties. It could have only benefited the UNP in the south and the rivals of the FP, the TC, in the North. As was expected, strong denials were issued by Senator A. P. Jayasuriya on behalf of Mrs Bandaranaike and S. J. V. Chelvanayakam for the FP. The *Daily Mirror* of 23 May, however, while publishing the denials in its front page, insisted that its report 'was unimpeachably true and incontrovertibly correct'. On 24 May in a strongly worded statement, Mrs Bandaranaike condemned the report as 'being malicious and a diabolical invention calculated to influence the result of the general election this week'.[41]

On the same day, Mrs Bandaranaike in election addresses claimed that the UF had united the people of the country and that Buddhists, Christians, Hindus and Muslims were with her.[42]

As if to prove her bona fides, earlier, on 12 May, Mrs Bandaranaike visited the Roman Catholic Mission House at Wennappuwa, which is a predominantly Roman Catholic constituency, and had tea there with the reverend fathers. A photograph of this 'encounter' was published in the CP daily *Aththa* and thousands of copies were released for public consumption. The Mission House later, to relieve itself of the embarrassment, issued a statement on 20 May to explain what happened. This statement maintained that the Prime Minister himself had visited the Mission House on 7 March in the company of Festus Perera, the UNP sitting member for Wennappuwa and subsequently the UNP candidate for that constituency.[43] But whereas the Prime Minister's visit was taken for granted, Mrs Bandaranaike's visit had greater significance, because her Government had dispossessed the Roman Catholics of their schools in 1960-1.

The *Catholic Messenger* of 17 May, the official organ of the Roman Catholic Church in Ceylon, published a message to all Catholics exhorting them to vote, and to vote wisely at the fothcoming election. It called on them to express the country's firm opposition to any regime which 'does not believe in religion, nor in the dignity and freedom which are the birthright of every citizen in this country'. The *Ceylon Daily News* of 23 May 1970 gave front-page publicity to this news item, evidently expecting the electors to interpret the call to vote against regimes opposed to religion as an appeal to Catholics to vote against the Marxists, or those parties having the support of the Marxists.

Felix Dias Bandaranaike

Some of the controversial pronouncements of Felix Dias Bandaranaike on the Marxists and the Tamil problem were given prominence in the pro-Government daily press as proof of dissension in the ranks of the UF. On 11 May the *Ceylon Daily News* carried an editorial entitled 'Strange Shibboleths' in which it drew attention to the pronouncements in the UF manifesto on the Tamil language, and contrasted these with some of Felix Dias Bandaranaike's denunciations of the Regulations framed under the Tamil Language (Special Provisions) Act 'by the UNP–FP Government.'

The pro-Government daily press also highlighted Felix Dias Bandaranaike's well-known dislike of Marxists and consequently his own public statements about his position *vis-à-vis* the Marxists. In an election address at Dehiowita, alluding to the UNP's comment about the LSSP being 'wiped out', he replied that if the 'key' (the LSSP's election symbol) were given to the 'hand' (the SLFP's symbol) it would remain there permanently.[44] On 14 and 15 May, Felix Dias Bandaranaike riled the CP when he urged the voters in the three-member electorate of Colombo Central to cast all their votes for the SLFP candidate. Pieter Keuneman, the CP general-secretary who had been one of Colombo Central constituency's representatives since 1947, was discomfited, because it was not certain that he would emerge a victor this time.[45]

The UNP drive against the traditional Marxists

The UNP concentrated its attack very heavily on the LSSP and CP, hoping to convince the electors that the presence of Marxists in the SLFP would constitute a danger to freedom and to parliamentary institutions. Their view was that the Marxists would infiltrate the SLFP and in the end overthrow Mrs Bandaranaike or make her simply a figurehead. The people were told of the Stalinist terror, the suppression of the Hungarian uprising of 1956 and the 'rape' of Czechoslovakia, and were warned that a similar fate would overtake Ceylon, if the 'Reds' gained a foothold here.

In particular, the UNP leadership went for N. M. Perera, slated to be the Minister of Finance in a UF Government. There was a general fear of Dr Perera's reputed abilities as a financial wizard, a constitutional expert and a political strategist.

Leading UNP spokesmen reminded the electors that the late S. W. R. D. Bandaranaike had in his public utterances condemned the Marxists as enemies of religion and of democratic institutions and that he had refused to have any dealings with them. (This view is, of course, open to question.) They also stressed that the LSSP in particular had harassed the late S. W. R. D. Bandaranaike during his premiership with their massive politically motivated strikes. The electors were reminded of Mrs Bandaranaike's denunciation of the LSSP and CP during her election campaign of February–March 1960, and the LSSP's criticisms of Mrs Bandaranaike and the SLFP during this phase. In this campaign, the UNP was strongly backed by the national press, in particular by Lake House.

The LSSP countered Lake House by putting out a booklet entitled *Why Lake House Seeks to Destroy the Coalition*, which contained the important portions of speeches of the two LSSP leaders, N. M. Perera and Leslie Goonewardena, and that of the SLFP's spokesman, Felix Dias Bandaranaike, on its allegedly illegal foreign exchange deals. This booklet also reproduced photostat copies of letters of some of the directors of Lake House relating to various foreign exchange transactions with European banks (*vide* Sessional Paper. No. VIII – 1971).

All-out efforts were also made to secure the defeat of the CP leaders, Pieter Keuneman in Colombo Central, and Dr S. A. Wickremasinghe in Akuressa in the south. A family feud was exploited by the UNP to press into its service one or two of Dr Wickremasinghe's relatives, and the UNP claimed that Dr Wickremasinghe faced certain defeat.

The UF's response

The LSSP and CP in their defence protested their loyalty to Mrs Bandaranaike and the Common Programme. Mrs Bandaranaike for her part visited almost all the electorates in the Sinhalese areas which the LSSP and CP were contesting and asked the electors to give their support to her allies. She had one simple answer to the UNP's charge that she was endangering democracy by her alliance with the Marxists. 'If the Marxists are such a danger, why', she asked, 'did Senanayake team up with Philip Gunawardena, the "father of Marxism" in Ceylon, and why did Senanayake welcome into his camp renegades and defectors from the Marxist camp?' What was good for him, she claimed, was also good for her. The UNP did not answer this question in any satisfactory manner.

Generally speaking, LSSP and CP spokesmen campaigned in those constituencies where they could influence votes where SLFP candidates contested. In particular the LSSP and CP were active on behalf of the SLFP in the constituencies in the Kelani valley area, in some of those in the Western and Southern provinces and in the Badulla district. In the last-mentioned especially, LSSP men campaigned to make up for any loss of support caused by the defection to the UNP camp of its leader there, Jack Kotelawala.

On the side of the SLFP, some of its leading men spoke on CP and LSSP platforms and appealed to the voters to support the candidates of these Marxist parties. Further, LSSP men appeared on CP platforms and CP men on LSSP platforms. There was in general cooperation among the three parties. The two Marxist parties in particular preferred to submerge their identity in the UF. This helped them to ward off the UNP's attacks.

'Scare' stories

From nomination day (23 April) onwards reports of tension and violence received publicity in the daily press. The pro-UF *Sun* in its issue of 23 April reported that the Inspector-General of Police had alerted his men concerning attempts that might be made by 'Che Guevara-type terrorists' to disrupt the elections – an obvious reference to the PLF. The *Weekend Sun* of 13 May gave much more detailed information of the plans of the PLF, and quoted a high police official as stating that 'it is like a volcano ready to erupt'. The *Ceylon Daily News* of 23 April also gave front-page headlines to PLF insurgent activities in the province of Uva. Needless to say, UNP speakers tried to identify PLF tactics as part of the Marxist strategy of seizure of power, directing their attacks more on the LSSP and CP than on the PLF itself. The pro-Government *Ceylon Observer* in its issue of 25 May asked why the SLFP journal *Sirilaka*, beginning on 25 August 1969 and ending on 10 November 1969, had serialised the diary of Che Guevara in its entirety. The implications of course were obvious. At meetings during the first two weeks after nomination, Mrs Bandaranaike as well as other senior spokesmen for the UF said that they did not need the support of the PLF to come to power. They stoutly denied any affiliation with this organisation. Some of the junior members of the UF however supported the PLF's programme of action.

The pro-Government daily press presented news of sporadic outbreaks of violence in order to convey the impression that instability would accompany a UF victory. Also, the UF feared that violence could be engineered by the UNP and used as a pretext to cancel or postpone the elections. This was in fact one of the matters mentioned to the Governor-General by a UF delegation led by Mrs Bandaranaike that saw him on the night of 8 May.[46] What is more, the delegation informed the Governor-General that they had received information, the accuracy of which they could not altogether vouchsafe, that moves were afoot by the army or a section thereof 'to take over the administration of the country either just before the general election, if there are clear signs of an electoral defeat for the present government, or immediately following the election in the event of an actual defeat for this government at the polls'.

The Prime Minister was prompt to reply to the UF's allegations. In his official statement addressed to the Governor-General, he called on the UF leaders to place any evidence they had, either accurate or otherwise, before the Governor-General or the Inspector-General of Police. He added that he was satisfied with 'the absolute loyalty of the armed services and the police to the institutions which they are duty bound to protect'.[47] But he also invited the attention of the Governor-General to various incidents since 1966 of subversive action on the part of 'extremist elements' to undermine the constitutional and parliamentary processes in the country.

Pre-polls optimism

With the day of the general election drawing near, both leaders in their public statements claimed victory. Even other sources with whom the Prime Minister had discussed his prospects indicated that he was greatly encouraged after his tour of the southern electorates, where the UNP was considered vulnerable.

Mrs Bandaranaike was just as confident. By 21 May she had visited a hundred electorates and addressed over 250 meetings. She claimed that she was 'absolutely certain of the verdict of the people' whom she believed were solidly behind the UF.[48] But she warned her supporters not to be over-confident and therefore complacent.

Sinhalese fears

Despite the optimism of the two rival leaders, there was a feeling among Sinhalese nationalist elements that the results might be inconclusive and that Tamil parties, especially the FP, would try to exploit the situation.

These considerations prompted the Maha Nayake Thero (the Chief High Priest) of the main Buddhist sect, the Malwatte Chapter, along with the Maha Nayaka Theros of the other two Buddhist sects, and a number of leading Buddhist monks to write to the leaders of both groups on 7 May about the need for them to unite in a national Government in the event of a stalemate. 'The Sinhala race', they stressed, was 'now facing a severe national calamity.'[49]

The Prime Minister replied that for the UNP 'to consider combining with the United Left Front would pose the problem of reconciling profound divergences in economic policies and ways of life.' He added that 'two strong elements of the UF are Marxist parties, and opposition to religion is a basic tenet of Marxism'. His objective was to win a sufficient number of seats to form a stable Government.[50]

Mrs Bandaranaike expressed similar hopes *vis-à-vis* the Front she was leading in her reply to the venerable Maha Nayake Theros and their associates.[51] She chided the Prime Minister for his condemnation of her alliance with the Marxists. She expressed wholehearted agreement with the views of the reverend gentlemen that 'it is very clear to every right thinking person true to his convictions that the Sinhala race is now facing a severe national calamity'.[52]

The religious dignitaries intervene

A few days before the election, the national dailies published pre-polls messages from the leading religious dignitaries in the country; the main theme was that democracy should be ensured at all costs and totalitarianism of any kind is unacceptable.[53] Such, for instance, was the message of the senior Bishop of the Church of Ceylon, the Right Reverend Harold de Soysa. The messages gave the impression that the Marxist allies of the SLFP should not be countenanced. Mrs Bandaranaike was obliged to issue a statement allaying such fears and offering guarantees of the freedom to vote and freedom of expression, of worship and of other democratic rights under any Government she would form.[54]

The UF counter-attacked by publishing a statement from the leader of the main Buddhist sect of the island, the Venerable Maha Nayake Thero of the Malwatte Chapter, in the dailies that were backing them (the *Sun*, *Dawasa* and *Sirilaka* of 26 May) expressing his support of 'the socialism of the UF headed by Mrs Sirima Bandaranaike as against the "conservative" policies of the UNP headed by Dudley Senanayake'. The same issue of the *Sun* also referred to a statement of the Venerable Maha Nayake Thero that Mrs Bandaranaike 'is a mother to us all', a view which served to reinforce the mother-image charisma of the UF leader.

The following day (27 May) the pro-Government national dailies carried a full front-page rebuttal from the Maha Nayake Thero to the effect that he had never uttered the words attributed to him regarding the UF and Mrs Bandaranaike. He appealed to the voters not to be duped, and added that 'a socialist dictatorship fashioned according to the Marxist philosophy will not guarantee democratic freedoms and protect national and religious interests.'[55] The Maha Nayake Thero's rebuttal was also relayed over the Government-controlled Ceylon Broadcasting Corporation's network on 26 May.

A measure of confusion was thus introduced as a result of these statements and counter-statements. Those who read only the Opposition newspapers would have been influenced by the original message. The rebuttal, further, would not have carried much weight because voters during the election phase, especially those who were opposed to the UNP, did not believe all that was published in the pro-Government national dailies, or what was relayed by the Ceylon Broadcasting Corporation.

The universities

As the campaign drew to a close, every effort was made by both sides to draw the crucial youth vote to its camp. The growing numbers of educated unemployed and the harassment practised on the university population by the UNP's Minister of Education gave the UF a commanding advantage.

On 13 May students from all four universities held a successful rally in the electorate of the Minister of Education. They as well as the people of Kuliyapitiya (the electorate concerned) were addressed by their more radical mentors, some of them national figures in the world of Sinhalese drama and Sinhalese literature.[56] On 26 May, the day prior to the election, the *Sun* published a statement from 15 professors, 12 senior lecturers, 102 lecturers and 7 librarians and assistant librarians of the four universities condemning the educational and other policies of the Government. It concluded by appealing to the voters to support the candidates of the UF.

The weight of opinion in the universities was in favour of the UF, and the UNP could do little to counter it. Some UNP academics appeared on platforms but they represented only a minority view.

Film idols

A better idea to attract the teenage vote for the UNP was to have the popular film idols of the Sinhalese screen appear on their platforms. Some of the best-known film artists (including Gamini Fonseka) agreed to help the UNP. But they began their campaign rather late, in the last two weeks, when it seemed as if the UNP was an unpopular cause. They gave the impression of being hired for the purpose. As mentioned earlier, the UF had staged their film actors in the mid-phase of their campaign.

Minor Sinhalese parties

MEP   The UNP had an ally in the Mahajana Eksath Peramuna (MEP) led by Philip Gunawardena, reputedly the founder of Marxism in Ceylon. It put up four candidates, two of whom were husband and wife, the Gunawardenas. In all the other constituencies, it declared its support for the UNP. Philip Gunawardena spoke at a number of UNP meetings bitterly denouncing his former Marxist colleagues as traitors to the cause of socialism. The MEP's position was negatived by Gunawardena's son, Indika, joining the CP. Mrs Bandaranaike capitalised on Indika Gunawardena's decision to support the UF. She laughed at Philip Gunawardena's stigmatisation of her as a *radalaya* (feudalist) and added that his son had accepted her *radala* leadership.[57]

SMP A new party which entered the contest in a rather impressive way was the Sinhala Mahajana Peramuna (SMP) of R. G. Senanayake, the cousin of the Prime Minister. The SMP ran 48 candidates, frankly declared its anti-Tamil objectives, urged the Sinhalese to unite, and announced that it would assume the role that the Tamil FP had played in the past in deciding the fate of Governments. To fight the Tamils in their 'fortress', as it were, R. G. Senanayake contested Trincomalee, as well as his own seat in Dambadeniya. The symbol that his party adopted, the 'bell', he said signified danger 'to warn against the rising tide of Tamil power.'[58] R. G. Senanayake courted Muslim support for his party; he alleged that the Muslims had also suffered as a result of the control of commerce by Indian and Ceylon Tamil traders. A leading Buddhist monk, the Venerable Matale Sasanatilleke Thero, gave the new party his support and presided very often at meetings held under its auspices.

The SMP was obviously designed to fill the vacuum created by the absorption of the Sinhalese chauvinistic husband-and-wife combination of the Rajaratnes, the now inactive Jathika Vimukthi Peramuna (JVP), by the UNP. But while the JVP may have fulfilled a need during a time of Sinhalese insecurity when it was feared that S. W. R. D. Bandaranaike would give in to the pressure moves of the FP, there did not appear to be a *raison d'être* for a Sinhalese communal organisation in the contemporary setting. If there still were lurking fears, these were stilled by the UF's stance on language and by the fact that the Sinhalese language had to a fair extent replaced English in the administrative life of the country. The SMP therefore, as far as the militant Sinhalese voter was concerned, was not a necessity.

In its election manifesto the SMP put forward a 21-point programme for protecting the Sinhalese language, culture and race.[59] It urged a racial quota for employment and for entrance to the universities, colleges of higher education, and technical institutions. To symbolise its extreme position in regard to Sinhalese nationalism, the leader and all SMP candidates on 25 April proceeded to the ancient capital, Anuradhapura, where they took an oath before the statue of King Dutugemunu at the Ruwanveliseya *dagoba* that 'they will continue the battle for Sinhalese rights until victory'.[60]

The SMP leader in his campaign was vehement in his denunciation of both the UNP and the UF. He alleged that both parties were after the Tamil FP. He accused the UF of insidiously trying to re-introduce district councils through the device of people's committees. He claimed that it was only his party that was following the policies of the late S. W. R. D. Bandaranaike.[61]

The UF alleged that the SMP was a party organised by Lake House to take away the votes of nationalist-minded Sinhalese who were supporting them. Mrs Bandaranaike alleged that the aim of R. G. Senanayake and the SMP was to protect Dudley Senanayake and to ensure the return of a UNP government.[62] This view gained support with the defection of Siripala Hettiarachchi, president of the SMP youth front and its candidate for Bulathsinhala, a few days before the election. In a statement, Hettiarachchi alleged that R. G. Senanayake's activities would safeguard the UNP and result in inroads on the UF vote. He called on all SMP candidates to resign from the party.[63]

Although UNP supporters hoped that the SMP would encroach on UF votes and in close contests help UNP candidates to win, the UF as a whole did not regard R. G. Senanayake as a serious threat.

The revolutionary Left

Two minor Marxist parties of little consequence were also involved in the general election but in a minimal and negative way. Both were led by Ceylon Tamils, which was further evidence of the hopelessness of their electoral prospects. The CP (Peking) led by N. Sanmugathasan put forward a single candidate, S. D. Bandaranayake, who claimed that his role in Parliament would be to expose 'the so-called socialists in the UF' and 'bare their artifices'.[64] Sanmugathasan in speeches and in statements to the press called for a boycott of the polls. Addressing plantation workers, mostly Indian Tamils in Hatton, he accused both the SLFP and UNP of anti-Tamil communalism. 'The general election', he said, was 'a fancy dress competition'.[65] In an appeal to the Tamils on 15 May, Sanmugathasan urged them to realise that they could not win their rights either by raising the communal cry against the Sinhalese people or 'by coming to terms with a section or sections of "the reactionaries" of the Sinhalese people'. He added, 'There is nothing called Tamil hunger or Sinhalese hunger' and the way out was to first find a solution to the common economic problems facing both Tamils and Sinhalese.[66] A few days before the general election, Sanmugathasan warned workers of Indian Tamil origin not to cast their votes for either the UNP or the UF. The choice, he claimed, was like that offered by the fisherman to the fish he had caught: 'Do you wish to be eaten fried or boiled?'[67]

Sanmugathasan in earlier statements denounced the two Marxist allies of the SLFP. He alleged that 'the LSSP-led reactionaries and the revisionists of the CP' had 'politically betrayed the workers to the capitalists'.[68] In a press statement on 26 April, Sanmugathasan stated that his party rejected 'the fraud of bourgeois parliamentary elections' and instead he called upon the people of Ceylon 'to follow the path of revolution illuminated by the radiance of Marxism–Leninism–Mao Tse-tung Thought.'[69]

The Revolutionary Sama Samaja Party [LSSP(R)], which had splintered from the parent LSSP, was led by another Ceylon Tamil (Colombo-based), Bala Tampoe, who controlled a very urban middle-class union of white-collar workers in the mercantile sector, the Ceylon Mercantile Union. The LSSP(R) did not put forward any candidates but issued a manifesto a few days before the day of the general election in which it reiterated its faith in revolution and ridiculed the democratic socialism of the UNP and the socialist democracy of the UF.[70] Like Sanmugathasan, Tampoe in his public utterances denounced the LSSP and CP for their collaboration with the SLFP.

Election-eve appeals

On the day before polling, both leaders made appeals to the electors. The Prime Minister asked parents who had enjoyed the right to vote in the past, and the young 'who are perhaps enjoying it for the first time now' to ensure that this would not be their last chance to vote. He assured the electors that 'our country stands poised for a period of even greater achievement than in the past five years'. He claimed that in the five years of his Government, Ceylon had become a model for developing countries.[71]

Mrs Bandaranaike in her message angrily rejected all the claims made by the Prime Minister.[72] 'The common man', she said, 'is the forgotten factor of this period;' 'squandermania' has characterised it; foreign and monopoly capital have been entrenched; future generations mortgaged; and a spurious national unity claimed while the real problems have been avoided. She asked 'the suffering people' to rid themselves of 'this incubus that has deceived the nation, betrayed its democratic values and undermined social justice' and concluded with the hope that a new era will dawn not for 'one community' or for 'one class' but 'for all to whom this island is a home'.

The contest in the Tamil-speaking areas

The principal contestants in the Tamil-speaking areas of the Northern and Eastern provinces were the Tamil FP and TC. The DMK put forward two candidates but they made little impact. A lone SLFP candidate contested in Kopay, and a UNP candidate in Mannar, but they were not regarded as a serious threat by the FP to its position in the Northern province. A number of Independent candidates also presented themselves.

A new party which demanded self-rule and sovereign independence for the Tamil-speaking provinces also put forward candidates against the FP and the TC. It was called the Thamil Suya Aadchi Kadchi (TSRP – the Tamil Self-Rule Party) and was led by a former FP stalwart, V. Navaratnam. But Navaratnam possessed neither the qualities of leadership nor the resources to do battle with the FP and his party therefore fared miserably. He raised many embarrassing questions on federalism, language, the Indian problem and acceptance of portfolios by the FP to which FP spokesmen were compelled to respond.

In the Tamil-speaking Eastern province, the FP concentrated on winning the constituencies of Trincomalee, Kalkudah, Paddiruppu and Kalmunai, in all of which its position was not secure. It won only Trincomalee. In the two other constituencies where it contested (Batticaloa and Mutur), the outcome was not in doubt.

The FP concentrated on two issues in its campaign. It claimed to be the party that would defend the Tamil-speaking people and their rights in the hour of crisis, as it had done in the past. It declared that it would not hesitate to use the extra-constitutional weapons of satyagraha and civil disobedience, should occasion demand it. More importantly, the FP professed to be the Tamil party contesting the largest number of seats which also had the possibility of capturing them. The results in the Sinhalese areas would be inconclusive. The party would therefore hold 'the balance of power' and could be depended on to obtain the best possible terms for the Tamils. The party also claimed that it was not interested in portfolios but in obtaining autonomy for the Tamil-speaking provinces and official recognition for the Tamil language.

The TC contested twelve seats in the Northern province. In two other constituencies, Trincomalee and Mannar, it decided to support the UNP. Its leader,
Ponnambalam, commanded a fair measure of support among the Tamils of
the Jaffna Peninsula as well as those in the Sinhalese areas. Ponnambalam
sought to capitalise on what he called 'the barren record' of the FP and its
failure 'to deliver the goods'. He contrasted their record with the phase, 1947
to 1956, when his party in cooperation with the then UNP Government had
developed the Tamil areas. He accused the FP of antagonising the Sinhalese
and of dividing the Tamils. 'Federalism', he insisted, 'could never be achieved.'
The FP responded by claiming that it had united the Tamils, prevented the
state-aided colonisation of the Tamil-speaking areas by Sinhalese persons from
the south, made and unmade Sinhala Governments, and 'forced' the Dudley
Senanayake Government to amend the Sinhala Only Act with the Tamil
Regulations of January 1966. It scoffed at the TC's paucity of candidates and
accused the leader of letting down the Ceylon Tamils, the man it alleged who
had surrendered to the UNP.

The main lines of debate in the two Tamil-speaking provinces were between
the TC and FP. Both parties organised mammoth rallies and processions as part
of their propaganda campaign. The TC however suffered in that, though its
campaign was ably organised, senior UNP Sinhalese leaders did not appear on
its platforms. Obviously, the UNP did not wish to antagonise the FP, for the
latter's support would be vital in the event of an inconclusive result.

TC and FP manifestos

Both the FP and TC put out manifestos which sought to explain their positions
and give an account of their achievements. In one instance – the granting of an
extension of three years by the Dudley Senanayake Government to those new
entrant Tamil public officers recruited since 1956 (the year of the passing of the
Official Language Act) to gain proficiency in Sinhalese – both parties claimed
the credit. The TC manifesto was released on 24 April.[73] It condemned federalism and accused the FP of seeking to confine the Tamil language and the rights
of the Tamil-speaking population to only two of the nine provinces of Ceylon.
It pledged that the TC would work for the Tamil language 'to be to the Tamils
what the Sinhalese language is to the Sinhalese', to be the compulsory medium
of instruction for children of Tamil parents, and for the incorporation of a
charter of fundamental rights in the constitution, among other things. But the
manifesto was mostly a diatribe against the FP and its 'misdeeds' rather than an
account of the TC's achievements, or of the means it proposed to adopt to
achieve its aims. The TC expected the public to assume that it would be a constituent partner of the next UNP Government, obtain portfolios, and from
within work towards its objectives. Ponnambalam in his public utterances
promised that if his party failed to implement its pledges within two years of the
new Parliament's meeting, all its elected members would resign their seats.[74]

The crux of the FP's position was stated in the opening lines of its manifesto
released on 4 May. The party expected an inconclusive verdict in the general

election, and hoped to be the deciding factor (as it had been in 1965) in the formation of a Government and to effect a bargain which would be to the advantage of the Tamil people.[75] The party then proceeded to list its achievements under various categories such as language rights, the preservation of the Tamil-speaking areas, the position of public servants *vis-à-vis* the implementation of the Official Language Act, amendments to the Indo-Ceylon Pact of October 1964 and the district councils bill. From there, it proceeded to list the objectives it would strive for – federalism, Tamil language rights, citizenship rights for Indian Tamil workers, the compulsory use of the mother tongue in the education of Tamil children, the nationalisation of Tamil schools in the plantation areas, the use of the Tamil language by all public servants so as to enable Tamil people to transact business with the Tamil public in any part of Ceylon.

The LSSP and CP

These parties for obvious reasons did not seek the support of the SLFP in the Tamil areas. The two parties of the Left helped each other in general, except in one constituency, Udupiddy, where candidates from both parties clashed.

Both parties had to face the barrage from the FP, in particular, that they were 'agents' of the SLFP and were no longer interested in upholding Tamil rights. To this they replied that the FP could no longer claim to be spokesmen for the Tamils because they had 'sold' the Tamils to the UNP in the larger interest of protecting 'the bourgeois class' to which the leadership of the FP belonged. V. Ponnambalam, the CP candidate for Kankesanturai, for instance, accused the FP of opposing 'progressive steps' such as the nationalisation of the bus services, the schools, and petroleum distribution, and the enactment of the Paddy Lands Act.[76]

The Left insisted that the FP in joining the UNP had accepted the principle of Sinhalese as the only official language. They warned the Tamil voter that no useful purpose would be served in supporting communal parties isolated from the mainstream of national politics which were only interested in making 'bargains' and 'behind the door secret deals'. They exhorted the Tamil voters to join the poor and underprivileged in the Sinhalese areas. They (the Tamils) could not, according to the Left leaders, hope for separate solutions to their problems. These were common to the whole of Ceylon and their solution only lay in the path of socialism.

Some of the Left candidates at this election (in the Tamil areas) were able men, known for their dedication and public service. In particular, V. Ponnambalam, the Communist candidate contesting FP leader S. J. V. Chelvanayakam in Kankesanturai, had a hold on the electorate for the reasons mentioned. But he had too formidable an opponent to hope to win. The LSSP candidate for Uduvil, V. Karalasingham, was nationally known. But he again faced a wealthy FP landowner whose influence in the electorate was widespread. Further, Karalasingham was not a resident in the electorate, but a Colombo-based Tamil.

The overall impact of the Left in the Tamil Northern province was minimal.

The majority conservative Hindu *vellala* voters knew that the Marxists stood for equal rights for the so-called depressed castes whom the more extremist *vellalas* oppressed. Besides, their leadership failed to inspire confidence. They were regarded as 'agents' of the 'anti-Tamil Sinhalese nationalist SLFP'. Above all, the Tamil voter did not expect the UF to win. The general view was that the UNP would gain a plurality of seats, and thereafter enter into a coalition with the FP and the TC. A vote for the Left would therefore be a wasted vote. The votes that the Marxist candidates received were, therefore, apart from family supporters, those of the depressed castes and of the Tamil working classes in the constituencies concerned. But even here, they did not receive an undivided vote. The FP, in particular, had a measure of support among the depressed castes in view of the stand it had taken for temple entry for the latter. The FP had support also among sections of the workers.

There was finally the impression that some of the Left-wing candidates were not serious in their intentions about winning. In Udupiddy, for instance, the depressed caste voters who normally supported the Left, on this occasion, worked very hard for an FP victory because they wanted to ensure the defeat of the TC nominee, M. Sivasithamparam, Deputy Speaker of the dissolved Parliament, as he had not actively campaigned for them on the temple entry question. In Kankesanturai, many believed that V. Ponnambalam was only wishing to establish his claims for victory at the next election, as it was widely felt that he could not hope to win against Chelvanayakam. The Left's lack of seriousness was evidenced by neither Mrs Bandaranaike nor senior Sinhalese leaders of the LSSP and CP appearing on Left platforms in the Tamil Jaffna peninsula where the main contests took place.

The campaign in retrospect

The Sinhalese areas

The UNP obviously suffered from having been the governing party responsible for many unpopular decisions. As well, to the ordinary mass of Sinhalese voters, it was the party of the 'haves' and of vested interests in alliance with 'anti-national' groups such as those among the Indian Tamils, Ceylon Tamils and the Roman Catholics. To the 'have-nots', the frustrated job seekers and the disgruntled rural and urban Sinhalese-educated intelligentsia, it was a party with no 'grass-roots'.

The Prime Minister had to fight an extremely difficult campaign, first in seeking to remove these impressions, secondly in justifying some of the more unpopular measures of his Government, and lastly in endeavouring to convince his audiences that on the positive side there was a great deal that he could claim for his term of office, especially the reasonable prosperity and the relative calm following his efforts at national reconciliation. He had placed excessive emphasis on his food campaign. Together with his frontliners and the other candidates he expected too much from the charismatic aspects of his personality. Consequently, other important details in the art of campaigning were neglected.

The Prime Minister himself believed that he was having the necessary effect on his audiences. This was indeed a fact, judging from the 1,892,625 votes the UNP obtained which was 37.9 per cent of the total poll in comparison with the 1,840,019 votes or 36.8 per cent of the vote the SLFP obtained. But the latter had the support of the two leading Left-wing parties which between them supplied an additional 602,423 votes or 11.9 per cent of the total vote. And their combined organisation functioned effectively.

The UNP leadership was hopelessly out of touch with the times. They were mostly men who were basking in the Senanayake image. But they were not united among themselves. There were continual bickerings and jealousies. Some eagerly sought the mantle of succession. This discouraged others, especially a few earnest and dedicated men who had devoted their time and resources in the party's difficult times to revive its electoral prospects. The Prime Minister failed to sense the dangers emanating from these divisions. Instead, he relied on the broad umbrella of his own all-embracing personality.

There was a certain buoyancy that seized Dudley Senanayake in all his robust electioneering. He seldom felt he was fighting, in a sense, a fairly successful rearguard action. From the beginning until the end of the campaign, he thought and perhaps he was made to believe that he was on the upswing. In previous general election campaigns, he had been known to fall ill when he seemed to realise the difficulties he was encountering. On this occasion, his health did not desert him. It was no wonder that when the results came out he was completely taken aback.

In contrast, Mrs Bandaranaike and her colleagues worked as a united team with clockwork precision. They were determined on victory and they believed that they would win. The single issue they concentrated on – the Government's rice cut – they were certain would provide them with the richest harvest of votes. But there were many other unanswered or inadequately answered questions on the UNP side such as employment, the cost of living, the alliance with the FP and CWC, that gave the UF added strength. The UF were careful to choose the occasion and the audience when they laboured on the Tamil problem.

Mrs Bandaranaike's personality was just as pervasive as if not more so than that of the Prime Minister. The frenzied crowds that greeted her placed a pathetic reliance on her 'magic wand' to conjure for them what they wanted – rice, jobs, and the advancement of the Sinhalese Buddhist cause.

A considerable amount of enthusiasm was generated among the Left's support bases as well in view of the united effort that the anti-UNP forces were involved in and the certainty that the traditional Marxists would be partners in the Government that was to come.

Above all, the UF was the party of the 'have-nots' and of the 'toiling masses'. The SLFP had its quota of rich men and feudalists, and the Left its intellectuals and rich professionals. But to their supporters they seemed to identify with the ordinary man.

The only doubt the UF entertained was the possible disruption of the campaign or subversion at the polls. But this had been a recurring theme at all elections and their fears in the end proved groundless.

The Tamil-speaking areas

In the Tamil-speaking areas, the two dominant parties were well organised. But the FP had an advantage because of its superior resources and the popularity of its leader, Chelvanayakam. Large sections of the Tamil voting public, especially its middle classes and the farmers, believed that he would not let them down, that he could be relied on to make a decision which was in their best interests.

Chelvanayakam, however, was in poor health and could not exert himself with the same vigour as on earlier occasions. He therefore concentrated his efforts in the constituencies of the Jaffna Peninsula and in a few of the outlying ones. He did not tour the constituencies in the Eastern province as often as he had in previous elections. Had this been done, the FP could very well have saved at least the constituency of its President, S. Rasamanickam, at Paddiruppu.

There were other factors as well which explain the failure of the FP to fare as well as on earlier occasions. Its leadership was stale and the new generation of youth voters was not willing to entrust them with the same good sense and responsibility that their elders would. The young people, especially, wanted jobs and this the FP was in no position to provide. The Prime Minister stressed this point when he campaigned against the FP President in the latter's constituency at Paddiruppu.

The TC bent all its efforts in the Jaffna Peninsula. But its leader, G. G. Ponnambalam, was involved in the desperate bid to save his seat. The TC apparatus was better suited to harnessing funds for its election effort and it had new and more energetic candidates in the field than the FP.

One factor which emerged from the election campaign in the Tamil areas was the recession to the background of the burning issues of yesteryear – federalism, colonisation, parity of status for the Tamil language with Sinhalese, voting and citizenship rights for the Indian Tamils. All these were thrown into the melting pot of a much hoped-for Tamil front or a single coalescent Tamil party which would be in a position to parley on equal terms with the Sinhalese parties and extract the maximum concessions from them. The question uppermost was whether the FP or the TC should be vested with the task or whether it should be entrusted to a united front of all Tamil parties. The campaign of the two parties did not directly address itself to this issue. The TC preferred such a front in its own interests, but wanted it formed before the election, presumably so that it could be assured its quota of seats. The FP wished to have it deferred until after the elections. Indeed this ultimately happened. About a year after the election, the TUF was forged under Chelvanayakam's leadership.

7. The issues

So many issues were raised in the course of the campaign that it is impossible to deal with each of them separately. For convenience, therefore, we have classified them under three headings: economic, political and constitutional, and cultural. Broadly speaking, the campaign was conducted on these lines between the two major contenders in the Sinhalese areas. The classification sounds artificial because all issues raised ultimately have political significance, but owing to their plethora, we have arranged them in the order listed.

Among the Ceylon Tamils, the issues were on a different plane and they will therefore have to be dealt with as a separate category. Though many of their problems were similar to those of the Sinhalese, the Ceylon Tamils generally believed that the issue of language which concerned them most was central to the question of their entire future, while all other issues were incidental to or arose from the prime one.

Economic questions

On all the important economic questions that the UF raised, the UNP was placed very much on the defensive. Their leader, the Prime Minister, was characterised by UF propagandists as unsympathetic to the ordinary man, affluent, 'slinging expensive cameras on his shoulder', a bachelor unaware of the problems of running the home.

Furthermore the UNP wrote off a section of the people when it insisted that the halving of the ration had benefited the farmer class and would, if restored, affect him adversely. It had very little to offer by way of compensation to the non-farmer class – the large numbers of workers, the urban dwellers, the land-less, the drifters from the countryside, the unemployed, and the disillusioned youth.

The rice subsidy and the food drive

The UNP called their period of rule the era of prosperity (*perakum yugaya*) and their leader the modern version of one of the greatest of the ancient Sin-halese kings, Parakrama Bahu. But the UF struck an echo in the hearts of the ordinary people when they referred to the past five years as the age of wheat flour (*panpiti yugaya*) where the poor people had to forgo their staple rice for bread and other edible food made from flour.

To the UF's offer of another measure of subsidised rice, the UNP had only tangential and contradictory answers, such as that finances would not permit it, the pledge was merely intended to deceive, that it was an acceptance of the success of the UNP's food drive and that if it were done the price of rice in the open market would be depressed because then rice would have to be imported.

They could not face the question directly. Many UNP candidates asked the Prime Minister, at the conferences that were called from time to time to take stock of the campaign, how they should answer. They were told that they should not place themselves on the defensive and should expatiate on the success of the food drive, the prosperity in the country, the danger to democracy from the Marxists, etc.

The Prime Minister's excuse that the cut in the rice ration became necessary owing to a world shortage of rice was, according to the UF leadership, a deliberate 'lie'. On the contrary, they argued that it was effected at the request of the World Bank, the same organisation which they alleged had imposed humiliating terms relating to the Mahaveli project which were an insult to the sovereignty of Ceylon and perilous to the poor peasant. This, they stated, was only the prelude; it would soon be followed by the undermining of other welfare services such as medicare and free education. The UF argued that they would not accept dictation from any outside agency. To the Prime Minister's question as to how the UF would provide the extra measure, the UF leadership offered different answers on different occasions.

The Prime Minister staked everything on the success of his agricultural campaign. He exploited this goodwill to the utmost. At an election meeting in the heart of the dry zone in Ceylon, in the North Central province at Anuradhapura on 25 March, he said:

Earlier people of the North Central province were dormant. When my father was the first minister of agriculture, he started development schemes ... But the Opposition even at that time went round the country saying that a colossal amount of money had been wasted. It is evident that the colonisation schemes initiated by my father had boosted the food drive in the country.[1]

This theme was repeated over and over again at public meetings and rallies throughout the country as a reminder to the people of the services that father and son had rendered the nation.

What was more, the Prime Minister developed a whole 'philosophy' on the subject of paddy production. In Ukkuwela in the Matale district, he said that the past civilisations of Ceylon had been built on the base of the irrigation tank and the *dagoba*. 'The people', he said, 'drew the water which gave them their material needs from the irrigation tanks, and for their spiritual needs they turned to the *dagoba*.'[2] 'The one was complementary to the other', he stressed. At Anuradhapura, he said 'our forefathers built their great civilisations on the *balaya* (power) of *jalaya* (water).' This theme was expanded, embellished and illustrated with examples from the ancient period and the recent past at UNP propaganda rallies.

At Puttalam, the Prime Minister explained his government's economic strategies. Owing to the shortage in foreign exchange, they decided to reduce as much as possible the exchange spent on imports by producing as much of these requirements as possible locally. At the same time, they organised a drive to export more and more of non-traditional goods and developed the tourist industry. The food drive arose from the compulsion to cut down on imports and as a result much of the Rs. 1,000 million that Ceylon used to spend annually on food imports had been saved.[3]

To the Opposition's pledge to restore the rice cut, the Prime Minister stated there were two ways of doing this. One was compulsory acquisition of all the surplus paddy produced by the farmer as in the war days, with the state fixing the price that would be paid for it. 'Is this what the UF proposes to do?' he asked. The other was to increase rice imports from abroad. This would drain exchange and push down the price of locally grown paddy. His Government had given the farmer the freedom to sell his produce to the state's guaranteed purchasing scheme, or in the open market. There was no compulsory acquisition of crops.[4] At another place, the Prime Minister asked whether the Opposition intended giving both measures of rice free.[5]

The Prime Minister repeatedly dwelt on the fact that his Government gave a measure of rice free to the people. But even if this claim to be the people's benefactor was accepted as valid by a section of the people, the possible electoral goodwill resulting from it was eroded when the UNP's deputy leader stated at a public rally that if the country was to be developed fast, the other measure of rice also should be cut. Mrs Bandaranaike seized on this to expose what she called the UNP's 'real intentions'.[6]

Towards the end of the campaign, the Prime Minister stated that the promise of the two measures of rice by the Opposition was a lie, and that if the latter came to power they (the UF) would create a situation which would make it impossible for the people to question them about their promises.[7]

The UF were shrewd enough not to make an issue of the food drive. Instead, they supported it, thus seeking to deprive the UNP of any credit. But they questioned its success, calling it all 'paper growth' based on exaggerated statistics, and alleged that the benefits, if any, went not to the peasant, but to the big farmers, middlemen, and dealers in agricultural equipment. The UF leadership repeatedly asked why, if the food drive was a success, the Government could not increase the ration of subsidised rice to two measures.

N. M. Perera ridiculed the placing of 'cardboard crowns' on selected *govi rajas* (farmer kings) for their prize harvests in the 'grow more paddy' campaign. T. B. Subasinghe alleged that vast acreages of valuable forest had been leased out under the guise of the food drive to big capitalists, ministers and M.P.s. He added that 'there were bogus farmers who went around the country in luxury cars and jeeps imported for agricultural work' and that out of the 97,000 acres leased out for agricultural purposes not even 5,000 acres had been cultivated. Although the UNP Government had increased the guaranteed price of paddy from Rs. 12 to Rs. 14 per bushel, farmers had to pay high prices for agricultural equipment, fertilisers, and the essential commodities relating to their daily food.[8] The LSSP's Senator D. G. William accused the Government of importing 'minimokes', jeeps and tractors under the guise of the food drive and giving these to their friends and relatives.[9] Felix Dias Bandaranaike rebuked the Government for distributing *itti haal* (unpalatable sticky rice). He admitted having proposed a rice cut when Minister of Finance in the last SLFP Government, but at the present time he would bow to public opinion and fully support the proposal to restore the second measure of subsidised rice. This was not a change of principles, but 'respecting the will of the people'.[10]

There was strong feeling in the country against the need to consume food made of wheat flour to compensate for the loss of the second measure of rice. UF speakers did not hesitate to exploit this situation. In a number of constituencies when ministers of the Government went around canvassing votes, and asked voters whether they remembered the services rendered to them by the UNP, they were told that they certainly remembered them three times a day when they had to eat food prepared from wheat flour.

To the UNP's question as to how the UF planned to provide the two measures of rice, many and sometimes contradictory explanations were proffered by UF spokesmen. On this matter, it was evident that they were caught unprepared and they had not thought out carefully beforehand the economic and financial implications of their promise. Mrs Bandaranaike at first was reported to have said that she was not prepared to tell the Prime Minister how the UF proposed to do it.[11] Shortly thereafter, N. M. Perera is reported to have pledged that the UF would give two measures of rice at 25 cents a measure within a month of their being returned to power.[12] Mrs Bandaranaike when pressed further by the Prime Minister said that as soon as they came to power, they would take stock of the existing supplies of local and imported rice, as she did not know whether the UNP would cause a scarcity, and then decide on the date when the subsidised rice would be issued. They would pay more for the farmer's paddy and they would not allow his interests to be affected adversely.[13] Mrs Bandaranaike came as close as possible to giving an answer when she declared at a meeting on 15 May

This is not the time to conduct classes to teach the Prime Minister and his allies as to how I would restore the rice ration. As such the only simple answer I could give him is that the United Front will give the people the two measures of rice in the same manner it did so from 1956 to 1965.[14]

At another rally on 17 May she said

It is futile to talk of development projects when farmers and workers are starving. Since development projects succeed only when the toiling masses are well looked after, the United Front has decided to issue an additional measure of rice for the ration as soon as it comes to power.[15]

Tied up with the rice issue and the food drive was the question of the condition of the peasantry. The UF asserted that the peasantry was worse off than before in view of the price rises in agricultural equipment and fertilisers, and the rising cost of living. The UNP scoffed at the UF's concern for the peasantry. Nimal Karunatilake, who was general-secretary of the SLFP during S. W. R. D. Bandaranaike's term as Prime Minister and was now in the UNP, alleged that Mrs Bandaranaike vehemently opposed the implementation of the Paddy Lands Act enacted by her husband's Government. This Act, among other things, sought to provide security of tenure for the peasant. Her husband told him that 'the strongest protests to the Paddy Lands Act came from our kitchen'.[16] Further, Philip Gunawardena, who had been responsible as Minister of Agriculture in S. W. R. D. Bandaranaike's Government for the formulation of the Act alleged that Mrs Bandaranaike's father, Senator Barnes Ratwatte, led the *radala* opposition against the implementation of the Act.[17]

The water tax

Next came the issue of the proposal to raise the water tax. Maithripala Senanayake, the SLFP leader of the North Central province and its outlying areas (referred to as the Rajarata) warned that the Minister of Lands, Irrigation and Power, C. P. de Silva, who was the UNP leader for the province, would have 'to charge this exorbitant water tax over the dead bodies of the Rajarata farmers'.[18] He said that, if the World Bank by some chance refused the loan, they would act in the same way that President Nasser acted when aid was refused for the Aswan Dam project. They would get the necessary aid from elsewhere.[19]

C. P. de Silva, replying on behalf of the UNP, alleged that the previous SLFP Government had decided to levy a water tax of Rs. 40 as far back as 1962 under its three-year development program 'without even making available the necessary facilities for cultivation', whereas the present Government hoped to do so only after sufficient water was ensured for paddy cultivation during two seasons in the year and 'after peasant incomes had been stabilised at comfortable levels'. 'The Government', he explained, 'would have to spend a substantial sum of money to effect improvements to peasant colonies.'[20] The SLFP did not answer the charge that they had themselves contemplated the Rs. 40 tax per acre in 1962.

The cost of living and unemployment

These were major issues in the election battle. UF spokesmen made much of the fact that the Prime Minister as a bachelor was unaware of the problems of the home, and ignorant of the requirements of children. Mrs Bandaranaike, they said, as the mother of three children and a housewife, could therefore view with sympathy the hardships that the common people were undergoing.

A very effective piece of UF propaganda was the distribution of a leaflet which showed how various items relating to the cost of consumer goods, agricultural equipment, and building materials had risen between 1965, the last year of the SLFP–LSSP coalition Government of Mrs Bandaranaike, and 1970, the last year of UNP rule. The figures, except in one or two instances, were a correct reflection of the situation then and now.

The UF's remedy for the prevailing situation was a socialist programme which envisaged a fair measure of nationalisation. Their chief spokesmen on this subject were T. B. Subasinghe and T. B. Ilangaratne, Left-wingers in the SLFP. Ilangaratne said that the UF believed in four agencies – the state, the cooperatives, the corporations and the private sector. If the last-mentioned failed to serve the people, the state would have to step in.[21] Subasinghe said that the UF proposed nationalising the external trade and the inland wholesale trade to bring down the cost of living.[22] Not all the means of production, distribution and exchange would be nationalised, but the vital sectors in the economy would have to be. They would however encourage a free retail trade.[23]

The Prime Minister said in defence of his Government that, although prices of goods had gone up, there were no scarcities as in the days of the last SLFP Government. That was, he said, 'the age of queues'. 'The only queues today', he claimed, 'were the usual ones in front of the cinema houses and those at rural banks where prosperous farmers flocked to deposit their money.'[24] 'Goods', he insisted, 'are in plentiful supply and though prices have gone up, people have plenty of money to purchase even the goods they could not purchase before.'[25]

Mrs Bandaranaike replied that there are no queues because there are no goods. She said that the Prime Minister had not seen the long queues that gathered daily at government hospitals for medicare due to malnutrition and at the central employment exchange. There were also queues at bus halts. The state-run Ceylon Transport Board was being mismanaged. 'What we started', she deplored, 'they have ruined' and she added that the nationalised services had deteriorated in the last five years.[26]

The Prime Minister further claimed that his Government had provided certain relief measures to help people meet the increased cost of living by sanctioning salary increases to public servants costing Rs. 250 million and compelling employers in the private sector to give wage increases. N. M. Perera, as Minister of Finance in Mrs Bandaranaike's last Government, could not implement a salary report which would have cost the state only Rs. 60 million. Referring to the UF's leaflet on the cost of living, he said that it would be more pertinent to compare salaries and incomes of people then and now, adding 'I say without fear, increases in incomes have kept ahead of increases in prices.'[27]

The UF made maximum use of the unemployment situation among graduates and the youth especially, to embarrass the Government. 'Never did I promise to solve the unemployment problem completely', said an indignant Prime Minister to the UF's charge that he had gone back on his general election pledge of March 1965. The only solution to 'this grave problem' was to develop the country, and in this he had achieved a measure of success because of the national unity he had established in the country. Mrs Bandaranaike's Government had instead 'sowed the seeds of hatred and jealousy,' a reference to the communal and religious troubles during her term as Prime Minister.[28]

Both the Minister of Finance and the Minister of Education stated that 3,000 graduates would be given employment in May, the month of the general election, in the Ministry of Education.[29] Some 7,000 graduates had applied for the posts.[30]

The UF claimed that they had a ready-made solution to the problem, though N. M. Perera added that it could not be solved overnight, but it would be done in about three months.[31] Among their many solutions was to take over the entire banking system, resurrect the nationalised sector, and train job-seekers and fit them into positions where their skills would be utilised.

The problem of landlessness and its consequence, the drift of unemployed youths from the villages to the towns and cities, was another aspect of the problem. Subasinghe opined that unless some of the estates in the coconut-growing areas and even those in the tea- and rubber-growing areas were taken over, the problem of acute land hunger in Ceylon could not be solved,[32] but the UNP's Minister of Trade and Commerce, Hugh Fernando, ridiculed the proposal, stating that the biggest landowners were in the UF.[33]

Mrs Bandaranaike felt that under 'the capitalist system' the unemployment problem could never be solved. The UNP had tried it for five years and failed; only a socialist Government could solve the problem.[34]

UF spokesmen condemned some of the UNP's plans to alleviate unemployment. One of them accused the Senanayake Government of 're-surrendering Ceylon' to foreign countries and 'virtually making it a trade centre as under the old East India Trading Company of the British'.[35] The UNP's much-publicised tourist drive, also aimed at relieving unemployment, was held up as a grave danger to the nation, its culture and religion, owing to its 'unintelligent promotion'.[36]

Education

The Minister of Education, I. M. R. A. Iriyagolle, was at the centre of criticism. The UF had stated in their manifesto that education had been reduced to 'an utter mess', that the free education scheme had been 'consistently undermined on the instructions of the World Bank' and that the universities are in 'constant turmoil'.

The downgrading of schools, the UF alleged, had denied proper education to thousands of children and the opportunities the poor had of entering universities under the earlier Bandaranaike Governments had been greatly restricted. The number of teachers in schools in 1968 was less than in 1965 and the average annual increase in the number of children attending school had fallen very low in the years 1965–8 when compared with the period 1956–64.

The Minister's action in dismissing teachers who had been politically involved against the UNP in the general election of 1965 was yet another issue. Most of these teachers were active in the UF campaign.

Further, the Minister's scheme for the sale of lottery tickets by school teachers and school children also came in for considerable criticism. Opposition speakers alleged that money had been extorted from the school-going population. Though the proceeds were utilised to improve facilities in the schools and to establish school libraries, none of these good works added to the stature of the Minister.

In sum, it was the UF's contention that the rural children and children of poor parents had suffered under the UNP Government's educational system.

They asserted that only the rich had opportunities of becoming doctors, engineers and lawyers. There were large numbers of children who for want of opportunities had to abandon their education half way. The Minister's move to make a knowledge of English compulsory for university students, they alleged, was a subtle attempt to avoid increasing the number of educated persons in the country.

A youth organisation of the four universities and other major educational institutions – the Sinhala Taruna Sanvidhanaya (the Sinhalese Students' Association) – in a ten-point memorandum to all the major political party leaders called for a special living allowance for all unemployed youth and an end to 'the disgusting discrimination' now prevailing in the country's educational system, while the Ceylon University Teachers' Front condemned the educational policy of the 'National Government' in no uncertain terms.

The iniquities of the Higher Education Act of 1966 promulgated by the 'National Government' was a live issue in the campaign. It was a focusing point for all student ills and problems of higher education in the country.

The Minister's defence was a constant repetition of the merits of his national system of education inaugurated in January 1968, which would solve the unemployment problem and improve the lot of the rural child.[37] He claimed that 500 schools which did not have facilities to teach science had been given these facilities during the last five years.[38] His scheme for the teaching of English in all schools, particularly in the rural areas, would give all children a broad education and enable them to obtain good jobs.[39] 'They would not', he said, 'merely end up as bus conductors, clerks or pupil teachers, as had happened in the past.' UNP spokesmen repeatedly accused the UF of denying the school-going population opportunities of obtaining a knowledge of the English language while they (of the UF) themselves sought to educate their children in the best educational institutions of the West.

With regard to the universities, the Minister made charges ranging from immorality to Marxism against the academic staff, and claimed that under his Higher Education Act he had disciplined both students and staff. The UF leaders replied that there was no student unrest during their term of office.

Political and constitutional questions

Marxism and democracy

The SLFP's alliance with the two Marxist parties, the LSSP and CP, gave rise to several issues in the course of the campaign. The UNP seized on these to warn the electors of impending totalitarianism in the event of a UF victory. Mrs Bandaranaike was well aware of the embarrassments that would arise as a result of her accommodation of the Left, but she had made up her mind to face the issue boldly at the election. At a meeting on 12 May, she told her audience that the UNP had at the 1965 general election misled the people by spreading 'false propaganda' to the effect that if the SLFP–Marxist coalition were returned to power, they would 'ruin the country, the nation and the Buddhist religion'. Because a section of the press had given prominence to this matter, rural womenfolk had entertained great fears against her coalition.[40]

The UNP adopted the posture of being the only party dedicated to the parliamentary system of democracy. The chief protagonists of this view were the Prime Minister and his deputy, J. R. Jayawardene. The Prime Minister at several meetings exhorted the voters to preserve their right to vote, and their freedom to express their opinions in public and to associate in political parties. He warned them that they would lose these rights if the UF were elected to power. He said that they of the UNP were prepared to safeguard these rights even at the expense of 'sacrificing our dear lives'.[41] The country was reminded of the numerous bills Mrs Bandaranaike's previous Government had presented to Parliament to control the press. On the contrary, the Prime Minister believed in a free press which would have even the freedom to publish slanders and falsehoods. R. Premadasa asked for a categorical statement on Mrs Bandaranaike's attitude to the freedom of the press.

As further evidence of Mrs Bandaranaike's alleged anti-democratic tendencies, the Prime Minister said she 'clung on to power' after the general election of 1965 when it was clear that she could not continue in office, whereas he had resigned on every occasion when it became clear that he did not have the confidence of Parliament or the people.

But more than Mrs Bandaranaike, the immediate target was the Marxist parties, and of the latter the LSSP was singled out most of the time. Various phrases were used to describe their policies and motivations, and the electors were treated to a detailed and vivid account of their activities since independence. Those who had defected from their ranks were paraded on UNP platforms to give the people an 'inside view' of what went on behind the barred doors of party conclaves. The burden of the UNP's thesis was that Mrs Bandaranaike in her 'craze for power' had let herself into something the consequences of which she was hardly aware.

The Prime Minister was most vehement in his denunciations. Explaining why Mrs Bandaranaike had joined hands with 'the two totalitarian parties', he said that both groups (the SLFP and the Marxists) were reactionary, the one (SLFP) tried to consolidate the antiquated *nindagam* system (feudal land tenure), the other sought to consolidate totalitarianism.[42] He reminded voters of the alleged attempts of the SLFP–LSSP Government of Mrs Bandaranaike to do away with the democratic system step by step in the second half of 1964, and added that democracy was saved in Ceylon because of C. P. de Silva and thirteen of his followers deciding to defect from the SLFP as a protest against these moves.

At election meetings in south Ceylon on 10 and 11 May, the Prime Minister told his audiences about the 'anti-national' positions taken by the LSSP on the issue of Indian citizenship and language whereas they were now accusing him of betraying the country to the Indians and betraying the Sinhalese language. He scorned their new-found love for Buddhism, stating that when he was

Prime Minister in 1952 he had arranged to make a grant to a Buddhist celeb-
ration in Burma and though his proposal was approved by non-Buddhists both
in his Cabinet and in Parliament, the LSSP leader, N. M. Perera, had disagreed,
on the ground that state funds should not be utilised for religious purposes.[43]
But now the LSSP accused him of striking at the Buddhist clergy.

The Prime Minister said that the LSSP organised some 300 strikes in a year
when S. W. R. D. Bandaranaike was head of the Government, and harassed
Mrs Bandaranaike in the first four years of her administration. Now they
profess to want to protect the Bandaranaike principles and speak in glowing
terms of the lady's 'noble programme'.[44] 'What', he asked, 'had become of the
twenty-one demands that N. M. Perera had formulated along with his colleagues
on behalf of workers and peasants when they formed the United Left Front
in 1963? I've seen political parties in action in Ceylon, I've heard of political
parties abroad and I've read about them, but never have I heard of any party
which has done as many somersaults as. the LSSP.'[45] He likened them to
political chameleons and condemned them as 'debased, cunning and treacherous'.[46]

But coupled with all the virulence of these attacks was also the firm conviction that the LSSP would fare disastrously at the elections and cease thereafter to be a political force of any consequence. Both in his private observations
and in his public utterances, the Prime Minister stuck to the view that the LSSP
was 'finished' and that its leader (N. M. Perera) and deputy leader (Colvin R.
de Silva) would definitely lose. At many meetings, he said 'Do not believe me,
but just pay a visit to those constituencies and see things for yourselves.'[47]

J. R. Jayawardene presented a systematic exposition of Marxist techniques
for the seizure of power, giving the examples of East European countries and
of Indonesia, Malaysia, Bengal and Kerala to drive home his point. He reminded people of Stalin's liquidation of thousands of kulaks. The LSSP and CP,
Jayawardene claimed, had tried for thirty years and realised that they could
never capture power on their own. That was why they had aligned themselves
with the SLFP in the hope of having a share of office in a SLFP Government.
When Mrs Bandaranaike took the LSSP into her Government in 1964, one of
the first proposals of the LSSP was to restrict speeches of Members of Parliament to only twenty minutes. 'But W. Dahanayake (the Southern UNP leader)
had thwarted this move', he added, 'by threatening to speak non-stop until
he died on his feet in defence of free speech.'[48] 'Wherever Marxists came into
power with the help of another party, they saw to it', said Jayawardene, 'that
they were given power over such key portfolios as those which had to do with
the police, finance and local government. They would', he added, 'cut the ground
under the feet of the party with which they came into power.'[49] It was his view
that 'if the Communist Party becomes strong, they will first of all throttle our
party, and they will restrict our freedom; they will next throttle the SLFP and
then they will snuff out the freedoms of democarcy in our country.'[50] Jayawardene argued that the SLFP had jettisoned the democratic principles which the
late S. W. R. D. Bandaranaike enunciated when he founded his party.

What the Prime Minister and his deputy said on almost every platform was repeated by other UNP stalwarts and candidates at their meetings. From the campaign speeches, it appeared quite clear that apart from the fact that the SLFP's acceptance of the two Marxist parties gave the UNP an issue on which they could raise the greatest amount of controversy, the UNP tended to regard the Marxists as a greater danger to them than the SLFP itself.

Philip Gunawardena in his appearances on UNP platforms and at his own MEP meetings raised questions on language and religion with a view to embarrassing his former comrades of the LSSP. He accused the latter of trying to betray the masses to a feudal leader, and of helping feudalists to enter Parliament with their kith and kin. The LSSP had no future in this country and were in a state of dissolution.

But while damning his one-time colleagues, Philip Gunawardena had also to explain why he, as a 'Marxist', had joined Dudley Senanayake and the 'capitalist' UNP. Philip Gunawardena argued that Dudley Senanayake had agreed to form 'a National Government in 1970' which he (Philip Gunawardena) had advocated as far back as March 1960, owing to the disturbed conditions in the country. This Government had followed 'a democratic path towards socialism', which objective he was confident would be reached in a few more years.[51]

Philip Gunawardena's contribution to the UNP's effort however was minimised, if not nullified, by his son's appearance on UF platforms. Mrs Bandaranaike dismissed him as a man in search of Cabinet office which she alleged was his sole motivation for joining her husband's coalition in 1956, and Dudley Senanayake in 1965. 'He would never have otherwise', she said, 'become a minister.'[52]

While Philip Gunawardena made his excuses for joining Dudley Senanayake's 'National Government', the Peking-Wing communists and the revolutionary Trotskyists aimed their attacks with equal fervour on the UNP, SLFP, LSSP and the CP.

The UF's response was a detailed account, from their point of view, of what the UNP had done to undermine the democratic processes. There was prolonged rule by emergency regulations. The 'National Government' had suppressed a great many democratic freedoms. Mrs Bandaranaike cited the instances of her husband's assassination, the 'incitement' of the Roman Catholics in 1961 against her Government's nationalisation of the schools, the attempted *coup d'état* by high officers in the armed forces and the police in early 1962, and the 'engineering' of the defection of members of her party in late 1964 resulting in her parliamentary defeat, as evidence of the impatience of 'the reactionary forces' (the UNP) with the constitutional processes of government. At one or two of her election rallies, Mrs Bandaranaike hinted that the code name of 'Shelly Silva' used by the *coup* conspirators of January 1962 referred to none other than Dudley Shelton Senanayake himself who was then the leader of the Opposition.[53] 'If they were dedicated so much to the democratic system,' asked Mrs Bandaranaike as well as most of the other leaders of the UF, 'why did the "National Government" give high appointments to the *coup* leaders in the public and private sectors?'

As for the alignment with the Marxists, Mrs Bandaranaike complained that when Dudley Senanayake took Philip Gunawardena into his Cabinet or indicated his desire to have the LSSP in his Government under certain conditions, the pro-Government national press had no criticisms to make or editorials to write on the subject, but they adopted a different and hostile attitude when she did the same thing. Her Marxist allies for their part maintained that they were committed to working within the parliamentary system. Colvin R. de Silva stated that they were all for democracy, while N. M. Perera, replying to the UNP's taunts about his twenty-one demands, said that 'underhand methods, manipulated cross-overs' prevented him from implementing them. He was minister only for six months, but had he succeeded in implementing them, the UNP, in his view, would never have been able to come back to power.

The UF had realised that the attempts of the SLFP–LSSP coalition Government of Mrs Bandaranaike in the latter part of 1965 to take control of Lake House had given its opponents an opportunity to organise a great public agitation against what the UNP and its allies regarded as the threatened onset of dictatorship planned by the Marxists. They were therefore determined to avoid a controversy on this subject once again, but their pronouncements on the issue left room for much speculation. As early as 13 March, Leslie Goonewardena (LSSP) said at a seminar on 'Revolution, Democracy and Socialism' sponsored by the Roman Catholic Peter Pillai Institute of Social Studies in Colombo, that the LSSP had never stood for the *complete* takeover of the press, but then this did not provide any assurance that sections of the press would not be nationalised.[54] In fact, Goonewardena in explaining why the LSSP supported the bill to nationalise Lake House stated that the latter held a monopoly in the field and 'they present news as they see it, and views as they conceive them'. The UF would assist the growth of 'independent newspapers' operated for instance by mass organisations like trade unions and cooperatives so that there will be 'a healthy competition' among newspapers.

Felix Dias Bandaranaike for the SLFP deliberately held out a threat when he said on 23 March: 'We shall watch carefully the policy followed by newspapers in connection with the forthcoming general election. If the press tries to mislead the masses and functions in an unjustifiable manner we shall do what is necessary as soon as we come to power. Therefore the press should realise that its destiny lies in its own hands'.[55] And the UF manifesto released on 20 April left the entire issue in doubt again when it stated: 'The freedom of the press will be ensured. Independent newspapers will be encouraged as a means to end the present domination of the daily press by capitalist monopolies.'

One of the ways of ending this domination by capitalist monopolies would be to take them over and give them to mass organisations or cooperatives.[56] Another way would be to starve them of Government advertisements or newsprint quotas. In short, the big newspapers were left in doubt concerning their future.

Mrs Bandaranaike did not help to clarify the situation in her public pronouncements. She condemned severely the partisan reporting of Lake House and, in some of her later speeches, made it clear that the takeover of the press was not an issue with her. But in an earlier pronouncement on the subject, at a meeting in her own constituency, she dismissed Lake House definitions of a free press as being those of Western journalists, and added that the first duty of a free press is not to abuse its freedom.[57]

The pro-Government national dailies, especially those published by Lake House, continued with the controversy. An alleged statement made by one of the SLFP's lesser-known candidates, S. D. R. Jayaratne, to the effect that 'immediately after forming a Government, the UF would take steps to gag the capitalist press', was seized on by the *Ceylon Daily News* to editorialise on the subject of 'imprisoning the people's mind'.[58] It described the UF's pronouncement on the subject in its manifesto as being 'calculatedly ambiguous'.[59]

What the UNP leadership sought to achieve was to create doubt in the public mind about the veracity of the UF's pronouncements. The view was expressed in private by the Prime Minister to at least one newspaper proprietor that the UF had tried once and would try again, i.e. to nationalise the press, no matter what they might say in their public statements.

People's committees

However, on the question of people's committees, the UNP raised the greatest amount of controversy in the hope of creating public misgivings on the dangers of totalitarianism arising therefrom. And here once more the UF, caught unprepared, could not provide a straightforward answer – its spokesmen giving contradictory explanations at different times, with of course a hostile press occasionally seizing on incorrect versions to add to the discomfiture of the UF leadership. Mrs Bandaranaike stepped in ultimately to reassure the public with a carefully worded statement of what exactly these committees were intended to be. This statement was printed in thousands and distributed to the public.

The occasion for the UNP's outcry against these committees was the publication of the UF manifesto on 20 April and the references contained therein to these organisations. The Prime Minister described these as instruments which would be used 'to fasten the iron collar of totalitarianism on the people', adding that these were 'the forms of regimentation used in totalitarian regimes'.[60] The Prime Minister as well as other leaders emphasised that the fate of Kerala and West Bengal under communist or communist-inspired Governments awaited the people of Ceylon once these committees were established. J. R. Jayawardene went so far as to say that, under these committees, the judicial processes would be mocked; justice would be dispensed on the Galle Face green; and people would be hanged in full public view. As if to lend credibility to these assertions, some of the over-enthusiastic SLFP new recruits spoke intemperately. The alleged view of the SLFP candidate for Ratnapura that 'those who exploit the national wealth disregarding the democratic rights of the people will be skinned alive on Galle Face Green',[61] was used to great advantage by the UNP despite the candidate's denials.[62] The Prime Minister himself at election addresses on 3 May asked whether all this was 'civilised talk'.[63]

UNP spokesmen alleged that under the rule of these committees, public servants would face the prospect of losing their positions. The UNP's Minister of Local Government (R. Premadasa) wished to know why, when there were so many local bodies in the country which were 'real people's committees', the UF sought to establish other 'pseudo-democratic organisations'. A statement attributed to N. M. Perera and other UF spokesmen that the UF's election committees would be converted to people's committees gave the UNP an opportunity to accuse the UF of seeking to replace the democratically elected instruments of government with partisan bodies. In short, the UNP assertion was that these committees would usher in a party dictatorship and destroy democracy. The Prime Minister touched on a sensitive political issue when he asked whether the UF hoped with these committees 'to open the door' towards the very same district councils which they (the UF) had so vigorously campaigned against when he had attempted to introduce them.

There was obviously an unexpressed divergence of opinion on the nature and functions of people's committees between the Marxists and the SLFP. Both Mrs Bandaranaike and Felix Dias Bandaranaike thought of these committees as simple advisory bodies which would bridge the gap between ruler and ruled. Mrs Bandaranaike further claimed that these committees had been envisaged by her late husband. She stressed that they would be constituted irrespective of political, caste, religious, or racial considerations. She characterised the UNP's concept of democracy as 'the rule of a small clique of capitalists from above'.[64] She and N. M. Perera stated that they were at a loss to understand the UNP's opposition, when the UNP's own Minister of Finance had originally suggested the idea of people's committees in his first budget speech in August 1965.

The Left wing in the UF were more articulate and definite about what they thought these committees should do. LSSP spokesmen explained that through these committees 'the imperialistic system of *kachcheri* administration' would be changed and the poor masses rescued from 'the iron heel of the bureaucracy'.[65] T. B. Subasinghe said that these committees would eradicate inefficiency, bribery and corruption in the public service, adding 'when the people take part in the administration, the imperialistic framework of the state would be broken and the capitalist class would be deprived of all the privileges that they were enjoying today. The reason for their fear was only that and nothing else.[66]

By the first week of May, the issue had become so very contentious that Mrs Bandaranaike was obliged to issue a statement explaining in detail its implications.[67] 'I can categorically assure the country', she said, 'that it never has been our intention to convert election committees to people's committees, as maliciously misrepresented. Nor will these be partisan bodies packed with party cadres. These committees', she added, 'will consist of persons with a supreme sense of civic responsibility and unqualified acceptability to the people of the area.'

Financial corruption and nepotism

Other issues of subsidiary political significance raised in the course of the campaign were the question of the rupee fund, the presence of a fair number of Mrs Bandaranaike's relatives as candidates in the UF's nomination list, and allegations and counter-allegations of bribery and corruption in the ranks of the UNP and the SLFP.

UNP spokesmen asked why the UF should need an election fund when the election laws had been revised adequately to permit even the common man to fight an election. This was R. Premadasa's contention. 'Did Mrs Bandaranaike have any ulterior motive?', he asked, 'and would she give a full account of the money received and the money spent?'[68] Hugh Fernando raised similar questions and sought to create further doubt in the public mind by asking whether the country had been given a detailed statement of receipts and expenditure of the funds collected for the Bandaranaike memorial at Horagolla?[69]

Mrs Bandaranaike stated that funds were required to help their poor candidates who did not even possess loudspeakers. She alleged that the UNP had summoned 'capitalists and big businessmen' to 'Temple Trees' (the Prime Minister's official residence in Colombo) and demanded huge contributions to swell their funds. 'Why was it therefore only bad for her to launch a rupee fund?', she asked. She was prepared to account for every cent collected.[70] But Hugh Fernando retorted that some of the UF ex-M.P.s and ex-ministers lived in palatial buildings, a number of their candidates had applied to buy new cars at prices ranging from 20,000 to 30,000 rupees, and their appeal was therefore meant to deceive the people.

The presence of Mrs Bandaranaike's relatives in the UF's list of candidates gave rise to questions. The UNP argued that they (these relatives) were 'hardened feudalists' who had no concern for the problems of the people. Dudley Senanayake said that his endeavour was not directed towards consolidating either 'radala balaya' (feudal power) or 'pawul balaya' (family power) but in promoting the interests of the country. He had relatives who could win seats.[71] But instead he nominated 'young and energetic' candidates to contest seats. Mrs Bandaranaike retaliated with a pertinent counter-accusation. Most of D. S. Senanayake's relatives were members of his Cabinet and she reminded the public of his request to the then Governor-General, Viscount Soulbury, that in the event of his death, his son Dudley should succeed him.

The UF realised that further explanation was necessary. T. B. Ilangaratne said that Mrs Bandaranaike's relatives had come forward to save the country while Dudley Senanayake's relatives were only interested in amassing wealth and 'collecting commissions on business deals'.[72] T. B. Subasinghe stated that Mrs Bandaranaike had not selected candidates, but a committee of twelve members of which he was secretary. Loyalty and efficiency were the only criteria for selection. 'Some candidates may be relatives of Mrs Bandaranaike, but this could not be helped in a country where everyone was related to everyone else in some way or another', he added. 'If the people wished to elect them to Parliament, what right', he asked, 'has the Prime Minister to object?'

To the UF's repeated challenge that the 'National Government's' administration had been characterised by bribery and corruption, the Prime Minister reminded the SLFP of the Bribery Commission's Report of 1960 which found a number of SLFP Members of Parliament guilty of corruption. He further alleged that Mrs Bandaranaike's Government enacted a bill to enable those found guilty of bribery to escape. P. B. G. Kalugalle on behalf of the SLFP said that a UF Government would enact legislation to punish with life sentences persons found guilty of bribery and corruption during the term of the 'National Government', but R. Premadasa replied that such legislation should also apply to those found guilty in the earlier Bandaranaike Governments when bribery and corruption, he alleged, were at their peak.

The proposed new constitution

The question of a Constituent Assembly and a new constitution was not a major issue in the campaign, but the UNP tied it up with the general question of democracy, dangers of dictatorship and fundamental rights. Some UF spokesmen said that they proposed doing away with the parliamentary system, to which UNP leaders replied that there was a clear danger of dictatorship through constitutional change and that the UF meant business when they said that they would change the system of government if they won power. J. R. Jayawardene took the position that the proposal to establish a Constituent Assembly would in itself be an illegal act when there was a constitution in existence which prescribed the procedure for changing it. The UF leadership ignored these questions, but were proud that they were going to abolish 'the present outdated imperialistic constitution' and make Ceylon a republic.[73]

Communal questions

The Ceylon Tamils and the FP

The claims of the Sinhalese Buddhists and the problems of the minority groups – religious and ethnic – are intertwined in the cultural complex of Ceylonese politics. The UNP was vulnerable because of its private agreements with the two Tamil groupings, the FP and the CWC. The UF did not directly assail the UNP on this question by raising the Tamil cry as a naked political issue. It used more devious methods to undermine the UNP's standing in the Sinhalese areas. The crudities emanated more from Hema Basnayake's cohorts which the UF exploited to its own advantage.

There was also R. G. Senanayake's SMP with its extreme Sinhalese Buddhist stance. Its role was open to question in the whole campaign. Mrs Bandaranaike had lumped it with the UNP. Tied to the question of the UNP's concessions to the Ceylon and Indian Tamils were the fears and grievances of the Sinhalese Buddhists.

The Muslims and the Roman Catholics looked askance at the UNP. Both groups felt that they were being taken for granted. The UF leadership once more successfully traded on their grievances.

What was damaging to the Prime Minister and the UNP was the FP's exit from the 'National Government' because a major premise in Senanayake's claim to have ushered in national unity was the FP's participation in it. Naturally Mrs Bandaranaike and her colleagues scoffed at this national unity, but the UNP persisted in its claim to have reconciled the minority groups.

The UNP leadership insisted that there was harmony in the country. It was now possible for political leaders to visit the Tamil areas and to be welcomed by the people in those parts. The Tamils were, they claimed, satisfied that their language had been accorded a measure of recognition by the Tamil Regulations enacted by Parliament in January 1966. Peace and unity had helped to accelerate economic development.

The Prime Minister insisted that the UF had embodied, in their manifesto, his view that communal harmony was a pre-requisite for economic development. Also, whereas in their Common Programme of February 1968, they stated that they would replace his 'National Government's' Tamil Regulations with regulations of their own, in their manifesto they were significantly silent on this question. 'Had they accepted his Regulations?', he asked; 'If so, why had they created all the disturbances at the time Parliament was debating them?'

The Prime Minister dismissed contemptuously the UF's proposal to enact legislation to punish anyone instigating violence against any person or persons on grounds of race, religious beliefs, caste or language. In his opinion, they (the UF) would be the first people to be punished under that law.

The Tamil Regulations coupled with the abortive District Councils Bill of the 'National Government' made the UNP vulnerable vis-à-vis the Sinhalese and Muslim electors – especially the Sinhalese Buddhists. There were attacks both from the UF, and from Hema Basnayake and his companions.

The accidental death, caused by police firing, of the young Buddhist monk, the Rev. Dambarawe Ratnasara, on the day the UF organised public demonstrations against the Tamil Regulations – 8 January 1966 – wrought considerable damage to the UNP's position. A UF poster depicting in an inset the execution of a Buddhist monk in 1848 by order of the British Governor of Ceylon at that time, Viscount Torrington, with the larger illustration showing a policeman in 1966 firing at demonstrators, and a Buddhist monk lying dead on the road, was widely distributed in all the Sinhalese areas. There were words in Sinhalese on the poster to the following effect: 'In 1848 the imperial British Government murdered the Reverend Kudapola. After that it was on 8 January 1966 that such a thing happened again. This is what your Government did to your language and your religion. We don't want the Tamil Act.' The death of the Buddhist monk by police action was a recurring theme in UF speeches.

A poster on the District Councils Bill created just as much embarrassment. It showed the Prime Minister with J. R. Jayawardene holding a lighted candle, about to sign his 'secret agreement' with the FP leader, S. J. V. Chelvanayakam, at the hour of midnight. The caption to it ran: 'The service your Government rendered to the Sinhalese race – the secret agreement of 24.3.1965'.

Mrs Bandaranaike warned the country while on a tour of Muslim electorates in the Eastern province that the Prime Minister had not abandoned the District Councils Bill and that he had so far maintained discreet silence over it. Mrs Bandaranaike further alleged that though the Prime Minister was now attacking the FP, he would team up with them after the elections as he had done in 1965.

The Prime Minister was quick to reply to Mrs Bandaranaike's taunt about his silence on the District Councils Bill. He assured the country that he had abandoned it and he denied having any understanding with the FP.

Basnayake, explaining his present hostility to the 'National Government', alleged that it had turned anti-national and anti-Buddhist as evidenced in (*a*) its amendment of the Land Settlement Act to enable citizens by registration (Indian Tamils mostly) to own land, (*b*) its adoption of the Tamil Regulations of January 1966, and (*c*) its failure to settle Sinhalese colonists in the Tamil-speaking areas of north and east Ceylon. He also alleged that the District Councils Bill would be revived at the appropriate time.

The second prong of Basnayake's campaign was against the Government's agricultural policies. In his opinion, the farmers had not benefited, the people were poorly nourished and the economic situation was hopeless.

Replying to Basnayake, the Prime Minister said that he wished to remind him that he (Basnayake) had told him that Mrs Bandaranaike's alliance with the Marxists should be opposed because it was a danger to Buddhism.[74] K. M. P. Rajaratne, leader of the JVP, assured the Sinhalese that though Dudley Senanayake accepted FP support to set up a Government in 1965, the rights of the Sinhalese people had not been affected by so much as even 'the size of a grain of mustard seed',[75] while the Buddhist monk orator, the Rev. Devamottawe Amarawansa, carried the war into the enemy's camp, as it were, when he accused the late S. W. R. D. Bandaranaike of giving unlimited rights to the Tamil language by his Government's enactment of the Tamil Language (Special Provisions) Act in 1958.

The Indian Tamils

The support of the CWC was more consistent than that of the FP. But again, the UNP was faced with one more embarrassment. There had been an understanding between the CWC leader, S. Thondaman, and Prime Minister Senanayake regarding the way in which the Indo-Ceylon Agreement of October 1964 (Sirima–Shastri Pact) should be implemented, and Thondaman was satisfied with the outcome.[76]

The CWC of all the plantation workers' organisations was thought to be the closest to delivering the Indian vote to the rival bidders. But once more, the timing of the decision and the publicity given to it could not but have had adverse effects on the UNP's propects *vis-à-vis* the Sinhalese voters. The CWC made known its decision on 11 May 1970. This gave the UF ample time and opportunity before election day on 27 May to tell the voters who 'the culprits' were in the business of 'selling the rights of the Sinhalese' to the Tamils. The Kandyan Sinhalese had already developed hostility to the manner in which Senanayake had proceeded to implement the Indo-Ceylon Agreement of 1964 – especially their elites. And the decision of the CWC to support the UNP merely reinforced their convictions.

The UF once more played a skilful game in exploiting anti-Indian sentiment, while not alienating the Indian Tamils altogether. For the DWC had decided to support the UF, and DWC votes in a number of constituencies were thought to be crucial. There were besides other Indian Tamil workers' organisations under Left-wing control – the LSSP-sponsored Lanka Estate Workers' Union, the CP's United Estate Workers' Union – which were supporting the UF. All these organisations condemned Thondaman for supporting 'the capitalist UNP'. There were, above all, the decisive factors of the rice ration and the soaring cost of living. Indian workers were just as affected as the Sinhalese and Mrs Bandaranaike took the opportunity to explain to the Indian workers the benefits they would derive from a UF victory.

The Muslims

Where the Muslims were concerned, the UNP was once more on delicate terrain. The UNP no doubt had strong Muslim support – but this was mostly from the older generation and the vested interests among them. The younger Muslim intelligentsia, who wanted recognition, felt that this was not forthcoming from the UNP. This section of Muslim intelligentsia felt that under UNP Governments the Ceylon Tamils gained at their expense, whereas with the SLFP they would stand to gain. The senior men of standing among the Muslims urged them to support the UNP, but the disaffected among them, as well as the poor Muslims, were well organised under Badiudin Mahmud's ISF which was affiliated to the SLFP. The ISF's impact on the Muslims was far from marginal; our investigations indicated that in the Sinhalese areas sections of Muslim opinion had been weaned away from the UNP as a result of the ISF's campaign.

The chief political spokesman of the UNP Muslims was M. H. Mohamed, Minister of Labour. Mohamed represented essentially the urban affluent and mainly Colombo-based Muslims but the rural tradesmen and others among them were expected to support the UNP – an altogether baseless calculation.

While problems of education and economic survival beset the Muslim community, Mohamed followed the UNP lead of decrying 'materialism' and 'ungodly communism'. Mahmud denied that his ISF stood for communism, but protested that Islam is a socialist doctrine – 'therefore while we will tread the path of socialism, we are not communists', he insisted.[77]

The attitude of the anti-UNP Muslims was best depicted by the former UNP

Muslim M.P. for Batticaloa, A. Latiff Sinna Lebbe, who resigned from the party some weeks before nomination. He said,

It is common knowledge that the Muslim voters of this country in 1965 voted practically *en bloc* for the UNP. This, it must be admitted, they did in spite of the many advantages they derived during the two Bandaranaike Governments. They were led to believe that if the coalition (SLFP–LSSP) came to power, it will spell doom on their livelihood and destroy their religion.[78]

Sinna Lebbe deplored the fact that the same kind of propaganda was continuing, while the 'National Government' had 'taken away many of the benefits they (the Muslims) enjoyed under the successive Bandaranaike governments'.[79] Rightly or wrongly, this was the impression left in the minds of sections of the Muslim intelligentsia, generally.

The debate within the Muslim community was how much or how little the SLFP or UNP Governments had done for their well-being. A. C. M. Ameer, Q. C., another prominent Colombo UNP Muslim, listed the hardships that the Muslims experienced under SLFP Governments in the course of his countrywide campaigning – especially their take-over of the leading Muslim secondary school, Zahira College. But the grievances he listed were not ones which directly affected the poor Muslims. He stated that Felix Dias Bandaranaike as the first Finance Minister in Mrs Bandaranaike's Government permitted only once-in-a-lifetime pilgrimages to Mecca for the Muslims, while Ilangaratne as a minister of the same Government, by legislation, made it obligatory for all Muslims to prove they were citizens of Ceylon when involved in the purchase of landed property. Against this list, however, Mahmud had concrete evidence to show his fellow men the benefits that had accrued to them during the period of the Bandaranaikes, in particular in the field of education. The eve-of-election message of the ISF to all Muslim voters contained an impressive list of the educational and cultural amenities they had obtained under the Bandaranaikes.[80] Under the last UNP Government, on the other hand, Mahmud complained that instead of the promises given to the Muslims being implemented, that Government had given more benefits to the FP and 'was dancing' to the latter's tune.

The rival party leaders also made their own appeals to the Muslim community. Dudley Senanayake warned the Muslims during his electoral tour of Muslim constituencies in the Eastern province that when the UF had 'finished with the Tamils, they will finish you next'. He cautioned them against the UF tactic of courting the Muslims by telling them 'the Tamil is your enemy'. 'My advice to you', he said, 'is not to get drawn into the same old game of divide and rule.'[81] Mrs Bandaranaike, on the other hand, called on the Muslims to support the UF because the UNP which had promised to safeguard their rights had 'cheated' them, while N. M. Perera assured the Muslims that the UF had also provided for a programme of work for the upliftment of the Muslims.

The question of foreign policy, especially Arab-Israeli relations, and the attitude of Muslims towards communist states were expected to influence the Muslim vote. The UF manifesto favoured the Arab position. Mrs Bandaranaike reiterated this in her addresses in Muslim majority constituencies. Similar if not more strongly worded sentiments were expressed by other UF spokesmen.

Minister Mohamed protested that the 'National Government' had at all times championed the Arab cause and would continue to do so at all times, while another Colombo-based UNP Muslim Queen's Counsel, Izzadeen Mohamed, alleged that Mahmud's ISF was 'a political device to entrap the Muslims in the communist net'.[82] He added that many belonging to the Muslim faith in the Soviet Union had suffered indignities at the hands of the Soviet authorities and three million of them had fled to Iran, Pakistan and other Arab countries since 1917. He asked whether it was not a fact that all the Islamic states such as the UAR, Pakistan, Indonesia and Malaysia had not outlawed the communists.

The Roman Catholics

The Roman Catholics on this occasion were in no mood to be led into voting for the UNP because of the 'dangers' of communism or prospects of harassment from an allegedly militant Buddhist United Front. And the supreme hierarchy of the Church maintained a stubborn, if not conspicuous silence. For one thing, they realised they could not strongly influence their flock who were undergoing the same economic hardships the rest of the country was undergoing. For another, they were bitter and very resentful of the way in which the Prime Minister had gone back on his commitment to provide a measure of relief to those schools privately maintained by the Church after the nationalisation of schools in 1960–1 by Mrs Bandaranaike's SLFP Government.

The Roman Catholics had other grievances. During the first half of the 'National Government's' term of office, no Roman Catholic had been included in the Cabinet. But, more importantly, the sabbath holiday was replaced with *poya* holidays without the Roman Catholics being adequately consulted. The Roman Catholics had recorded their protests at two by-elections in the Catholic belt when UNP candidates won, but with their majorities reduced. But the UNP and its own Catholic leadership was apparently unaware of the developing situation. At least one UNP Catholic M.P. informed the Prime Minister that there was no need for him (the Prime Minister) to visit his constituency. He was so certain of victory. At the count he lost by 10,000 votes to the UF candidate.

The UF campaign in the Catholic areas was well managed by Felix Dias Bandaranaike. Quite pertinently he told them that they had lost their *buth* (food) and their sabbath, that the UNP had gone back on their promises to the hierarchy, that for the first two odd years of the 'National Government', not a single Roman Catholic had been included in the Cabinet, that in short the Catholics had been 'taken for a ride' by the 'National Government'.

The questions of the sabbath and the nationalisation of schools were important issues on which both the UF and UNP speakers dwelt in their campaign in the Catholic areas. Ilangaratne accused the Prime Minister of acting 'dictatorially' in abolishing the Sunday holiday, while Leslie Goonewardena accused the UNP of going back on its promises to the Catholics. 'The ten commandments have been destroyed', he said, 'because of the *poya* holidays.'[83]

A Buddhist chief priest's (the Venerable Dhammaratana) announcement at a coalition rally in Kelaniya that the UF would restore the sabbath holiday for the Catholics and have the full moon day as a *poya* holiday for the Buddhists was the occasion for protests from the All Ceylon Buddhist Congress and from leading Buddhist monks. But the controversy did not go any further, though Lake House was eager to raise it to the level of a national debate with a view to embarrassing the UF leadership.

Hugh Fernando, the only Roman Catholic minister in the 'National Government', endeavoured to explain that Catholicism did not require that the sabbath day should be observed only on Sunday.

The UF denied that the nationalisation of schools was specifically directed against the Roman Catholics. 'The real purpose was', they protested, 'to give an equal education to everybody alike.'

Against the UF attack, the UNP retaliated with accounts of the past humiliations and hardships suffered by the Roman Catholics during the period of the two Bandaranaike Governments. The chief UNP Catholic spokesmen were Hugh Fernando, who accused Mrs Bandaranaike of feigning pro-Catholicism only 'to capture' the Catholic votes, and Denzil Fernando, the sitting Roman Catholic UNP M.P. for Negombo at the time of dissolution and Mayor of that city, who kept reminding his co-religionists of all the indignities inflicted on them by the Bandaranaike Governments. Denzil Fernando urged the incorporation of a bill of rights in the constitution as a safeguard for the future.

The UF leadership was shrewd in trying to wean off the Catholic vote from the UNP. Mrs Bandaranaike played the leading role in the effort to convince the Catholics. Towards the end of her campaign, she asserted that in spite of the UNP charges of anti-Catholicism, the Catholics were 'turning to the UF with a massive show of support never seen before'. She attributed this change in attitude to the economic hardships felt by the Catholics.

The Protestant Christians

The Protestant Christian leaders in general urged support for the UNP directly, and sometimes indirectly. The statements of the Church of Ceylon's Bishop of Colombo and a former President of the Methodist Church in Ceylon on the day prior to the general election could not but have left any reasonable person with the impression that they were not in sympathy with the UF, and cautioned the Christian man to beware of its political ideologies.[84]

The debate in the Tamil-speaking areas

The arguments and counter-arguments of the chief spokesmen of the main Tamil parties, the FP and TC, referred to earlier, became bitterly personal and acrimonious as the campaign drew to a close. None of the important economic questions, such as those relating to rice and the cost of living, which engaged the attention of the people in the Sinhalese areas, appeared to bother the Tamils. Part of the reason for this was the over-concentration by the Tamil leadership on constitutional formulae as solutions to the problems confronting the Ceylon Tamils. But there was also the fact that paddy and onion cultivators in the Northern province and paddy cultivators in the Eastern province had gained from Senanayake's food drive. There was considerable unemployment among qualified Tamil people, but it was all blamed on the discriminatory policies of the Sinhalese-oriented Governments, their nationalisation policies which the Tamil leadership equated with 'Sinhalisation' and the rigours of the Official Language Act.

The Tamil youth were tired of listening to these oft-repeated excuses. Sections of them therefore broke off their support of the traditional parties, especially the FP, and switched to other groups.

C. Rajadurai, one of the FP leaders of the Eastern Province, claimed that the unemployment problem is not only found among the Tamils. In his view, it was common to all the 145 electorates in Ceylon, including those of the Prime Minister and all ministers. Chiding the impatience of people who kept asking what the FP had done in all these years, Rajadurai drew attention to the long-drawn-out freedom struggles of India (150 years), Fiji (87 years) and African countries. 'A great deal of sacrifice and suffering would have to be undergone', he said, 'before freedom could be won by the thirty-five lakhs of Tamils who formed one third of the population of Ceylon.'[85]

Chelvanayakam said that after the general election of March 1965 both the UNP and the SLFP sought the support of the FP because neither of these parties were in a position to form a Government of their own. 'Since the SLFP deceived us in 1960, we helped the UNP to form the Government', he said.[86] It was his view that the Tamil community 'had gained something' by joining the UNP-led 'National Government'. Chelvanayakam insisted that if the people supported the nineteen candidates that the FP had put forward 'any Sinhala party will seek our help'.[87]

These were in effect replies to the taunts of the TC leader, G. G. Ponnambalam, who said that since both the SLFP and UNP had publicly disavowed the FP, the Tamil electors would be wasting their time and resources in supporting the FP. 'The only path left for the Federalists is to fight with the Sinhalese', argued Ponnambalam, and he posed the question over and over again whether Chelvanayakam was prepared to follow such a course of action.

The Federalists dismissed Ponnambalam's contention that only his Congress could successfully put across the grievances of the Tamil people to the Sinhalese leaders and win for them their 'lost rights'. Naganathan, one of the FP's senior leaders, argued 'time has revealed and proved that all parties in the south no matter what their professed ideologies, composition or colour ultimately develop into rabid Sinhala communal parties wanting to annihilate the Tamils in this country'.[88] Chelvanayakam insisted that the FP could, if necessary, use the satyagraha weapon to fight for the rights of the Tamils, and the general secretary of the party warned that 'as long as the rights of the Tamils were not granted and as long as the FP existed, no party would be able to run a government peacefully'.[89]

The TC countered the FP charge that it had 'betrayed' the Indian Tamils by supporting the citizenship legislation of the D. S. Senanayake Government in 1948, with the accusation that the FP had done worse by supporting the 'National Government's' implementation of the Sirima–Shastri Agreement of 1964 and had agreed to the plan to repatriate 525,000 Indians. The FP's answer was that this had been agreed to by the Indian Tamil leaders, Thondaman and Aziz, and that it was because of the FP's opposition that 'the obnoxious clauses' in the agreement were removed. Further the FP claimed that the agreement provided for 350,000 stateless Indians obtaining Ceylon citizenship, which in itself was an achievement.

The main accusation of the TC that the Tamil areas had gained nothing from the FP was not answered adequately. FP leaders referred to the sacrifices they had made to defend the rights of the Tamil-speaking people, their success in preventing further colonisation of the Tamil areas by the state, and the advances made in regard to securing recognition for the Tamil language, but these were not substitutes for roads, bridges, schools, hospitals, factories, employment, etc. From the results, evidently this is how sizeable sections of the Ceylon Tamil voters felt.

Conclusion

Most of the issues raised by the UF had been the subject of continuing controversy from the second year of the 'National Government' taking office. The campaign only brought these into sharper focus, producing the atmosphere of a national debate between the two opposing groups. But it is doubtful whether the respective arguments and defences did make any serious impact on the mass of voters who had already made up their minds several months before the election.

The only new issue was that of people's committees and the other instruments of participatory democracy that the UF proposed. But even this had been included in their Common Programme in 1968. Lake House and the UNP had tried to capitalise on it with a view to shifting votes from the UF.

What mattered more, therefore, was the technique of campaign management and the efficiency of the respective parties in organising support to ensure the maximum possible turn-out on election day. Here the UF, judging from the results, appeared to have had an advantage. Not only were its supporters anxious and enthusiastic to record their protest but its organisers at all levels made every endeavour to maintain excitement and interest till the actual day of the election. More importantly, there was the definite prospect that those who supported them would obtain certain benefits from their victory – the second measure of rice at a heavily subsidised price, other food items at subsidised prices and the possibilities of employment in an expanding public sector. Underlying all this was of course the resentment of the underprivileged and the 'have-nots' against a Government which they identified with the rich and the powerful.

The UNP had its solid base but was unable to mobilise the interest necessary to make certain that the entirety of its vote would be registered on election day. For one thing, its election apparatus was not as efficiently maintained as that of its rival. An excessive emphasis appears to have been placed on their leaders and candidates. For another, there was little or nothing that their supporters could hope to gain from their victory. The Government had run its course for five years, dispensed patronage and tried in its own way to improve living conditions and provide employment. The question naturally arose, what more could people gain from another UNP victory.

In the Tamil-speaking areas, the lines of debate between the two main contestants were not so sharply drawn. What either side was saying had been said many, many times over since 1949, the year in which the Federal Party was inaugurated in opposition to the TC. The question at issue was which of the two parties could be depended on to safeguard the interests of the Ceylon Tamils. There was no doubt that both parties would in the event of a UNP victory seek an accommodation with that party. Opinion was divided on this matter, a section of the electors feeling that the UNP's ally in the Northern province, the TC, and the UNP's Tamil candidates in the Eastern province could better provide the necessary benefits than an intermediary such as the FP. In a way it seemed therefore that TC and FP support was directed towards the UNP. Other issues were passed over for the one central question as to which party could be depended on to make the best deal.

8. The role of the national press and the Ceylon Broadcasting Corporation

There is a wide reading and listening public in Ceylon, especially as the literacy rate exceeds 80 per cent. Newspapers and the broadcasting system are the cheapest sources of information available in Ceylon.

Ceylonese newspapers sell within the price range of 4 to 5 pence per copy. Distribution figures at face value are not very impressive, though a Sinhalese weekly, the *Silumina*, claims to have the biggest circulation in south and southeast Asia. But often a single newspaper passes from one hand to another and from one family to another. On this basis, a reading public of approximately 1,400,000 in an adult population of 7,800,000 can safely be reckoned.

The national press

Ownership and biases

The three most important national press combines in Ceylon are the Associated Newspapers of Ceylon Limited, better known as Lake House, the Times Group, and the Independent Newspapers of Ceylon Limited. Together they publish five English, four Sinhalese and three Tamil dailies, besides many weeklies in the three languages referred to – all of which are very influential. (See Table 18.)

Ranjith Wijewardena, who has the controlling interest in Lake House, is (as already stated) the son-in-law of Robert Senanayake, brother of Dudley Senanayake. One of the principal shareholders of the Independent Newspapers of Ceylon Limited is the daughter-in-law of Hema Basnayake, who was one of Dudley Senanayake's bitterest opponents in the election campaign.

The Times Group of newspapers received no intensive proprietorial direction nor had they a direct interest in the outcome of the election campaign in the way that the other two groups were motivated, but its principal editorial directors had definite UNP sympathies.

Lake House in particular was expected to make an all-out effort to bolster the UNP's election campaign. Other than the family relationship, Lake House had reason to fear a take-over and refused to place any credence in the UF's assurances that they had no interest in this question any more. The directors of Lake House also had serious charges laid against them relating to alleged illegal exchange transactions by the leaders of the UF. The matter had already been debated in Parliament and figured in the course of the election campaign. The Times Group supported the UNP, though not in the open and deliberate way that Lake House did.

The Independent Newspapers of Ceylon Limited also operate important and influential newspapers, particularly in Sinhalese. They had supported the UNP

Table 18.   *Circulation of major newspapers, 1 January – 30 June 1970*

	Name of paper	Language	Average daily circulation
Associated Newspapers of Ceylon Limited (Lake House)*	*Ceylon Daily News*	English	72,403
	Ceylon Observer	English	12,509
	Ceylon Observer Magazine Edition (weekly)	English	86,777
	Dinamina	Sinhalese	123,892
	Janata	Sinhalese	31,015
	Silumina (weekly)	Sinhalese	355,020
	Thinakaran	Tamil	34,074
	Thinakaran Vara Manjari (weekly)	Tamil	37,329
Times Group*	*Daily Mirror*	English	17,217
	The Times of Ceylon	English	8,867
	The Times Weekender (weekly)	English	29,613
	Lankadipa	Sinhalese	57,769
	Sri Lankadipa (weekly)	Sinhalese	133,093
Independent Newspapers of Ceylon Limited†	*Sun*	English	6,800
	Dawasa	Sinhalese	58,600
	Weekend Sun (weekly)	English	‡
	Savasa (weekly)	Sinhalese	‡
	Dinapathy	Tamil	12,100
	Virakesari	Tamil	‡
	Eela Nadu	Tamil	‡

SOURCE: As stated below.
*Figures as published by the Audit Bureau of Circulation, Ceylon.
†Figures were obtained from investigations made by us. They are fairly accurate and are calculated to the nearest hundred.
‡Figures not available.

in the general election of 1965. But after 1965, they turned against the UNP, carried on a sustained campaign against the 'National Government' and were particularly critical of Dudley Senanayake and his Minister of Education, I.M.R.A. Iriyagolle.

Lake House and Independent Newspapers of Ceylon Limited provided wide coverage to the election news from as early as the first week of February in their English and Sinhalese newspapers. The Tamil newspapers published by them did not provide as much coverage to the election news in the Sinhalese areas, concentrating more on the campaign in the Tamil constituencies of north and east Ceylon.

Lake House Newspapers

Up to the date of Parliament's dissolution (25 March),[1] Lake House provided within limits fair coverage to meetings organised by the UF and speeches made by their principal spokesmen. An attempt appeared to be made to strike a balance between Government and Opposition. Speeches by the UNP leaders were given more prominence, but the Opposition was also provided with coverage. For instance, the *Ceylon Daily News* of 17 and 18 March had detailed and prominent accounts of speeches by Maithripala Senanayake on 'the People's Revolution' (17 March) and the Mahaveli river diversion (18 March), and by T. B. Ilangaratne on his views on Dudley Senanayake (17 March) and American imperialism (18 March). The *Ceylon Daily News* of 25 March had a further account of Ilangaratne's attack on Western imperialism, while that of 26 March contained a speech he made in a Roman Catholic constituency on Jesus Christ being a socialist. Of course, all these issues of the *Ceylon Daily News* gave wider coverage to speeches of UNP leaders. But it could be argued that statements of the Prime Minister and his ministers are more news-worthy than those by Opposition leaders and therefore deserve greater prominence.

After 25 March, the slant of news in the *Ceylon Daily News* was against the Opposition. For example, the *Ceylon Daily News* of 28 March had headlines in prominent type of a speech by N. M. Perera promising rice at 25 cents a measure, when in fact the UF had not made a decision on the economics of restoring the cut in the rice subsidy imposed by the 'National Government'. The same issue of the *Ceylon Daily News* in its front page carried a carefully edited account of Prime Minister Senanayake's review of his five-year term of office at a press conference he summoned for the purpose at his private residence in Colombo on 27 March. The Prime Minister's explanation of sensitive issues such as the FP, citizenship for Indian Tamils, the shortage of rice, were given in prominent type, as were the claims he made to establish that his administration had achieved a measure of success in the important sphere of national development. Thereafter, more often than not, the headlines were against the UF.

Further, from time to time, there were speeches that were not accurately reported. For instance, the *Ceylon Daily News* of 29 March reported that Anil Moonesinghe had said that the UF would change the parliamentary system in six months, while that of 18 April stated that N. M. Perera had declared that the UF's election committees would function after the elections as advisory committees to the new UF government.

The editing and reporting created a certain amount of uncertainty if not doubt and confusion in the public mind as to what would follow if a UF Government were installed in office. The *Ceylon Daily News* of 31 March reported T. B. Subasinghe as having said that the UF would take over the import, export and wholesale trade while those of 8 and 13 April reported Mrs Bandaranaike (8 April) and Colvin R. de Silva (13 April) as having said that the unemployment problem could not be solved within the existing capitalist framework. These may have been true, but the selective prominence given to them was intended to alarm middle-class susceptibilities. Felix Dias Bandaranaike was described as 'the lone ranger' in the UF fighting to safeguard democracy[2] while most of the speeches of the UNP leaders inclusive of the Prime Minister were reported from the anti-Marxist angle.

What is more, the racial and religious minority groups were warned of the dire consequences that would befall them in the event of a UF victory. The *Ceylon*

Daily News of 13 April gave prominence to a speech of the Prime Minister during his tour of Muslim constituencies in east Ccylon with the headlines, 'You will be Finished after Tamils, says Dudley to Muslims', while an earlier report of a speech by the Prime Minister carried the headline: 'Opposition Leaders Speak with Double Tongues – Tailor their Speeches to Suit Religion and Race'.[3]

Two other big headlines sought to create doubts on the race issue. They read as follows: 'Two Measures – Coalition's Last Trump – To Deceive People and Win Votes'[4] and 'Coalition will Promise, then Stop Democratic Elections – Says Prime Minister'.[5]

Similar headline reporting was repeated in the evening English language publication, *The Ceylon Observer*, and its weekend version, *The Ceylon Observer Magazine Edition*. The *Observer* also had an enterprising cartoonist, Wijesoma, who through his caricatures, depictions and short sentences sought to portray the UF, its leaders and its policy statements in an adverse light.

Our examination of the Sinhalese-language publications of Lake House, particularly the daily issues of the *Dinamina*, its weekend version, the *Silumina*, and the evening daily, the *Janata*, of this period indicates that especially in the case of the first two, wider coverage than was given in the English-language publications was provided for meetings addressed by R. G. Senanayake, the leader of the chauvinistic Sinhalese Buddhist-oriented SMP. It gave substance to Mrs Bandaranaike's charge that the SMP was a Lake House creation intended to draw away votes from the UF. Wide publicity was also given to UNP speeches, but the reporting was of cruder quality – no attempt being made to clothe the abusive expressions in finer language, as was done in the English-language dailies.

There was occasionally extensive reporting of speeches by UF leaders, but this was far from the general rule. The pattern was true of the English-language dailies and truer of the Sinhalese dailies. The UF's Kurunegala rally was given wide publicity in the *Ceylon Daily News* of 1 April, as was its rally in Polgahawela in the *Ceylon Daily News* of 7 April and in Gampaha in the issue of 24 April. A few other meetings and speeches by Mrs Bandaranaike were also given adequate publicity.

Sometimes the reports of speeches of UF leaders were given *in extenso* in the hope that these would discredit them more than do them any good. This was especially so with regard to their references to the Prime Minister. For instance, the *Ceylon Daily News* of 16 April carried the detailed report of a speech by Maithripala Senanayake in the headline; 'The Reason why P. M. is Called a "cad" and "Pacha Bahu"', while his references earlier to the Prime Minister's 'political caddishness' also received prominence. Presumably it was felt that these unconventional epithets hurled at a personage who had a reputation for correct behaviour in public life would outrage the sensibilities of those, especially the non-committed, who had faith in his integrity.

After nomination day – 23 April – Lake House all but declared war against the UF. The attempt at maintaining appearances as a national press was continued, but the reporting of UF meetings more often than not seemed to have the purpose of exposing differences in its ranks and raising doubts as to the validity of its promises.

The *Ceylon Observer Magazine Edition* of 21 April carrying the front-page banner headline on the UF manifesto, 'People's Committees will be Watchdogs' gave the signal for the attack, as it were. Its Sinhalese counterpart, the *Silumina* of the same date, carried similar headlines emphasised in red type. Thereafter between 50 and 60 per cent of the reporting was on the dangers facing democracy from Marxists, people's committees, proposals to change the constitution, etc.

As against the hostile headlines given to the UF manifesto, the *Ceylon Daily News* of 29 April carried the UNP manifesto with the caption 'Peace and Stability', obviously directed more at its staid and sober middle-class reading public than at its other readers. But Lake House's Sinhalese-language weekend publication, the *Silumina* of 28 April, gave the headline 'Further Benefits to Cultivators' to the same UNP manifesto, which was of course meant for the rural public and the large numbers of peasants that form the highest component of Ceylon's agricultural complex.

The following headlines were typical of the reports of speeches made by UF leaders, as edited and published in the *Ceylon Daily News* (our examination of its sister publications reveals that similar headlines appeared in the *Ceylon Observer* and the *Dinamina*):

> 'People's Committees will Govern Country' – issue of 27 April
> 'Committees will Rescue Masses from under the Iron Heel of Bureaucracy' – issue of 30 April
> 'We'll wipe out UNP when we come to Power – Ellawala' – issue of 4 May
> 'First Power by the Ballot. Then we will Rule through People's Committees: Check on Bureaucrats' Activities – Ilangaratne' – issue of 4 May
> 'No Changing of Governments after we Come to Power – Gunasekera, People must Ensure that for all Time' – issue of 9 May
> 'If Coalition is Returned, end of UNP for ever: No Chance to Form another Government – N. M. Perera' – issue of 10 May
> 'Parliamentary System will be Changed Says Gnanasiha Thero' – issue of 11 May
> 'Nanda Ellawala Warns: Struggle will be Carried on outside Parliament' – issue of 12 May
> 'After 27th we will Take Revenge: Dhanapala Weerasekera Warns those who Bark at Coalition Now' – issue of 12 May

The reports of speeches by UNP leaders of Marxist attempts to subvert the democratic processes were also given similar headlines. A speech by J. R. Jayawardene carried the following banner headlines in the *Ceylon Daily News* of 29 April: 'People's Committees will make mockery of justice: Government Servants, Grama Sevakas (village officials) will lose their jobs: Public Hangings on Galle Face Green?' and a speech by Professor Stanley Kalpagé, a UNP senator, carried the headline 'Danger of Dictatorship through Constitutional Change' in the *Ceylon Daily News* of 26 April.

The spectre of defeat facing the Marxists was a constant theme of speeches by the Prime Minister and senior leaders of his party, and these again were blown up into headlines. A special column captioned 'From the Electorates' which appeared from time to time in the *Ceylon Daily News*, and another column called 'Campaign Politics' in the *Ceylon Observer Magazine Edition* highlighted statements by UNP leaders of how poorly the LSSP and CP candidates were faring in their electorates, among other things.

Speeches of former members of the LSSP and CP against their ex-comrades were given publicity, especially attacks against the LSSP made by Philip Gunawardena and the revolutionary LSSP, and the broadsides directed against the CP and LSSP by the Peking-wing CP.

Reports of speeches by UNP leaders and their allies also made out that the Buddhist clergy and Buddhism faced grave danger in the event of a UF victory. Typical were the headlines which appeared in the *Ceylon Daily News* of 24 May: 'Slave Labour Threat to *Sangha* (the Buddhist clergy) from Coalition: Malwatte Monks Threatened'. Another headline in the *Ceylon Observer Magazine Edition* of 5 May which sought to cause embarrassment to the UF over alleged promises made by some of their leaders that they would restore the sabbath holiday read as follows: 'No, say Buddhist monks to Coalition plans to change *poya* holidays'.

On the day of the general election itself, the *Ceylon Daily News* had the following front-page banner headline: 'Coalition Fake Shattered: Mahanayake "Do not be duped: Marxist Philosophy won't protect national and religious interests"'. Similar headlines appeared in the *Dinamina* of that day and in the *Ceylon Observer* of the previous evening (26 May). These statements by the Head of the main sect of Buddhist monks in Ceylon were intended to contradict reports which appeared in the English and Sinhalese newspapers of the Independent Newspapers of Ceylon Limited, the *Sun* and the *Dawasa* respectively, as well as in *Sirilaka*, the official daily of the SLFP. These had stated that the Buddhist prelate had extended his good wishes to Mrs Bandaranaike and her UF. The venerable monk, some time after the election, said that he had issued this contradiction under duress.

On the day before the general election, the *Ceylon Daily News* had in its first column on the front page the word VOTE set out in prominent type, listing seven reasons why people should use their vote. In substance, it was an appeal to the electors to vote against the UF because it said that, if the latter came to power, people would lose their right to vote.

The *Dinamina* of the same day was even more specific. It carried an editorial entitled 'Supreme Day, Supreme Duty' in which it exhorted the electors to cast their votes, regardless of the weather, as a sacred duty for the party which would safeguard their democratic rights and freedoms – the UNP. What is more, the same issue of the *Dinamina* carried a four-page election supplement in which, by pictorial representation and engaging phraseology, an effort was made to link Buddhism closely to the economic and especially agricultural progress made during Dudley Senanayake's premiership. The first page of the supplement (page

9) had various portrayals from the history of Buddhism with the caption: 'The country (Ceylon) to which the Buddha entrusted the protection of Buddhism. See that Buddhism which was here for 2,500 years is not destroyed. This is the duty of the people.' The second page had photographs of the Prime Minister depicting his identification with Buddhism and with the reconstruction of some of the most important Buddhist shrines in Ceylon. The third page illustrated 'the philosophy of the irrigation tank and the *dagoba*' with pictures of the Gal Oya and Uda Walawe irrigation schemes, and of the Oruwela site of the State Steel Corporation, presumably to emphasise the UNP Government's interest in industrial development as well. The last page had photographs of the Prime Minister participating in various Buddhist ceremonies and a picture of the Prime Minister almost waist deep in a fully grown paddy field. It carried the key sentence: 'When we have the tank and the *dagoba*, why should we go after the hammer and sickle?'. (Note, the *Dinamina* of 25 May also had an illustrated page with the caption 'What the Leaders of the "National Government" did to Help Buddhism'.)

The reports of UF speeches by the Lake House press were slanted to indicate that religious and linguistic minorities would not be treated fairly. Rather they would be persecuted once more under a UF Government.

Attempts were also made to give the electorate the impression that the UF's policy on the Tamil language was no different from that of the UNP. On 27 April a headline in the *Ceylon Daily News* read: 'Big Fuss then, but now they've Accepted "Tamil also Laws" – Dudley Senanayake'. The issue of 6 May had the headline: 'Parity of Status for Sinhalese and Tamil Says Leslie Goonewardena up North'. But on 5 May the *Ceylon Observer Magazine Edition*'s 'Campaign Politics' column referred to the 'subtle' anti-Tamil line being followed by UF campaigners in the Sinhalese areas, while on 9 May the *Ceylon Daily News* carried the following headline: 'Tamil Language Regulations a Betrayal: Sinhala Officers will Have to Know Tamil Claims Felix Dias Bandaranaike'. The intention of all this was to set the Sinhalese against the UF, on the one hand, and the Tamils against the UF, on the other.

In the weeks after nomination day, it seemed very clear that the reporting and news coverage in the English and Sinhalese newspapers of Lake House were deliberately aimed at putting the UF on its defence. Those speeches of UNP leaders and their allies which were attacks on the UF and its policies were given greater prominence while UNP explanations on the reasons for the high cost of living, unemployment and other embarrassments in the economy, which were also recurring themes, though not emphasised, were hardly reported – not even their claims of success in the food drive. Most of these receded to the background. On the other hand, Lake House reports of speeches of UF leaders could be interpreted mainly as defences to ward off UNP attacks. From the point of view of election strategy, the UF's situation (as depicted by Lake House) was by no means enviable, and this is precisely what the press sought to achieve by its partisan reporting.

Our examination of the reports of UF meetings sent by various reporters of

Lake House to the head office indicate that in many instances they were not adequately reported, or were published if the effect would have adverse consequences for the UF. Both Mrs Bandaranaike and her deputy, Maithripala Senanayake, complained to senior journalists that reports of their speeches were distorted and sometimes fabricated. Mrs Bandaranaike further complained that speeches never made by UNP leaders were reported in the papers published by Lake House.

Lake House had its own field staff reporting back to headquarters from time to time about the progress being made by UNP candidates in the various constituencies. These reports (private information) indicate the direct and immediate interest that the proprietors of the most powerful press in Ceylon had in the outcome of the election.

The reports dwelt on the activities of the candidate, his success or shortcomings in canvassing, the effect of speeches made at meetings by leading party figures, the need for other important party personalities to address meetings in order to excite caste or religious groups as well as youth in the cause of the UNP, the shortage of transport, and lack of party literature for distribution to the electors in several named constituencies.

But as the campaign progressed, the field staff informed the head office that the UNP would come out victorious – a mistaken assumption as the final results indicated – and perhaps this optimism, among other reports, made the UNP general staff itself confident of the outcome. The specific questions that these reports sought to answer leave us with no doubt that the information thus gathered was passed on to the UNP's campaign managers for necessary action.

Lake House reports from the Tamil areas indicated that the FP would emerge as the party with the largest number of seats. Though the Lake House field staff were confident that the UNP would hold its ground, there was uncertainty as to whether that party would gain a clear majority. Whatever the Prime Minister may have thought on the subject (and it was evident that he was piqued by the FP's attitude), some of the policy-makers of Lake House felt that in the end it would become necessary for the UNP to seek the assistance of the FP. The Lake House papers therefore were not entirely against the FP, despite the fact that the latter had broken its ties with the UNP and was taking an independent stand, and often an anti-UNP position, in its campaign for the Tamil vote.

In other words, Lake House did not wholly support the UNP's Tamil ally, the TC. For instance in its issue of 6 May, the *Ceylon Daily News* gave detailed coverage and favourable headlines to the FP's manifesto while the same paper in its issue of 25 April provided only a detailed summary of the TC manifesto. In fact, those high up in the TC protested with no results to Lake House over this specific instance of what they felt was discrimination against them.

All in all, reportage of FP and TC meetings in the *Ceylon Daily News* was fair to both groups. However, FP speeches on the UNP's 'secret undertakings' to them were not given publicity and were seldom reported; yet, speeches by FP leaders, such as those of Chelvanayakam, on the approaches made to the FP by the SLFP were given prominence. So were speeches made by Tamil politicians reminding the Tamil electors of the hardships and indignities they (the Tamils) suffered during the periods of SLFP rule. Such reportage (on the SLFP's approaches to the FP) was for the Sinhalese electors, while publicity of FP and TC condemnation of the SLFP's Sinhalese chauvinism was evidently for the benefit of Tamil voters in the Sinhalese areas.

TC speeches which were critical of FP policies *vis-à-vis* the Sinhalese parties, especially the UNP, and of FP leaders were given due publicity. The speeches of the leader of the new Tamil Self-Rule party were also publicised. These were embarrassing to the FP leadership. But they nevertheless were reported.

In the Tamil-language daily of Lake House, the *Thinakaran*, which had the largest circulation among the Tamil public in Ceylon, the campaign was directed more towards the Tamil voting public in the Sinhalese areas. FP and TC meetings were reported but not extensively or prominently. There was no obvious evidence of discrimination in favour of one or the other of the two parties. But for a Tamil newspaper with such a large circulation, more adequate coverage would have been expected for these parties.

Speeches of the Prime Minister and J. R. Jayawardene on the theme of national unity were usually given banner headlines (see, e.g., the *Thinakaran* issues of 14 and 28 April, and 1 and 26 May), as were the appeal of the CWC to the Indian Tamil workers to support the UNP (14 May) and the statement of Dr M. C. M. Kaleel, the Muslim elder statesman, on why he had always supported the UNP (26 May). Similar appeals and speeches by Indian Tamil and Muslim leaders were reported in other issues of the *Thinakaran*.

The *Thinakaran* of 26 May for obvious reasons contained a middle-page feature article by C. Eesvaranathan under the following headlines and sub-headings: 'Was it Government? The Kind of [Mob] Rule that Took Place in 1958: the Pathetic Death of a [Tamil] Person who Went to Purchase Milk: the Young [Tamil] Girl who was Raped in a Sugar Cane Plantation'. The same issue of the *Thinakaran* expressed the indignation of Tamils in Ceylon over the alleged reports of the FP's secret discussions with the SLFP.

In addition to these reports of the speeches and statements of spokesmen from the contending parties, Lake House newspapers published a series of articles and editorials critical of the SLFP and condemnatory of its Marxist allies. These were generally repeated in the Sinhalese-language *Dinamina* and *Silumina* but not as frequently in the Tamil *Thinakaran*. Appendix 1 gives a detailed and representative selection of the material that was published in the *Ceylon Daily News* and the *Ceylon Observer* during the period of the campaign.

The Times Group

The Times Group did not identify itself as actively with the UNP as the Lake House press, but its sympathies nevertheless were undeniably with that party. Of its papers, its morning English-language daily, the *Daily Mirror*, and its Sinhalese-language daily, the *Lankadipa*, took a greater interest in the election campaign than the older and more restrained evening English daily, *The Times of Ceylon*.

On 17 March the 'Opinion' column (really another name for its daily editorial) of the *Daily Mirror* stated that it would set aside a special page in its daily issue to be called 'On the Election Front' for the publication of election speeches. It added: 'We are allocating the same proportion of space to every party so that we will hold the scales evenly, at least where speeches are concerned, and let the readers judge the merits of the parties involved, from their verbal displays.' Broadly, it could be said that this paper stood by this arrangement, though in political sympathies it was more with the UNP than with the UF and more with the TC than with the FP.

The paper has a fairly wide reading public among the Tamils and Roman Catholics, especially among lower-grade public servants and their counterparts in the mercantile sector. Its general reading public is of the lower-middle-class level, but also comprises some sections of the middle class.

The *Daily Mirror*'s presentation of news may have been fair in the general context of things. But through its 'Opinion' column, through its political commentator, Maithri, and its cartoonist, S. C. Opatha, it made no effort to conceal its dislike of the UF, especially of the latter's Marxist component. Further, the way in which some of the news was presented leaves us with no doubt that the intended effect was to alienate voters from the UF and the FP.

The *Daily Mirror*'s viewpoint, in its 'Opinion' of 27 May (the day of the general election) set out on its front page, in large headlines, 'Now or Never, So Vote for Your Nation and Your Future', was indicative of its sympathies. The following lines, among others, by implication, asked the people to vote UNP:

The choice is as simple as investing one's money in a bank. Does one deposit one's earnings in a reputed, solid, established and secure bank or in a bank of hazardous, dubious reputation? None but the mentally unbalanced should not know the right answer. The consequences of ill-considered vote deposits in the ballot box are suicidal.

In fairness to the *Daily Mirror*, its 'Opinion' did not always support the UNP. In fact, on many occasions it was highly critical of UNP policies and personalities.

Maithri, the *Daily Mirror*'s political commentator, chose the occasion of the election period to start a series (commencing 4 May) on political parties in Ceylon. His interpretation of party development and party policies indicated a bias in favour of the UNP, and a hostility to the SLFP. The instalment which appeared in the issue of 15 May was accusatory of S. W. R. D. Bandaranaike's Prime-Ministerial ambitions and his conversion from Christianity to Buddhism. Appearing so close to the date of the general election, it cannot but be assumed that it was intended to have some effect on the *Daily Mirror*'s *petit bourgeois* reading public who would have been swayed by appeals to prejudices of this kind. Maithri rounded off his series with a contribution on 27 May entitled 'The General Elections 1970, Points to Ponder', printed in prominent type. It asked a number of questions of the voter which carried obvious answers, the substance of these being that he should exercise no other option than that of voting for the UNP. These comments and 'Opinions' were, towards the closing stages of the campaign, backed by news which would have had adverse consequences on the electoral prospects of the UF and the FP.

On 14 May, the *Daily Mirror* carried a report of headlines that had appeared in the FP's weekly *Suthanthiran* lashing out at the UF and calling it 'a blood-thirsty, man-eating tiger'. It was said at the time that Tamils in Sinhalese constituencies dissatisfied with the policies and actions of the 'National Government' were contemplating voting for the UF. A report of this kind would have made them think again.

Similarly on 25 May the *Daily Mirror* reproduced by courtesy of the *Catholic Messenger* an article entitled 'Using Your Vote'. This was couched in rather vague terms and the unquestioning faithful could have interpreted it as an appeal to vote for the party of stability, for the party which stood for freedom, for private initiative and for national solidarity. To its reading public, such a party was none other than the UNP.

On the day of the general election, the *Daily Mirror* carried a picture of the Hindu high priest, Shri Sharma, a Tamil-speaking brahmin, who had, in the *Daily Mirror* of the previous day, issued an appeal to the public to return a party that 'would safeguard freedom of worship and communal concord' (which from his point of view was the UNP) with a report to the effect that the priest's brother was killed by a Sinhalese mob during the racial riots of May 1958 – in the time of S. W. R. D. Bandaranaike. Obviously the purpose of this news item on that day was to canvass the support of the Tamil public for the UNP.

The *Daily Mirror* of 26 May carried an 'eve of election call to voters' by heads of the Buddhist, Church of Ceylon, Muslim and Methodist religious confraternities. The message was clear in the case of the last three mentioned – in effect, vote UNP.

In its issue of 19 May, the *Daily Mirror* carried a front-page report of exploratory talks between the UF and the FP regarding the possibilities of a *rapprochement* between the two groups. This seemed a reversal of the position of the FP, as was reported in the *Daily Mirror* of 14 May (referred to above). But evidently there were more weighty considerations at stake. Tendentious reports of this nature could damage the prospects of both the UF and the FP, nullifying sometimes the purposes of their respective campaigns. Further, the *Daily Mirror* was sympathetic to the TC, and the TC leader was known to be in difficulties in his constituency (Jaffna) where he faced a powerful FP rival and an equally powerful Independent candidate. A report of a proposed UF–FP agreement at this stage would possibly alienate the Roman Catholic and some of the Tamil support of the FP candidate in Jaffna, and these votes would, hopefully, go to the TC leader and not to the Independent candidate, for the latter was definitely identified with the SLFP. The *Daily Mirror*'s reports of the UF–FP talks must therefore be considered against this background.

In its issue of 23 May, the *Daily Mirror* carried front-page banner headlines to the effect that the UF–FP talks *did* take place, while it also gave publicity to denials issued by the FP leader, S. J. V. Chelvanayakam, and by Senator A. P. Jayasuriya, a senior vice-president of the SLFP. The *Daily Mirror* insisted that its information was absolutely correct. Presumably, FP men who had no mandate from the party *did* engage in exploratory talks with equally non-accredited UF leaders. When we interviewed Chelvanayakam, at this time, about the veracity of these reports, he replied 'We have not at this stage even thought of what we should do after the elections'. When we asked whether there was any truth in the current rumour that one of his chief lieutenants, M. Tiruchelvam, had been involved in unofficial talks with SLFP men, Chelvanayakam replied that he had asked Tiruchelvam about these rumours, that Tiruchelvam denied them and he (Chelvanayakam) had every reason to trust the word of Tiruchelvam.

The *Times of Ceylon* was subdued in contrast to the *Daily Mirror*'s aggressive journalism. But it was well-known that *The Times of Ceylon* was the organ of conservative interests and had, therefore, nothing to conceal. This paper too gave publicity to the alleged talks between the UF and the FP and was lukewarm in its publication of the denials. On the eve of the general election in its 'Focus' (editorial) column (on 26 May), it made clear its stance when it cautioned the voter not to 'permit himself to be led up the garden path by slick sales talk which promises the sun and the moon'.

Our investigations indicated that the Sinhalese-language daily of the Times Group, the *Lankadipa*, was, until the day of the general election, comparatively speaking, the most impartial of the national newspapers in Ceylon. *Lankadipa's* editorial staff is usually recognised for its record of independent journalism.

With one or two exceptions, which seemed to favour the UNP especially in headline reporting, we found that *Lankadipa's* presentation of the election speeches of the rival groups was fair and balanced. Generally on a single page in its middle sheet, the *Lankadipa* devoted roughly one half to important speeches by UNP leaders and the other half to speeches by UF leaders. Sometimes a whole page contained UNP reports, but on such occasions there was substantial space in another page devoted to UF reports. The reporting we found was straightforward and direct, not devious or intended to discredit one side or the other.

Nor did *Lankadipa* have the usual run of middle-page feature articles, until a few days before the election, warning electors of the dangers that may follow victory by one side or the other. It did not even, generally speaking, editorialise on such matters. We noted that one editorial, that of 25 March under the caption 'Historic Date', was complimentary of the 'National Government's' five-year term, but this we thought was giving praise where praise was due. Most editorials however were of a non-partisan character dealing mostly with national problems.

Not even the *Lankadipa*'s skilful cartoonist, 'G. S. F.', used his brush to tar either political grouping. Usually his cartoons were in good humour, making fun of the election gimmicks of political parties, and the strategems and artifices of rival candidates seeking votes.

The activities of the Ceylonese 'Che Guevarists', the PLF, were given great prominence, particularly in *Lankadipa*'s issues of 20 April and 15 May. In both issues the banner headlines ran across the entire front page. But a careful reading of the reports that followed did not indicate any evidence of an attempt to link the activities of these extremist Marxist revolutionaries with those of Mrs Bandaranaike's Marxist allies, as for example some of the Lake House newspapers had tried to do.

Lankadipa's independence began to erode with the approach of the elections. In its issue of 22 May, there appeared a feature entitled 'Regarding the Friendly Talks between the UF and the FP' in which an attempt was made to establish the fact that there had been talks between the two in the past and there was no reason why the UF should be 'shy' of having discussions with the FP. It argued that if the SLFP has 'pacts' with the LSSP, CP and ISF, why should it not have a similar arrangement with the FP? This would bring communal peace to the country, it insisted. In substance, this article was more or less a repetition of what the *Daily Mirror* had been dwelling on for a long while.

In its issue on election day (27 May), *Lankadipa* came out openly on the side of the UNP. In an editorial which was inserted in its first page, and not in the middle page, as is its practice, *Lankadipa* reproduced almost verbatim what the *Daily Mirror* had stated in its 'Opinion' column of the same day, already referred to earlier. It was an open invitation to the voters to choose the UNP, the party which it said had given peace and stability to the country and promoted its economic development. Readers were asked to vote for their country and their religion, not merely to bring a party or an individual to power. The editorial was captioned 'Think Before You Leap'.

The Independent Newspapers of Ceylon Limited (the Dawasa Group)

The national dailies of the Independent Newspapers of Ceylon Limited – the *Sun* (English) and *Dawasa* (Sinhalese) – maintained a sustained campaign against the UNP while their Tamil counterpart concentrated on the FP. In effect, the publications of the Independent Newspapers of Ceylon Limited supported the Sinhalese Buddhist nationalist stance adopted by representative sections of SLFP opinion while giving grudging support to the SLFP's alliance with the Left-wing parties. Their position was best expressed by the columnist writing the 'How's That? How's That? How's That?' feature in the *Sun*. On 26 May, the columnist said that 'Many of the leftists are rather old men, and the major strand in the party is by no means committed to extreme measures' and that 'there are also strong elements in the party (SLFP) specially concerned to preserve and restore Sinhala culture and Buddhism', adding that 'these are wholesome values'. But he cautioned that, in the UNP, 'there are threats to true religion' and he suggested that 'greater threats to true religion' emanated more from 'the naked secularism imported from the West' by the UNP than from 'dogmatic Marxism's plain materialism'. In its pre-election-day editorial of 26 May entitled 'The People's Verdict', the *Sun* expressed the hope that the UNP would be defeated.

The *Sun*'s antipathy to the UNP was, in addition, expressed in its headlines and its presentation of news, in its editorials and feature articles, including letters to its editor, and through its daily cartoonist-type commentator 'Pukka Sahib', who below a humorous sketch expressed opinions on the burning questions of the day in rather caustic verse.

The slant in the presentation of news sometimes corrected the imbalance and the distortion of UF activities in the Lake House press. The *Sun* presented a different point of view – thus rendering a useful service. But from time to time, its headlines were misleading and its news stories were obviously incorrect. This was however true of Lake House as well.

The *Sun* and the *Dinamina* (Lake House) gave wide coverage to the activities of R. G. Senanayake and his SMP, quite out of proportion to its infinitesimal strength in the country – but for different reasons. The *Sun* presumably wished to prepare R. G. Senanayake for a future role as the protagonist of the rights of the Sinhalese. There was talk of a constellation of the Sinhalese Buddhist forces in the country led by Hema Basanayake, R. G. Senanayake and the former army commander, Major-General Richard Udugama. Lake House, on the other hand, as stated earlier, hoped that R. G. Senanayake would drain away votes from the SLFP.

The headlines of the *Sun* were critical of the 'National Government', but not as a daily feature. However, when they did appear, they were deadly in their intent. For instance, in its front-page headlines of 28 March, the *Sun* reported: 'P.M. Confesses at Press Conference: National Unity Not Achieved'. This was not exactly what the Prime Minister had sought to convey, though he may have spoken some dubious words to that effect *en passant*. Earlier, on 18 March, the headline 'FP and TC Pledge to Back UNP' appeared. It was plainly incorrect where the FP was concerned.

Both the *Sun* and the *Dawasa* concentrated more on discrediting the UNP over its alleged neglect of Sinhalese as the official language and its 'excessive' concern for the rights of the Tamil-speaking groups in the country. Thus on 7 April the front-page headline was 'Old Entrants to Public Service; Premier Rules Sinhala not Necessary' and two days later 'Mrs Bandaranaike Informed Official Language Act Sabotaged' – both of which were intended to alienate from the UNP the support of Sinhalese-conscious electors and public servants. On 11 May the front-page report read: 'Dudley–Thondaman Secret Pact' – which was mere conjecture – while in the inner page of its issue of 27 May, a headline reported 'Another UNP–FP Secret Pact', which was not true.

The headlines were sympathetic to the SLFP, and sometimes to its Marxist partners. This was not unusual – and was only to be expected, given the political slant of the Independent Newspapers group. Thus the *Sun* of 22 April reported (with much truth) in its front page, 'United Front Meeting at Kandy: Vast Crowds Greet Mrs Bandaranaike,' which was a news report of the UF's most important election rally preceding nomination day. The same issue reproduced the UF programme under the heading 'Manifesto Gives Top Priority for Common Man'. The *Sun* of 3 May had the headline, 'Mrs B. Issues Statement:

People's Committees Explained,' while the issue of 24 May gave prominence to Mrs Bandaranaike's denial of UF talks with the FP. A headline of 25 May stated that the Muslims, an important electoral factor on this occasion, 'were Better Off under the SLFP' – according to Badiudin Mahmud, the ISF leader. The issue of 26 May had a full front-page banner headline: 'I am for the United Front, Says Maha Nayake of Malwatte' with the subheading 'She [Mrs Bandaranaike] is a Mother to us All'.

But unlike the general reporting of UF activities by Lake House, which was not disinterested, and directed towards putting the UF on the defensive, the *Sun* and *Dawasa* were straightforward in the coverage given to UNP election meetings. On the whole most UNP meetings were fairly well reported, except for occasional headlines which may have misled readers who did not trouble to read the details.

The coverage of election meetings in the Tamil areas of north and east Ceylon, as was stated earlier, was directed against the FP. The latter's opponents, the TC, and the newly formed TSRP were provided with adequate news space for their attacks on the FP, somewhat out of proportion to their actual political potential in the country. The TC manifesto was reported in greater detail by the *Sun* (26 April), no friend of the Tamil political parties, than in the *Ceylon Daily News* (Lake House), despite the TC's alliance with the UNP. On the other hand, the reporting of many FP speeches was done in such a way as to embarrass the UNP. To mention but a few instances, the *Sun* of 31 March reported the FP general-secretary as having stated at a meeting in Trincomalee that the UNP adopted the Tamil Regulations in January 1966 under pressure from his party and had Parliament approve it 'at the cost of the life of a bhikku'. The issue of 4 April reported Chelvanayakam as stating that the Tamils 'had not suffered' by joining the 'National Government' and that in fact they had 'gained something'. While that of 11 May had a report of a speech by the FP general-secretary describing the events that led to the FP's decision to support the UNP in the forming of a Government in 1965. Thus, while FP speeches were reported reasonably well, with the occasional inaccuracies, the purpose was quite obvious – to cause maximum embarrassment to the UNP. On the other side, Lake House in its reporting avoided as best as it could giving publicity to such speeches.

The *Sun*'s editorials were generally more restrained than those of Lake House. What it had to say of the UNP, it said in a language which though partisan conveyed the impression of a decision arrived at after careful consideration of the issues. Nor were such editorials fired in rapid succession as was the practice with the national dailies of Lake House. Typical of the *Sun*'s approach was its editorial on 'People's Committees' in its issue of 10 May. It ended:

We are not either for or against People's Committees. Much depends on their composition, powers and functions. We would however hope that the leader of the United Front, Mrs Bandaranaike, will explain these committees further because certain leaders of the United Front have spoken of them with their tongues in their cheeks.

The *Sun*'s feature articles were more forthright and hostile to the UNP – but these too did not appear frequently as in the case of the Lake House dailies – presumably owing to lack of sufficient editorial skills for the purpose. Mention was made earlier of the two articles by F. R. Jayasuriya. Their captions provided unconcealed evidence of the *Sun*'s hostility to the Prime Minister himself. On 28 March, Jayasuriya in 'A Review of Last Five Years: Sinhala is Forced to Take a Back Seat' blamed Dudley Senanayake for the activities of his Government on the cultural and economic fronts, while on 22 May the same writer published an article entitled 'The Greatest Threat to Democracy Comes from the Premier Himself'. Earlier, in the *Sun* of 31 March, a correspondent had a feature on 'The Prime Minister's Credibility Gap', while on 24 May E. H. de Alwis, retired Director of Education, in his 'The Choice before the Voter', berated the UNP on its five-year record.

The 'letters to the editor' page of the *Sun* had a carefully selected assortment of criticisms, attacks and harangues against the UNP and the 'National Govern-ment' – some of them written by informed and well-known personages such as university dons and public figures. The headlines given to the 'letters-to-the-editor' page indicated clearly whom the *Sun* was critical of. To mention but a few examples, on 2 May it was 'Central Bank Data Belie P.M.'s Claims Made for Food Drive'; on 26 May, 'Devaluation, *Feecs* and Soaring Living Costs: The Common Man Never Had it so Bad'; on the day of the general election it was 'Plight of Tea Small-Holders: UNP's "Democratic Socialism" Subordinated to World Bank Demands'. Such headlines were the usual rule during the months of the election campaign and even the two or three months preceding the dissolu-tion of Parliament.

Other national newspapers

Udaya   A post-1965 Sinhalese-language daily, the *Udaya* specialised in the problems of the country's youth and showed evidence of developing circulation and influence. In the early stages, it was controlled by Esmond Wickremasinghe, formerly one of the principal directors of Lake House. He had helped the UNP in its general election campaign of 1965 and had immediately thereafter identi-fied himself very closely with the 'National Government' and its leading person-alities. Wickremasinghe soon fell out with Dudley Senanayake and the *Udaya* proved particularly critical of the Prime Minister and his policies, as well as of those ministers close to him.

The *Udaya* performed the useful service of focusing attention on the problems of young people and in this way bringing to the attention of the authorities and the general public their grievances and complaints. The *Udaya*'s correspondents in the different towns and villages made it their task to investigate the needs of this sector of the population. The *Udaya*'s important shareholder besides Esmond Wickremasinghe was J. R. Jayawardene, Senanayake's second-in-command in the Government. When Wickremasinghe quarrelled with the Prime Minister, the latter, because of the embarrassment to his Government from *Udaya*'s news coverage, had Wickremasinghe ousted from his position of editorial influence in that paper.

Virakesari   Along with the *Udaya*, J. R. Jayawardene did have some interest in the Tamil-language daily, the *Virakesari*, which had earlier been owned by an Indian businessman and had its circulation mainly among the Indian community in Ceylon, particularly among the plantation workers of Indian origin.

Surprisingly our investigations show that the *Virakesari* despite its proprietorial connections did not adopt an excessively pro-UNP approach in its reporting of election news when compared even with some of the other national dailies. In fact, the *Virakesari* editorial of 25 May claimed that a balanced reporting had been precisely the objective of the newspaper throughout the campaign. The claim was however a mild exaggeration. Given the fact of its UNP influences and its large circulation among the Indian Tamil community, the *Virakesari* gave greater publicity to the utterances of S. Thondaman and his CWC spokesmen, who were supporting the UNP, and much less space to Abdul Aziz and the DWC, who backed the UF. Further, the TC which was the UNP's Ceylon Tamil ally was given slightly more prominence, the minimal as it were, in relation to the FP. But the latter could not complain too much; given the newspaper's affiliations, the FP had its reasonable share of news space.

Between the major parties, the *Virakesari*, given its background, was far from being altogether partisan in its reporting of election news. UF meetings received due coverage. But editorial comment was hostile to the UF. That of 21 May was typical: the *Virakesari* stated that reliance should not be placed on the programmatic arrangements of parties with contradictory policies which come together for specific purposes.

The prominence given by the *Virakesari* to the UF's sympathetic pronouncements on the problems of the Tamil-speaking peoples is difficult to explain. For instance, the UF's programme was given front-page headlines in the *Virakesari* of 21 April with the caption: 'The Mother Tongue is the Medium of Instruction – Estate Schools will be Nationalised'. In the news paragraph which followed, it was stated that Mrs Bandaranaike would make these announcements when introducing the UF manifesto at the election rally in Kandy on the afternoon of 21 April. Both these problems concerned the Ceylon Tamil and Indian Tamil populations.

The UNP manifesto was introduced with the uninspiring headline 'Income of Cultivators will be Increased Further' in the *Virakesari* of 28 April. No attempt was made to publicise what the UNP claimed to have done to improve communal harmony, etc. Likewise prominence was given to the pronouncements of Badiudin Mahmud on behalf of the ISF. But here however similar publicity was also given to the speeches of UNP Muslim leaders.

Eela Nadu   The other Tamil national daily, the *Eela Nadu*, was the Jaffna Tamil counterpart of the Indian Tamil *Virakesari*. The *Eela Nadu*'s ownership was not in sympathy with the FP, but it sought to maintain its impartiality *vis-à-vis* the Tamil political parties. Fair coverage was provided for both the leading Ceylon Tamil contenders, the FP and TC, as well as for the smaller Tamil parties such as the TSRP and ATM. The coverage was of course in relation to the popularity of these parties, determined presumably on their parliamentary positions. The FP gained thereby. Our examination of the reporting indicates that the FP obtained more news space than other parties, but not quite in proportion to the influence it wielded in the Tamil-speaking areas, while the TC had a little more than was its due.

The *Eela Nadu* ran features in the form of question and answer discussions between its staff correspondent and the better-known Tamil leaders. The FP benefited from this. Particularly an interview with the FP leader, S. J. V. Chelvanayakam, which covered three full columns and two half columns of the eight columns of the last page of the *Eela Nadu* of 26 May, the day before the general election, enabled the FP to clarify its stand on some of the issues which had raised strong controversy between itself and the TC. On the previous day (25 May) the *Eela Nadu* carried in front-page headlines a message from S. J. V. Chelvanayakam to the Tamil voters in the seven 'Sinhalese' provinces on how they should vote in the forthcoming election. This could have created the impression that Chelvanayakam's word was important to the Tamil voters.

The *Eela Nadu* carried little news of political activity among the Indian Tamils or Muslims. It had some news of the UNP and UF, but its main focus was the two Tamil-speaking provinces.

The party press

Left-wing dailies

Unlike the general elections of 1965 and before, the years after 1965 saw the emergence of two very articulate and forceful Left-wing Sinhalese-language dailies which developed a fairly wide circulation despite the fact that in the public mind they were definitely identified with the two leading Marxist parties in Ceylon. The *Aththa* (CP) has the larger circulation, in the area of some 40,000 to 50,000 readers, while the *Janadina* (LSSP) has approximately 20,000 to 30,000 daily readers.[6] Both newspapers in the years 1965 to 1970 became noted for their enterprising journalism, their vitriolic criticisms of the Government and their front-page eye-catching headlines which usually ridiculed the leading personalities of the governing party.

The *Janadina* was banned for a fair period of time under emergency regulations. Further, both Left-wing newspapers were not permitted carriage facilities in the state-managed omnibus transport system. They were besides denied commercial advertisements from Government departments and state-run corporations. But they survived nevertheless.

Others

There are, in addition to the above, the usual party newspapers and party weeklies published mostly in the Sinhalese or Tamil language. *Sirilaka* and *Sinhale* are SLFP, *Siyarata*, UNP, and *Suthanthiran*, FP.

The broadcasting system

Radio Ceylon is a state monopoly managed by a corporation. During the time of the May 1970 election, it was under the chairmanship of Neville Jayaweera, one of the country's ablest higher civil servants who was also Director-General of Broadcasting. However, in SLFP minds he was closely identified with Dudley Senanayake.

The listening public numbers some 3 million, and broadcasts are in Sinhalese, Tamil and English. The major share of time is allocated to the Sinhalese section, which has the most numerous listening public.

In 1969, the Federal Republic of Germany provided the Government of Ceylon with an outright gift for the installation of powerful medium-wave transmitters with a power factor of 50 kilowatts in two stations situated at Maho and Weeraketiya. A German engineer, a project manager from the firm of Siemens which supplied the transmitters, and a Herr Schmidt, representing the German Government, were in charge of the project, which was completed in April 1969. The aid component from the Federal Republic amounted to Rs. 4.5 million, while the Government of Ceylon contributed Rs. 2.7 million.

Arising from this project, which was utilised as an election boost for the UNP, a National Exhibition was launched, primarily depicting the expansion of medium-wave broadcasting in Ceylon as well as plans for its future expansion. A large map of Ceylon identified the various places in the entire island which would be covered by medium-wave broadcasting. The maps also indicated the intended location of the various regional stations, and the actual areas these stations would cover. Besides this, the exhibition was also used to advertise the success of the Government's 'grow more food' campaign and the plans for the organisation of the Mahaveli river diversion, with the benefits it would bring the people of Ceylon. It was an exhibition on wheels entirely organised by Radio Ceylon and was successfully staged in some of the leading towns of Ceylon. From the point of view of attendance, especially, the exhibition was a success. We visited most of the towns where the exhibition was conducted and noted the crowds present. But this could not be taken for support, as people in this country as in many other parts of the world are also given to enjoying circuses.

More pertinent were the responses we obtained when we interviewed the employees of the Ceylon Broadcasting Corporation who went to Maho and Weeraketiya for work connected with the installation of the medium-wave transmitters. Particularly in Maho, we were told that the village folk were hostile to the project. They felt it had no use or priority in respect of their immediate needs. A typical remark of villagers was that they had asked for rice and were given radios instead.

More lavish than the National Exhibition was the Mahaveli Ballet extravaganza prepared and organised again by the Ceylon Broadcasting Corporation. Part of the expenses for it was borne by the Government of Ceylon's Information Department, Rs. 192,535/72. Thevis Guruge, the Director of the National Service of Radio Ceylon, was in charge of the production. The troupe of more than 100 dancers was trained over a period of two months by Pani Bharata, Principal of the Government Fine Arts College. The ballet depicted the Mahaveli river diversion as envisiaged in the plans of the Government of Ceylon and referred to the grandeur of the ancient irrigation civilisation of the Sinhalese kings. The ballet was originally produced for Ceylon's Independence Day celebrations on 4 February 1970. But it was primarily intended as an election booster for the 'National Government' of Dudley Senanayake; it was staged in all leading towns in the Sinhalese areas during the period of the election campaign. The UNP, as already mentioned, placed much weight on this grandiose development project, but learned to its cost that 'elections are not won by plans alone'.

The National Exhibition and the Mahaveli Ballet were special undertakings of the Ceylon Broadcasting Corporation to highlight some of the 'National Government's' principal achievements during its five-year rule. But the normal channels of Radio Ceylon were also widely used to publicise these achievements. Normally Radio Ceylon would broadcast four main news bulletins in the morning, afternoon, evening and night. But starting from 1969, presumably in anticipation of the general election scheduled for May 1970, Radio Ceylon had its news programmes expanded by approximately 50 per cent. Apart from the four main news bulletins, a 'news in brief' item was introduced, nine of these, at hourly intervals. The 'news in brief' programme was utilised to provide information about agriculture. Really it was propaganda to advertise the success of the Government's 'grow more food' campaign.

In addition, Radio Ceylon set up a new establishment called the Rural Section, with new staff specially recruited to undertake field investigations on the 'grow more food' drive. This Section employed various methods to collect data relating to output in agriculture which were then put across in the form of various programmes, made specially attractive for the purpose, for public consumption.

For other programmes of a related nature, the Rural Section sent producers to the rural areas who sometimes travelled distances of beyond 200 miles. These producers had links with the *govi rajas*. They conducted on the spot interviews with different farmers, as well as with the *govi rajas* whose information they utilised for their special programmes. They had links with certain rural societies in different parts of the paddy-growing areas through which they conducted competitions among farmers and others in the form of radio quizzes etc. These competitions were made into recorded programmes.

The forms of propaganda organised by the Ceylon Broadcasting Corporation were highly elaborate and, for a country of Ceylon's rural proportions, even somewhat sophisticated. The intention was to convince the listening public that the food drive was becoming stronger, and that accompanying it was a fair degree of affluence and prosperity. Even the forms of music heard in the beginning-of-the-day programmes as well as the song and drama were altered to emphasise the importance of, and to cater to, the agricultural sector. All this propaganda, as could only be expected, was almost wholly in Sinhalese, with occasional allowance for Tamil.

Conclusion

This was the first election in Ceylon where the press was rather evenly divided in its support for the rival groupings. The UNP did not have the overwhelming support of the national press that it enjoyed in all previous general elections. The question arises whether this erosion of its support affected the outcome.

Voters read the newspapers they liked depending on their political attitudes. The Lake House and Times Group newspapers made their appeal to the conservative sections and to those who subscribed to the UNP's way of thinking. The *Dawasa* group addressed itself to the traditional Sinhalese Buddhist orientations of the SLFP in particular and to UF biases in general. The only difference was that Lake House newspapers were also read by UF supporters as well as by an uncommitted public who normally regarded these as providing reliable coverage of news. Here Lake House was guilty of excesses. By making its biases too obvious it opened itself to criticism and doubt. In the end, it achieved the opposite of what it sought to achieve. As for the *Dawasa* newspapers, it was clear that their support was solely for the UF. Other than these, the objectives of the rival newspapers were to maintain the enthusiasm of the opposing sides. The presentation of news was designed towards this end.

Given the fact that voters had already made up their minds months before the election, it is not possible to state with any degree of assurance that newspapers succeeded in swaying the electorate. At best they kept up the morale. At worst they were guilty of excess. The latter could have shifted marginal votes either way.

9. The result

In the island as a whole

The UF's majority was beyond all expectations. It won 115 of the 151 elective seats. The SLFP alone obtained an overall majority (90 seats) and an additional one at a by-election held later. The LSSP secured 19 and the CP 6. The UNP and its ally (MEP) fared disastrously. The latter lost in the four constituencies it contested. The UNP won 17 seats, of which only 3 were in the Sinhalese Buddhist areas, while 5 were in constituencies with minority concentrations. It nevertheless polled an impressive percentage of the total votes cast. In the Tamil-speaking areas the party's Ceylon Tamil ally, the TC fared just as poorly, winning 3 of the 12 seats contested. The FP did not fare as well either. It won 13 of 19 seats with its majorities reduced in many constituencies.

Of the nine general elections held in the island since the introduction of universal adult franchise in 1931, the election of May 1970 was the only one in which the economic theme dominated over all others. The outcome of the 1956 general election was also determined by economic issues, but the cultural factor was just as potent on that occassion. In 1970 Mrs Bandaranaike's UF presented a manifesto which was a considered programme of work for the economic and social development of the country.

The UNP preferred to fight the election on their old policies with few modifications. They spoke a great deal about their economic achievements and the social peace they had brought to the country. A perpetual theme of their election addresses was the dangers of Marxian totalitarianism and the imperilment thereby of true religion. All this was no different from what they had been saying through the years.

The SLFP in contrast presented the spectacle of dynamism. In 1956 it was cultural regeneration and economic benefit for the common man through the People's United Front (MEP) headed by S. W. R. D. Bandaranaike. In March and July 1960, Mrs Bandaranaike appealed for a mandate to complete the unfinished tasks of her late husband. In 1965 she led a coalition of her party and the traditional Left. In 1970 the electors were offered the Common Programme of a United Front. With every election there was a change of emphasis in the SLFP's stance. The UNP in contrast got bogged down in the quagmire of its own static ideology.

There were 794,141 new voters in an electorate of 5,505,028. The majority of these new voters belonged to the newly enfranchised 18-year-old age group. It is not possible to state exactly how the 18-year-old group voted for the rival contenders, but, taking all circumstances into consideration including our own field investigations, it can be reasonably assumed that the bulk of this vote went against the UNP.

The female vote was by and large hostile to the UNP. Women were faced with the problems of budgeting in the context of soaring living costs, the cut in the rice subsidy and the scarcity of essential commodities. Mrs Bandaranaike capitalised on the fact that she was a mother and a housewife and knew the problems of the home. 'Go to the kitchen', she repeatedly said, 'and you will know what the food drive is.' Our observers reported that her meetings were attended by large numbers of women. They were a committed crowd. Philip Fernando, the *Ceylon Daily News* correspondent who was specially assigned to cover all election meetings addressed by Mrs Bandaranaike throughout the island, wrote in his private diary on 18 May 1970: 'There is a carnival atmosphere at her meetings. People come not to hear but to cheer her. There is no speech making. What she says is immaterial. They are a committed crowd. She communicated in an invisible way. Women cheer her. Many of them cried in joy'.[1] In contrast, the major UNP meetings which we observed did not have as many women attending them. The deputy leader of the UNP (J. R. Jayawardene) confirmed this in his interview with us. We thought however that he exaggerated the position somewhat. It is not possible to state accurately how the female vote distributed itself.

The 1970 general election recorded the highest poll ever, 85.2 per cent compared with the previous record of 82.1 in 1965. Table 19 gives the details of the percentage polling in all the general elections held since 1947.

The outcome left the UNP stunned and almost paralysed. Eleven of the seventeen Cabinet ministers suffered defeat. Senanayake abandoned the parliamentary leadership of his party – an index to the gloom and despair that seized him and his immediate followers. Throughout the campaign, he had been certain of his ground, and was quite convinced that his party would win. He had told his closest advisers that he could sense the difference in the responses of his audiences in July 1960, when he suffered defeat, and on the present occasion. In the end, however, the UNP won only 17 of the 128 seats it contested and of these only three were in the 114 predominantly Sinhalese Buddhist electorates.[2] Even here, the members returned won on the basis of the large

Table 19. *Turn-out at general elections, 1947–70*

Date of election	Total electorate	Turn-out of voters at polls	Turn-out as percentage
1947	3,048,145	1,701,150	55.9
1952	2,990,912	2,114,615	70.7
1956	3,464,159	2,391,538	69.0
March 1960	3,724,507	2,889,282	77.6
July 1960	3,724,507	2,827,075	75.9
1965	4,710,887	3,821,918[a]	82.1
1970	5,505,028	4,672,656[b]	85.2

SOURCE: Reports on Parliamentary General Elections in Ceylon by the Commissioner of Parliamentary Elections.
[a]There was no contest in the two-member Colombo South constituency.
[b]Welimada constituency returned its member uncontested.

personal support they commanded and the national or local prestige they held. Of the rest, four were from Muslim majority constituencies, three from Roman Catholic (with their majorities slashed) and two from Ceylon Tamil constituencies. The other five constituencies had sizeable minority groups. But it cannot be argued that UNP victories in these last-mentioned constituencies were evidence of a confidence established among minority groups. For the party suffered reverses in other Roman Catholic and Muslim constituencies where it had usually taken its position for granted.

The UF victory was not unexpected. In fact from the UF point of view, this was the one occasion where the result of a free election was known months in advance. As far as the UF was concerned, the voters had made up their minds at least six months prior to the date of the election. There was only doubt as to the size of the majority it would obtain.

The outcome was noteworthy for another important reason. The UF made almost a uniform clean sweep of all the electorates in the predominantly Sinhalese areas. In previous encounters the results were somewhat criss-crossed. The rival parties had their traditional sources of strength. The UNP had been certain of the Roman Catholic belt, the Indian vote in the Kandyan Sinhalese constituencies, the bulk of the Muslim vote and of the Ceylon Tamil vote in the Sinhalese areas. On this occasion none of these marginal votes, even when they were available, could have substantially altered the result. There were 84 seats in which the UF candidates scored majorities of over 3,000 while in 58 seats their majorities exceeded 5,000.

The UNP's *débâcle* in terms of seats (from 66 to 17) should not, however, convey the impression that it had suffered a proportionate loss of strength from the point of view of votes. In fact, as Table 20 indicates, the party polled more votes than the SLFP, though the combined votes of the UF (48.7 per cent of the total polled) far exceeded those of the UNP and its electoral partners, the MEP and TC (41.1 per cent). Although the party polled 37.9 per cent of the total votes cast, it only secured 11.2 per cent of the seats in the House. In contrast, the SLFP polled 36.8 per cent of the votes but wrested 60.2 per cent of the seats. The UNP experienced a similar fate at the general election of July 1960 when it polled 38.1 per cent of the votes and obtained only 19.8 per cent of the seats. The SLFP's percentage of votes then was 32.9, but it collected as much as 49.6 per cent of the seats. (See Table 20 for further details.)

After making allowance for the fact that, on both the occasions referred to, the UNP had more candidates in the field than the SLFP, there is an obvious explanation for the SLFP's success, despite its lower percentage of votes. This is the instrument of the mutual aid pact between the SLFP and the traditional Marxist parties (the LSSP and CP).

After their electoral disaster in March 1960 (see Table 20) the traditional Left realised that their future lay in alliances and coalitions with the SLFP and not on any independent course of action. For the Left, this was the only way of preserving whatever position they had and, if possible, of gaining access to the corridors of powers. They realised both objectives. The returns of 1970 indicate further

Table 20. *All-Island position of parties in the four general elections*

Parties	MARCH 1960					JULY 1960				
	Votes polled	%age of total votes polled	%age of seats won	Candidates contesting	Seats won	Votes polled	%age of total votes polled	%age of seats won	Candidates contesting	Seat won
UNP	908,953	29.3	33.1	127	50	1,160, 971	38.1	19.8	128	30
SLFP	647,905	20.9	30.4	109[c]	46	1,004,561	32.9	49.6	98	75
LSSP	330,510	10.6	6.6	101	10	224,993	7.3	7.9	21	12
MEP	323,942	10.4	6.6	89	10	106,082	3.4	1.9	53	
CP	147,060	4.7	1.9	53	3	90,219	2.9	2.6	7	
FP	175,106	5.6	9.9	19	15	213,753	7.0	10.5	20[f]	16
TC	38,275	1.2	0.6	8	1	46,803	1.5	0.6	10	
Independents and other parties	521,546	16.8	10.5	393	16	197,859	6.4	6.6	55	1
Total	3,093,297	99.5	99.6	899	151	3,045,241	99.5	99.5	392	15

SOURCE: Compiled by the author from statistics contained in Reports of the Commissioner of Parliamentary Elections for March and July 1960, 1965 and 1970 and from *The Ceylon Daily News Parliaments of Ceylon* for 1960, 1965 and 1970.
[a] This excludes the UNP candidate for Colombo South who was returned without a contest.
[b] Exclusive of the UNP candidate for Welimada electoral district who was disqualified for not submitting his nomination papers according to the statutory requirements.
[c] There were two candidates with SLFP nomination for the Mawanella seat.
[d] Exclusive of the SLFP candidate for Welimada electoral district who was returned uncontested.
[e] Exclusive of the LSSP candidate for Colombo South who was returned uncontested.
[f] A Sinhalese obtained the FP nomination to contest the Chilaw constituency which is outside of the usual Tamil areas that the FP normally contest. Chilaw has a Ceylon Tamil population which is 10.9 per cent of its total population.

progress for the two Left-wing parties (see Table 20) in terms of both seats and votes. The improvement however is hardly significant.

The exception was 1965 when, despite the mutual aid common front of the SLFP, LSSP and CP, the UNP emerged as the largest single party. But there were other reasons for this. It is now axiomatic in the context of Ceylon's perilous economic situation that even Governments swept into office with the greatest amount of electoral goodwill flounder in the economic morass. The no-contest mutual assistance electoral arrangements can therefore be expected to

| | 1965 | | | | | 1970 | | | |
Votes polled	%age of total votes polled	%age of seats won	Candi-dates contest-ing	Seats won	Votes polled	%age of total votes polled	%age of seats won	Candi-dates contest-ing	Seats won
1,590,554	39.2	43.7	115[a]	65[a]	1,892,625	37.9	11.2	129[b]	17
1,221,999	30.1	27.1	101	41	1,840,019	36.8	60.2	107[d]	91
303,095	7.4	6.6.	24[e]	10	433,224	8.6	12.5	23	19
96,375	2.3	0.6	59	1	46,571	0.9	0·0	4	0
109,744	2.7	2.6	9	4	169,199	3.3	3.9	9	6
217,916	5.3	9.2	20	14	245,747	4.9	8.6	19	13
98,746	2.4	1.9	15	3	115,567	2.3	1.9	12	3
408,804	10.1	7.9	144	12	249,006	4.9	1.3	141	2
4,047,233	99.5	99·6	487	151	4,991,958	99.6	99.6	444	151

work only in alternate elections. Just as cogent a reason was the fact that the three parties concerned were thrown off their guard when parliamentary defections from the SLFP upset Mrs Bandaranaike's coalition Government in December 1964. They had little time between the date of dissolution and the general election to regroup their forces.

The results are significant for one other reason. It seems now established that through all the vicissitudes of rapid social, economic and political change effected since 1956, there persists a constant and inflexibly traditional base in Ceylon politics. This base is not seriously affected by the alternations of the parties *vis-à-vis* governmental power. The conservative vote since July 1960, as Table 20 shows, remains at over 35 per cent of the total poll. And from the point of view of votes, it is even more impressive. This vote is a cohesive one and has seldom been dispersed between rival parties.

In the rural areas

Approximately three-quarters of the country's population live in the rural areas. For the first time since March 1960, the SLFP, as Table 21 shows, secured the larger share of the rural vote. On all previous occasions the UNP had enjoyed

Table   21.   *The rural vote*

Parties	MARCH 1960					JULY 1960				
	Votes polled	%age of total votes polled	%age of seats won	Candi-dates contest-ing	Seats won	Votes polled	%age of total votes polled	%age of seats won	Candi-dates contest-ing	Seats won
UNP	640,885	28.3	27.3	100	32	821,987	37.0	17.9	100	21
SLFP	539,598	23.9	34.1	87	40	797,666	35.9	52.9	79	62
LSSP	197,226	8.7	5.9	80	7	114,520	5.1	5.9	14	7
MEP	268,949	11.9	7.6	78	9	93,826	4.2	2.5	41	3
CP	89,281	3.9	1.7	39	2	36,967	1.6	1.7	5	2
FP	123,388	5.4	10.2	15	12	153,107	6.9	11.1	15	13
TC	26,155	1.1	0.8	6	1	31,293	1.4	0.8	7	1
Inde-pendents and other parties	371,190	16.4	11.9	299	14	166,486	7.5	6.8	42	8
Total	2,256,672	99.6	99.5	704	117	2,215,852	99.6	99.6	303	117

SOURCE: Compiled by the author from statistics contained in Reports of the Commissioner of Parliamentary Elections for March and July 1960, 1965 and 1970 and *The Ceylon Daily News Parliaments of Ceylon* for 1960, 1965, and 1970.
NOTE: The total number of rural seats at each of the four general elections stood at 117. See Appendix 2 for note on rural and urban seats.
[a] Exclusive of Welimada electoral district which returned an SLFP member without a contest. We have therefore calculated the percentage on the basis of 116 seats.

a slight lead. On this occasion the SLFP obtained 41.0 per cent of the rural vote to the UNP's 35.8. In terms of seats, the UNP's defeat was even more devastating, but from the point of view of votes, the party did not fare so badly.

Unemployment in the rural areas, especially among the 18–24 age group, contributed measurably to the UNP's defeat. A memorandum on unemployment prepared by the Department of National Planning in June 1966 estimated the number of unemployed at 480,000, of whom 75 per cent were males. About 41 per cent of the latter belonged to the 18–24 age group.[3] But more pertinent was the fact that nearly 88 per cent of the total unemployed were in the rural areas. The largest number of unemployed (rural and urban) was in the Colombo district (32 per cent), followed by Kalutara (10 per cent), Galle and Kandy (9 per

| | 1965 | | | | | 1970 | | | |
Votes polled	%age of total votes polled	%age of seats won	Candidates contesting	Seats won	Votes polled	%age of total votes polled	%age of seats won	Candidates contesting	Seats won
1,139,437	37.6	40.1	91	47	1,311,760	35.8	6.8	103[a]	8
1,020,766	33.7	31.6	83	37	1,502,254	41.0	68.1	88	79
183,552	6.0	5.1	16	6	253,861	6.9	10.3	15	12
80,094	2.6	0.8	52	1	33,690	0.9	0.0	3	0
52,226	1.7	1.7	6	2	89,878	2.4	3.4	7	4
162,141	5.3	9.4	16	11	184,335	5.0	8.6	15	10
71,429	2.3	1.7	12	2	95,229	2.6	1.7	10	2
314,246	10.3	9.4	109	11	189,334	5.1	0.8	105	1
3,023,891	99.5	99.8	385	117	3,660,341	99.7	99.7	346	116

cent each), Matara and Kegalle (6 per cent each), Ratnapura (5 per cent), Kurunegala and Badulla (4 per cent each) districts. The UNP's performance in the rural electorates in all of these districts, as Table 22 indicates, was from the point of view of seats almost a total disaster.

Besides the fact that youth played a major part in the UF's electoral organisation, the UF leader herself was very much aware of the potentialities that this vote offered. According to the private notes of the *Ceylon Daily News* correspondent Philip Fernando who interviewed her during the course of the election campaign, she reportedly estimated the 21-year-old age group as being nearly a million and the 25-year-old age group as almost double that. 'We offer them', she said, 'this idea of a scientifically based development programme capable of providing a socialist answer to the ills of the country.'

The votes polled by the two Left parties demonstrate that they are more urban-based. There has been no significant increase in the rural Left-wing vote since March 1960 (see Table 21), though they continue to exercise a hold in those areas where their leadership initially organised their movement. This is the explanation for their rural support.

Table 22.   *UNP's performance in rural electorates with largest unemployment*

Districts	Total number of seats	Seats contested	Seats won
Colombo	14	13	1
Kalutara	5	3	nil
Galle	7	7	nil
Kandy	13	12	1
Matara	6	6	nil
Kegalle	8	8	1
Ratnapura	7	7	nil
Kurunegala	11	11	1
Badulla	7	6	nil
TOTAL	78	73	4

In the Kandyan Sinhalese Areas

The problems of rural indebtedness, landlessness and poverty are particularly felt in the Kandyan areas because of the vast acreages of tea (foreign and locally owned) covering this territory which the Kandyan Sinhalese peasantry feel belong to them. Further, the presence of Indian plantation labour in their midst, they allege, deprives them of the employment opportunities that are their due. The situation is most serious in the two Kandyan provinces of Uva and Central which cover the five districts of Kandy, Matale, Badulla, Nuwara Eliya and Moneragala. These two provinces account for one-fourth of the total land area of the country and contain roughly one-quarter of the island's total population. The three other Kandyan Sinhalese provinces of the North Central, the Kurunegala district of the North Western, and Sabaragamuwa have their problems, but are not as acutely impoverished as the two referred to. Sixty-six of the 128 electorates in the Sinhalese areas are in these five provinces, so they are definitely an important focus of electoral politics.[4]

The UNP's faring in the five Kandyan provinces was the worst ever experienced. All in all they won in only two of the Kandyan Sinhalese electorates. They failed to win a single seat in two Kandyan provinces, Uva and North Central. The UNP expected to make great headway in the North Central Province because this province was to benefit most from the Mahaveli diversion project, and the Minister responsible for its implementation, C. P. de Silva, was the UNP leader in the province. But in the end, even C. P. de Silva suffered defeat.

The proposed prohibitive annual water tax of Rs. 40 per acre to be imposed when paddy lands came under the Mahaveli scheme alarmed the peasantry there, if not angered them. In addition, the UNP was destroyed by the defection of some of its prime supporters in the province, particularly P. L. Bauddhasara, by the effective rhetoric of the Sinhalese film idol, L. M. Perera, the exploitation by UF propagandists of the shooting of a Buddhist monk by the police in January 1966 in a province in which was situated the sacred historic Buddhist city of Anuradhapura, and the overall election strategy of the respected SLFP deputy leader, Maithripala Senanayake.

Generally, the reasons for the UNP's failure in the Kandyan Sinhalese provinces can be attributed to the unpopularity of its social and economic policies. But there were factors peculiar to the Kandyan areas. In addition, the Senanayake Government's laxity in implementing the Indo-Ceylon Agreement of October 1964 and the openness of the Indian CWC in its electoral support of the UNP made the latter vulnerable in these areas.

Four seats in the Kandyan areas were annexed by LSSP candidates. These constituencies were usually associated with the LSSP. One seat (Kalawana) was won by a CP candidate, marking the first time a CP candidate won in a Kandyan constituency. All other seats (with the two UNP exceptions mentioned) were captured by the SLFP.

The Indian Vote

CWC officials in our interviews with them laid exaggerated claim to the strength of the Indian vote in the Kandyan Sinhalese provinces. One senior CWC official stated that in 40 of these constituencies the Indian vote could have affected the results. Our rough estimate is that in 15 constituencies in the Kandyan areas the Indian vote could have influenced the result, but only if the outcome was very close. In two other constituencies, however, Nuwara Eliya and Maskeliya, the Indian vote could decide the issue even in normal circumstances.

Thondaman, the CWC 'boss', was certain that he could win these two constituencies for the UNP. The UNP, however, was only able to secure one. The party failed in the other (Maskeliya) because a candidate to whom it refused nomination contested as an Independent and splintered its vote. Further, in both constituencies Indian labour leaders who had severed their ties with Thondaman contested and split the Indian vote. This was especially so in the Maskeliya constituency.

It has been suggested that sections of the Indian vote under CWC control had tended on this occasion to act independently. Indian labourers were as much affected by the cut in the rice subsidy as the Sinhalese. The UF's promise to restore it and to take steps to bring down living costs, it was said, drew away the Indian vote from the UNP. It is impossible for us to confirm or contradict this assertion. The CWC is in a near-monopoly situation in the plantation areas, and Indian workers did not wish to risk its displeasure by admitting how they had voted. The Left-wing trade unions among the Indian plantation workers and the DWC of Abdul Aziz backed the UF.

In the Low Country Sinhalese Areas

These comprise the Western and Southern Provinces and the Puttalam district of the North Western province. There are 58 constituencies here, of which three are Muslim majority, leaving a balance of 55 seats with Low Country Sinhalese majorities. In addition, two seats in the Kandyan Sinhalese areas (Kandy and Nuwara Eliya) have a majority of Low Country Sinhalese, making thereby a total of 57 Low Country Sinhalese seats.[5]

We are not suggesting a rigid distinction between Low Country Sinhalese and Kandyan Sinhalese seats. Many Kandyan Sinhalese seats have been won by Low Country Sinhalese and on occasion Kandyan Sinhalese have won in the Low Country. The distinction is made for social and political reasons. The Kandyan Sinhalese have their own economic problems, and as a rule have been traditional in their political attitudes, with the exception of the LSSP-influenced area in the Sabaragumuwa province. On the other hand, the Low Country Sinhalese areas have been more exposed to Western influences, especially the western seaboard from Negombo to Matara, and their radicalisation has been a continuing process since the beginning of the Marxist movement in the 1930s.

The UNP won both the Low Country Sinhalese seats in the Kandyan Sinhalese areas. But in the Low Country Sinhalese areas proper it suffered heavy losses. The party won only four seats in Colombo City (Western province). Its position here had always been strong because of its middle-class support and the success of its city bosses in organising for it the *lumpen* vote. In addition the large minority element in Colombo City, Muslim and Ceylon Tamil, is sympathetic to the UNP. Lower-middle-class white-collar workers as well as other workers who used to live in Colombo and were opposed to the UNP had moved to the suburbs. In two other constituencies in the Roman Catholic belt the UNP won, but with their majorities severely cut. In the past, the party had had no difficulty in winning in these areas. It won only one seat in the Southern province but this was because in addition to the party vote the winner, W. Dahanayake, had local popularity.

The LSSP and CP have been strongest in the Western and Southern provinces and both parties won more seats in these provinces than at any time previously. The LSSP annexed 10 seats in the Western and 4 seats in the Southern. The CP obtained 1 in the Western and 4 in the Southern. The SLFP won 29 seats. The UF therefore as a group captured 48 of the 57 Low Country Sinhalese seats.

In the paddy-growing areas

The UNP laid great store on the 'success' of its food drive and hoped to win the votes of the majority of small farmers and peasantry in the paddy belt. Mention has already been made of the total disaster they met with in the North Central province, referred to as the rice bowl of the country. It was the same in most of the other paddy-growing areas.

In the Sinhalese areas (Low Country and Kandyan), there are 24 electorates in the major paddy-growing areas.[6] The UNP lost in all of these electorates, except one, Hiriyala, where as stated earlier the candidate won mainly because of his local influence. In all of the 23 others, UF candidates won: 21 SLFP, 1 LSSP and 1 Independent (in the Nikaweratiya constituency) who had UF backing.

In the Tamil-speaking areas of the Northern and Eastern provinces, there are 9 such constituencies (one of which has two members). The UNP contested in 8 of these constituencies (5 Muslim and 3 Ceylon Tamil). It won in 4 (2 Muslim and 2 Ceylon Tamil). In all of these constituencies, however, there were other issues which were as relevant to the ultimate results as, if not more relevant than, the success or otherwise of the food drive.

Part of the reason for the UNP's failure in the paddy-growing constituencies in the Sinhalese areas was that the 'National Government' did not do anything significant by way of agrarian reforms or of alleviating the conditions of the peasantry in regard to the more urgent problem of rural indebtedness. Without action in these fields, the food drive would have brought only minimal results to the vast majority of the peasantry.

Rice in Ceylon is a smallholder's crop. About 85 per cent of paddy lands is below 2 acres each and 60 per cent is less than 1 acre.[7] In addition, many of the paddy lands are in fragmented ownership under what is called the *thattumaru* system, a system which combines co-ownership of a small area among the members of the family unit with individual cultivation. A micro-survey conducted by the Investigation Unit of the Water Resources Board in a paddy-growing area in the North Central province in 1968 had an interesting observation to make on this question of land fragmentation:

Paddy lands . . . under most tanks in the North Central province are owned by peasants in several isolated parcels varying in sizes, located not at one place but in several different places under the same scheme.

A cultivator whose holding is split up and dispersed in this manner dissipates his time and energy when he has to work isolated lots. His work capacity is greatly affected when he has to move from one parcel to another for cultivation of each in turn.[8]

The survey noted that the total of $2,176\frac{1}{2}$ acres under cultivation in the area investigated was owned by 815 farmers in 3,641 different parcels scattered all over.

During the first three years of its rule (1965–8), the 'National Government' undertook the settlement of 17,400 families on new land mostly in the dry zone areas of Ceylon, that is in the North Central and parts of the Northern and Eastern provinces.[9] Assuming 6 persons to a family unit, these settlement schemes would have benefited 104,400 persons and created a fund of goodwill for the UNP amongst friends and relatives of these persons. Similar schemes were put into operation in the next two years as well. But the electoral returns for the UNP in these areas indicated that there was not adequate appreciation of these efforts.

Our investigations indicate that the conditions of the peasantry did not improve significantly despite the 'National Government's' food drive meeting with a measure of success. The big farmers, dealers in agricultural equipment and middlemen gained most. The peasantry resented the vulgar ostentation of these new rich groups while they (the peasantry) remained in more or less the same state of impoverishment.

Table   23.   *The urban vote*

	MARCH 1960					JULY 1960				
Parties	Votes polled	%age of total votes polled	%age of seats won	Candi-dates contest-ing	Seats won	Votes polled	%age of total votes polled	%age of seats won	Candi-dates contest-ing	Seats won
UNP	268,068	32.0	52.9	27	18	338,984	40.8	26.4	28	9
SLFP	108,307	12.9	17.6	22	6	206,895	24.9	38.2	19	13
LSSP	133,284	15.9	8.8	21	3	110,473	13.3	14.7	7	5
MEP	54,993	6.5	2.9	11	1	12,256	1.4	0.0	12	0
CP	57,779	6.9	2.9	14	1	53,252	6.4	5.8	2	2
FP	51,933	6.2	8.8	4	3	60,646	7.3	8.8	5	3
TC	12,120	1.4	0.0	2	0	15,510	1.8	0.0	3	0
Inde-pendents and other parties	150,141	17.9	5.8	94	2	31,373	3.7	5.8	13	2
Total	836,625	99.7	99.7	195	34	829,389	99.6	99.7	89	34

SOURCE: Compiled by the author from statistics contained in Reports of the Commissioner of Parliamentary Elections for March and July 1960, 1965 and 1970 and from *The Ceylon Daily News Parliaments of Ceylon* for 1960, 1965 and 1970.
NOTE: The total number of urban seats at each of the four general elections stood at 34. See Appendix 2 for note on rural and urban seats.
[a] Exclusive of the two member Colombo South constituency which returned a UNP and LSSP member uncontested. We have therefore calculated the percentages on the basis of a maximum of 32 urban seats.

In the urban areas

According to our estimate (see Appendix 2) there are 29 urban or quasi-urban electoral seats in the Sinhalese areas and 5 such seats in the Tamil-speaking areas. The UNP, SLFP and its Marxist allies also contest some of the latter seats.

Compared with its performance in the rural areas in the four general elections since March 1960, the UNP, as Table 23 shows, has had more consistent support from the urban areas. It obtained more than 40 per cent of the total urban vote

	1965					1970			
Votes polled	%age of total votes polled	%age of seats won	Candidates contesting	Seats won	Votes polled	%age of total votes polled	%age of seats won	Candidates contesting	Seats won
451,117	44.0	56.2	24ᵃ	18	580,865	43.6	26.4	26	9
201,233	19.6	12.5	18	4	337,765	25.3	32.3	19	11
119,543	11.6	9.3	8	3	179,363	13.4	20.5	8	7
16,281	1.5	0.0	7	0	12,881	0.9	0.0	1	0
57,518	5.6	5.8	3	2	79,321	5.9	5.8	2	2
55,775	5.4	8.8	4	3	61,412	4.6	8.8	4	3
27,317	2.6	2.9	3	1	20,338	1.5	2.9	2	1
94,558	9.2	2.9	35	1	59,672	4.4	2.9	36	1
1,023,342	99.5	98.4	102	32	1,331,617	99.6	99.6	98	34

in the last three general elections, though in terms of seats, its success depended on the combination of forces against it and the vagaries of the political climate.

The statistics indicate that when its traditional opponents combine in a common front, the UNP's share of urban seats is halved, unless of course the former are strongly out of political favour. In March 1960 the UNP scored 18 victories due to the severe clashes between the SLFP and the traditional Left in a large number of urban constituencies. In July 1960 the UNP won in 9, this time because its usual enemies were in a mutual aid polls pact. In 1965 the UNP returned to its March 1960 position. Though the same anti-UNP forces were involved in a united effort on this occasion, the UNP's skilful manipulation of prejudices among sections of the electorate against Mrs Bandaranaike's coalition with a Marxist party such as the LSSP in June 1964 and the poor showing of her 1960–4 Government, especially on the issues of employment and cost of living, went against her. In May 1970 the UNP was down to 9 seats again. There was strong voter dissatisfaction. Besides, incredible enthusiasm was generated among the poor and 'have-nots' in these areas because of the formation of a united front of anti-UNP groupings.

When compared with the UNP, the SLFP is not strong in the urban areas.

Table 24.   *The urban vote in terms of percentage and seats – UNP and its principal adversaries (SLFP, LSSP and CP)*

General election	UNP	SLFP	LSSP	CP	Total SLFP, LSSP and CP
March 1960[a]	32.0(18)[b]	12.9(6)	15.9(3)	6.9(1)	35.7(10)
July 1960	40.8(9)	24.9(13)	13.3(5)	6.4(2)	44.6(20)
1965[c]	44.0(18)	19.6(4)	11.6(3)	5.6(2)	36.8(9)
1970	43.6(9)	25.3(11)	13.4(7)	5.9(2)	44.8(20)

[a]In March 1960 there was no mutual aids polls pact between the SLFP, LSSP and CP.
[b]The figures in brackets are the number of seats won; the others are percentages.
[c]The figures for 1965 are exclusive of the two-member Colombo South constituency which returned a UNP and LSSP member uncontested.

At the same time, however, our statistics (Table 24) contradict the commonly held view that it is the weakest of parties in the urban areas. It fared poorly only at the general election of March 1960 when there was confusion and division in its ranks after the assassination of its leader. Thereafter, at every general election, it polled a higher percentage of the urban vote than the LSSP and CP combined. However, an important factor for the SLFP's support in the urban areas is the push it receives from its two Left-wing allies when it is in a mutual aid polls pact with them. The LSSP and CP are doubtless better organised than the SLFP in the principal urban areas with their network of trade unions, party branches and cells, and this accounts for the popular tendency to overrate their strength there. In actual fact, if we look at Tables 21 and 23 together, it will be noticed that both Left-wing parties contest and win more rural seats than urban ones, which leads us to the conclusion that the UNP, of all the parties directly concerned, has the largest measure of urban support. Even if we group together the urban votes of its three principal adversaries, the SLFP, LSSP and CP, these have never exceeded the UNP vote by more than 3.8 per cent.

At the general election, the UNP contested 26 of the 29 urban seats in the Sinhalese areas and won 9. The UF contested all 29 seats and won 20. The UNP polled 43.6 of the votes in these constituencies while the UF polled only a percentage more. None of these parties was successful in the urban seats they contested in the Tamil-speaking areas.

An explanation for the UNP's strength in the urban areas is that these are cosmopolitan in their social composition, have more of the middle classes and the economically better-off sections of the community residing there, inclusive of members of the minority groups belonging to the latter category. All these groups are usually attracted to the more traditional party. It is also easier for the UNP to mobilise votes in the urban areas for its candidates.

The Muslim vote

There are 8 to 10 seats in which Muslim candidates could comfortably win. Five of these are in the Tamil-speaking Northern and Eastern provinces, and the other 5 in the Sinhalese provinces. In addition, there are 24 constituencies, of which 5 are in the Tamil-speaking provinces, in each of which the Muslim vote exceeds 7 per cent of the total electorate.[10] In as many as 13 of these, the Muslim vote exceeds 10 per cent of the total electoral strength. In 23 of these 24 constituencies, the Muslim vote would count especially if the contest was a close one. In 2 of the latter, the UNP (Borella constituency) and SLFP (Trincomalee) put forward Muslim candidates, even though the Muslim population was 7.8 per cent of the total in one (Borella) and 16.3 in the other.

Traditionally, the Muslim vote has been associated with the UNP, though on occasion some prominent Muslim leaders support the SLFP. Muslim leaders from the middle and upper classes in the urban areas were able to obtain these votes for the UNP. The conservative All Ceylon Muslim League and other associated organisations were generally inclined towards the UNP. The SLFP only succeeded in attracting some of the Muslim leaders in the rural areas, though not in appreciable numbers. From 1965, however, a growing body of influential Muslim opinion, taking their cue from the SLFP's Islamic Socialist Front, began veering towards the SLFP.

The ISF played an important role in the general election, but not to the exaggerated extent some of its protagonists claimed, if electoral returns are to be taken as a test. SLFP candidates won in 4 of the 10 Muslim constituencies and the UNP in four. In one two-member constituency (Batticaloa), UNP and SLFP candidates split the Muslim vote so sharply that this constituency which had always returned a Ceylon Tamil and a Muslim returned two Ceylon Tamils on this occasion. Three of the 4 SLFP victories (Mutur, Kalmunai and Puttalam) were due more to the local influence of their candidates than to the fact that they bore the party label. In fact, two of these candidates had at various times contemplated joining the UNP.

We cannot state with any accuracy how the Muslim vote influenced the verdict in the 24 constituencies where it may have counted. In 7 of these the UNP won while in 13 UF candidates won. In 4 constituencies the FP won despite the fact that the Muslim vote was generally hostile to it. The UNP and UF victories could however be attributed to other reasons as well, except in two constituencies where we have definite evidence of the victories being due to the Muslim vote.[11] These were in Udunuwara constituency (SLFP, 17 per cent Muslim) and Kalkudah (UNP, 30 per cent Muslim).

The Christian vote

The Roman Catholic vote matters more than that of the Protestant denominations. However, in some of the constituencies in the Tamil-speaking areas, particularly in the Jaffna peninsula and in Trincomalee and Batticaloa, the Protestant groups are of some consequence.

The Christian vote, like the Muslim, has come to be associated with the UNP. This is more true of the Roman Catholics who are closely knit. Protestant Christians do not usually go for group action, but those who belong to the middle and upper classes are staunch UNP supporters.

There are 41 constituencies returning 45 members, 31 in the Sinhalese areas (34 members) and 10 in the Tamil-speaking Northern and Eastern provinces (11 members) in each of which the proportion of Christian voters exceeds 7 per cent of the total electoral strength. In 33 of these (returning 37 members), of which 24 are Sinhalese (returning 27 members) and 9 are in the Tamil-speaking provinces (returning 10 members), the Christian vote could count if the votes between the main contenders are more or less evenly divided (see Appendix 3). In the other 8 (returning 8 members) the Roman Catholics are in a majority or constitute the largest single bloc of voters (see Appendix 3). Protestant Christians are not in a majority in any constituency.

Both the UNP and UF contested all 8 Roman Catholic seats. The UNP secured 3 of these while the UF won 4. The FP was successful in the one Roman Catholic constituency in the Tamil-speaking provinces (Mannar). The TC did not contest this seat, leaving it to its UNP ally. The UF put forward 32 candidates (one of whom was a sympathiser) in the other 33 constituencies, of whom 21 were victorious; the UNP adopted 25, of whom only 6 won, while the MEP's 2 candidates lost. The FP had 9 candidates in the 9 constituencies (returning 10 members) in the Tamil areas, of whom 8 won; its principal rival, the TC, contested 6 of these, winning 1, while an Independent candidate won in another.

It is not possible to state with any degree of accuracy how the Christians voted at the general election. There was resentment against the UNP on many matters – the substitution of *poya* days for the sabbath, the neglect of schools in the Catholic belt, the failure of the 'National Government' to honour its pledges to the Church to provide relief for the schools they were obliged to run on their own resources. In addition, the underprivileged Roman Catholic had just as much complaint about the economic policies of the Government as most others who were of their same economic level.

Besides all these relevant factors, however, there were also certain radical trends discernible in the social and political thinking of the Catholic clergy. The new recruits to the clergy belonged to a different social category to that of their seniors, who came from the better-off sections of the community or from abroad. Some prominent Ceylonese Catholic priests had also been active in creating opinion on some of the neglected but urgent issues of the day. The new recruits to the clergy, as well as the poor Roman Catholic laity and their intelligentsia, when exposed to these new lines of thinking could not but act in ways different from those that had been followed in the past. But underlying all this, in our opinion, was the fact that the Church was angered by the 'National Government's' breach of faith in going back on its pledges to provide relief to their schools.

In the Tamil-speaking areas

The contest here was in the main between the two Tamil parties, the FP and the TC. The UNP had 4 of its candidates contesting Tamil seats while the LSSP and

CP had 7 and the SLFP one. Reference has already been made to the contests for Muslim seats in the Tamil-speaking Eastern province.

The FP secured the largest number of seats, but with all but one of its candidates being returned with reduced majorities. It had 19 candidates and of these 13 won. Three of its leading stalwarts suffered defeats, in addition to the party losing one other seat (Kilinochchi) which it had previously held. However, the party gained 3 new seats including the prestigious constituency of Jaffna. This was the first time that the party was successful in these 3 seats. In securing these seats (Jaffna, Udupiddy and Vavuniya), it destroyed the traditional parliamentary leadership of its principal rival, the TC. It also ousted the leaders of one of its splinter groups (V. Navaratnam of the TSRP) from the seat (Kayts) he had held since September 1963.

The election saw the FP claim of having the support of sections of the Tamil-speaking Muslims of the Eastern province nullified. It contested only one Muslim seat (Kalmunai) where previously it used to put forward at least two, if not more, Muslim candidates. And this candidate received the third place instead of coming second or in fact winning the seat, as happened in the past. ,

The TC ran 12 candidates of whom 3 won. But its leader (G. G. Ponnambalam), his deputy (M. Sivasithamparam) and its youth league leader (T. Sivasithamparam) lost to FP candidates. The TC was really in alliance with the UNP and the latter did not therefore run candidates in constituencies which the TC contested.

The UNP won 2 of the Tamil seats it contested. Both were in the Eastern province. The SLFP's lone candidate in the Jaffna Peninsula of the Northern province forfeited his deposit, while its Muslim candidate for the Tamil majority Trincomalee seat was also defeated.

The two Left-wing allies of the SLFP failed to win any seat. What is more, there was a noticeable decline in support for the LSSP candidates, owing to the fact that that party was in alliance with the SLFP.

No definite trends could be detected in the pattern of voting in the Tamil areas. The FP did not fare as well as in the past, but part of the explanation for this could be attributed to the fact that most of its M.P.s had been in Parliaments consecutively from 1956 and the public had grown weary of them. The party also appeared to fail to capture the imagination of the youth whose support it had received on earlier occasions. Decline in youth support had started with the general election of 1965, but it dwindled considerably on the present occasion. It was also evident that the FP's message had grown stale with the years, as no new dynamic content was injected into it. The promise to achieve an autonomous Tamil regional area appeared to be devoid of meaning, if not content.

There was one other factor pertinent to the FP's declining support. Those who had backed the party saw the UNP as a quicker means of achieving parochial objectives. The UNP had succeeded in establishing a measure of confidence among the Tamil people so that sections of the Tamil voting public no longer saw any threat to the Tamil position from the UNP.

Conclusion

The results established two facts. Firstly, the electors in giving an overwhelming mandate to the UF chose to overlook the point that a reasonably strong Opposition is just as important for responsible Government. There had been this tendency in some previous general elections as well, particularly at those of 1952 and 1956, but it was never so evident as on this single occasion. A weak Opposition encourages arrogance and authoritarianism in the exercise of governmental power. This is confirmed by the behaviour of Government M.P.s in the present Parliament. Opposition members are sometimes heckled and at other times not permitted to freely articulate their views on issues which are important to them. The Speaker's task is thus rendered difficult. The electorate however cannot be wholly blamed for this unfortunate consequence. The system of electoral demarcation, with its imbalances in voter strengths in constituencies, tends to produce massive landslide majorities for the victorious coalition. At this general election a rural drop of only 1.8 per cent and an urban loss of 0.4 per cent for the UNP gave the UF a huge majority. Similar situations occurred at the general elections of 1952, 1956 and July 1960. The electoral system thus reflects only a fraction of the Opposition's real strength in the House. Consequently the main Opposition groups concentrate more on activities outside of Parliament. This causes problems for the Government in office.

A second fact made evident was the maturing of a two-party system comprising opposing coalitions in agreement on the broad foundations of the state. It had become a reality after twenty-three years of parliamentary government and thirty-nine years of universal suffrage. The electorate itself in successive general elections had vaguely indicated a desire for two recognised coalitions, between which it could choose. The main rival parties and their leaders perceived this preference and consequently brought into being their respective coalitions. That way, they realised, was the road to electoral success.

The monopoly of power by the two rival groups can have dangerous implications for a contracting and stagnant economy such as that of Ceylon. Inability on their part to regenerate the economy could persuade the electors that the system will not work. Other parties which advocate the destruction of Parliament could obtain a wider appeal. There are already signs of such a trend. Their development will be determined by the success or failure of Governments operating within the existing framework.

10. Epilogue

Post-election trends

General elections since 1956 have had a crucial relevance to the social, economic and political problems of the island. The issues raised indicate the direction along which the rival leadership wishes to lead the country. A further factor is that the political situation since 1965 has been considerably clarified with a gradual move towards a two-party situation with the smaller groupings tending to cohere around one or other of the major parties. Consequently the trend is for Governments in office to endeavour to pack in, in the limited and sometimes uncertain space of time available, a great deal of change which, depending on the circumstances, inevitably generates tensions from the groups affected.

The political concepts and ideologies of the opposing camps should not therefore be taken at their face value. The objective of 'democratic socialism' of the UNP and its allies and that of a 'socialist democracy' advocated by the SLFP and its Left-wing partners mean much more than what these terms imply to the Western observer.

In many respects, the SLFP has been responsible for stabilising the democratic system. While acting as a social and political catalyst, it has also provided a parliamentary alternative to considerable discontented sections in the electorate who might otherwise have reposed confidence in the island's traditional Marxist leadership. This may have imperilled the democratic system, as the Marxists in their earlier phase were unwilling to commit themselves to it. By allying themselves now with the SLFP they have also declared their willingness to work within the constitutional framework – the LSSP and CP realising that only in a merger, such as the UF, could they hope to achieve some of their goals.

However, it is significant that what the Common Programme of the SLFP and its parties seeks to achieve with its victory in May 1970 is not very different from what the SLFP had outlined in its policy statement when it was first inaugurated by its founder, S. W. R. D. Bandaranaike, as far back as in 1951.[1]

The party at the time called for industrialisation as a method of eliminating unemployment. With a view to effecting an equitable redistribution of incomes, it pledged itself to impose a supertax on all incomes in excess of Rs. 50,000, to introduce death duties and a progressive scale of income taxation. Accumulation of too much private capital by individuals or groups, it held, should be ended. It planned therefore to nationalise in a gradual way all essential industries inclusive of the large plantations and the transport, banking and insurance concerns. With the necessary controls, the party declared that it would be possible to gear private capital to a plan of national development.

In the socio-cultural spheres, the SLFP called for a switch to the national languages and for the protection of the national religions. With time, the emphasis tended to be more on the Sinhalese language and Buddhism.

179

Much of the SLFP's economic programme was taken from the LSSP and CP – both parties having advocated similar policies since their inception in the early 1930s. In this respect, therefore, the Common Programme that the UF Government of 1970 is implementing is a programme of action that had been discussed and debated in the country by opposing parties for several decades.

There is, however, one factor that the SLFP and its partners did not take into adequate consideration – what we choose to call the 'external constraints' that operate on the freedom of any Ceylonese Government to manoeuvre in the implementation of its economic policies. The vagaries of the international market expose the island's staple export products to price fluctuations which cause serious crises in its terms of trade and consequently its balance of payments. This results in a shortage of hard currency for capital development and more importantly for the import of essential consumer items. Recourse must therefore be made to foreign credit – and the more obvious sources are the international credit agencies and the countries of the West. The communist states have also provided assistance, but not as much as might be expected.

The provision of credit especially from the international banks carries with it definite obligations such as pruning of the welfare services. And assistance from Western countries implies abandonment of the pledge to nationalise foreign-owned concerns. Such obligations have worked to the detriment of Governments in office, especially those which are SLFP-oriented. Consequently in the latter instance there is a gap between expectations and results which in turn produces disillusionment, frustration and anger among those who built hopes on these Governments.

In a sense, this was the dilemma which faced the UF Government of 1970. Promises produced expectations and expectations in turn stimulated demand for further change in the direction of an egalitarian society. Presumably the SLFP's Marxist partners gambled on this latter fact. On the other hand, some of the radical changes already effected have postponed the need for the revolutionary transformation of the social order. The SLFP's own hard core hope for this kind of social equilibrium at the level of change effected and intended. They have apparently succeeded to date in their endeavours.

Such a limited exercise, however, has given rise to two other possibilities. There is a reaction against the increasing regimentation of society and the imposition of state controls, also a realisation that these would not produce the promised results. The UNP has stood to benefit from this.

Yet there is a growing impatience among the young with what they call the 'parliamentary game of musical chairs' and a conviction that the existing framework cannot solve the urgent problems of unemployment and economic development. These people seek a violent overthrow of the established order. The abortive Popular Liberation Front (PLF) insurrection of April 1971 was one such attempt and there is no guarantee that other such attempts will not be made in the future.

The UF Government

The Cabinet

Mrs Bandaranaike's own SLFP commanded an overall majority in the House (90 of the 151 elective seats), but in terms of the agreement with the two Marxist parties, portfolios were allocated to their leaders as well. The LSSP was given three key ministries – Finance, Plantation Industry and Constitutional Affairs, and Communications – and the CP, one – Housing and Construction. Two other important portfolios – External and Internal Trade, and Industries and Scientific Research – were vested in Left-wing socialists in the SLFP, one of whom (T. B. Ilangaratne) was among those mainly instrumental in forging the UF alliance, while the other (T. B. Subasinghe) had been earlier a prominent LSSP front-ranker before crossing over to the SLFP. In addition, 'two friends of the Soviet Union' were also included in the Cabinet. A leading CP man was made Deputy Minister of Education while another with Maoist leanings was given the junior Portfolio of Planning and Employment.

However, the Centrists and Right-wingers of the SLFP maintain their influence. The strongest of them, Felix Dias Bandaranaike, took three important ministries which are the key to the control of the domestic situation – Home Affairs, Local Government, and Public Administration. After the new Republican Constitution came into effect in May 1972, he was assigned a fourth portfolio, that of Justice.

Mrs Bandaranaike sought to make her Government as representative as possible of the ethnic, religious and social groupings. For the first time since 1956, an SLFP-oriented Government had in its ranks a Ceylon Tamil. He was not an elected Member of Parliament but a nominee of the Government in the Senate. He was given an inconsequential portfolio, that of Posts and Telecommunications. The Muslim leader, Badiudin Mahmud, was appointed Minister of Education. A Roman Catholic was nominated to the Senate and made Minister of Justice, while another from the House became Minister of Broadcasting the Information. The important non-*goigama* caste groups were given due consideration, while another caste group normally thought outside the pale had one of their number included in the Cabinet.

All in all, the Cabinet was a carefully balanced affair. Politically the Left-wingers were well poised but in actual fact the Centrists are now favourably positioned. Account must also be taken of the Prime Minister's advisers and close associates outside the Cabinet circle. They are mostly individuals committed to maintaining the existing social order, though not averse to changes which might promote its sustenance.

Foreign policy

Given the powerful Left-wing component in the new Government and Mrs Bandaranaike's own preference for closer association with the non-aligned and communist states opposed to all forms of Western colonialism, it was only to be expected that Ceylon would shift her foreign-policy orientation more to the Left. And this in fact was effected in the first flush of victory without very much forethought.

Diplomatic relations with Israel were severed until such time as the latter came to an amicable settlement with the Arab states. Diplomatic relations with the German Democratic Republic were established despite last-minute efforts by the Bonn Embassy in Colombo to have this deferred; West Germany was one of Ceylon's principal aid givers in the past. The Asia Foundation and the Peace Corps had to quit despite the fact that the U.S. was piqued over the decision on the latter. The Democratic Republic of Korea and the Provisional Revolutionary Government of South Vietnam were recognised – actions which hardly pleased the countries of the West. At the Lusaka Conference in September 1970, Mrs Bandaranaike joined other non-aligned states in calling for an economic boycott of the Republic of South Africa, a move which could very well have endangered Ceylon's annual 80 million rupee tea trade with that country. The call for the boycott was not implemented by Ceylon.

Some aid at first was forthcoming from a few Western countries. But the West German Government suspended assistance, and the United Kingdom followed suit in the second year of the UF Government's term of office as a protest against those revenue measures of the Government which had affected British interests in the island. The U.S. proved lukewarm. Finally, the LSSP Minister of Finance found it impossible to accept the terms laid down by the World Bank as conditions requisite for providing his Government with further financial accommodation.

The Government blundered over the stance it took on the Indo-Pakistan conflict concerning Bangladesh during the latter part of 1971. It was under pressure from local Muslim lobbies interested in supporting the territorial integrity of Pakistan. Ceylon received adverse press coverage in India despite the efforts of the Prime Minister to refute charges that Pakistani troop planes *en route* to Bangladesh stopped at Bandaranaike International Airport to refuel.[2]

On the other hand Ceylon obtained immediate military assistance to crush the Che Guevarist-styled PLF insurrection of April 1971 from the states of the different power blocs – the U.S.A. and U.K., India and the U.S.S.R. Mrs Bandaranaike claimed this as a vindication of her policy of non-alignment and neutralism.[3] But it was evident that in all the instances she mentioned, there was an interest at stake which would have been adversely affected if a Che Guevarist or Maoist junta had seized power.

But non-alignment failed to enlist appropriate recognition for Ceylon at the 1972 Georgetown (Guyana) Conference of Foreign Ministers of non-aligned nations. Ceylon wished to have Colombo as the venue of the next non-aligned meeting. Only Nepal and Singapore supported the Ceylonese claim while India remained silent and the African and Arab states opted for Algeria. Mrs Bandaranaike was obviously disappointed and stated in the National State

Assembly that 'some countries with whom we had been closely associated since the earliest days of non-alignment had shown a disregard for principle in this case'.[4]

Mrs Bandaranaike's efforts to have the Indian Ocean declared a nuclear free peace zone have also not received too enthusiastic support even from the littoral states involved. At the Commonwealth Conference in Singapore[5] in January 1971 and at the U.N. General Assembly in October 1971,[6] she pressed her proposal and expressed Ceylon's disapproval of the proposed Anglo-American communications base on the Indian Ocean atoll of Diego Garcia.

The frustrations that the UF Government met with in its efforts to obtain aid from the Western-oriented Aid Ceylon Consortium of powers and from the international credit agencies have led it to become increasingly dependent on the People's Republic of China. After the abortive PLF insurrection of April 1971, China provided Ceylon with a Rs. 150 million long-term interest-free loan in convertible exchange and five patrol boats for her Navy in February 1972. In June 1972, Mrs Bandaranaike visited China and received a warm and enthusiastic reception. Also a further interest-free loan of Rs. 265 million was made, repayable in 20 years with an initial 10-year grace period. Substantial project aid for a textile mill, for shipping, internal fisheries harbours and flood control was also pledged. What implications such Chinese assistance will have in the domestic sphere cannot readily be anticipated. It will improve the position of the small Peking-oriented CP in Ceylon and will enable the Chinese Embassy in Colombo to engage in various activities.

All in all, however, the Government's foreign policy exercises failed to produce the expected results – shoals of foreign aid and a measure of international recognition for Ceylon. There was not enough compensation from the non-aligned and communist states – China excepted – while the Western bloc has been increasingly alienated by the new policies pursued. In fact, the question arises as to whether non-alignment and neutralism have any significance in the present global context, considering the fact of India's and the U.A.R.'s close ties with the Soviet Union.

Economic policies

The most urgent problems facing the new Government were the removal of the rice cut imposed by the 'National Government' in 1966, unemployment, especially that of approximately 14,000 graduates, and the need for a development programme which would generate growth.

Soon after the Government took office, they decided to continue providing the first measure (two pounds) of rice per adult per week free of charge (as was done by the previous Government) and the second measure at a heavily subsidised price. In the first year, the cost to the exchequer was Rs. 377 million. It continues to be an increasing burden. In the second year, the Government raised the price of the second measure on the score that rice cost more to buy in the world market. Income taxpayers were required to pay for their rice. The Minister of Finance also made attempts to increase the prices of other subsidised items of food but was able to accomplish this only in an extremely limited form owing to stiff opposition from the Government's own back-benchers.

Meanwhile, there has been a continuing scarcity of essential foods and curry-stuffs. The cost of living has shot up and the Government is virtually helpless in the face of all this because of the shortage of hard currency to import the required items. In fact, bans have been imposed on the import of some items of food in the hope that this will stimulate local production.

On the employment front, the Prime Minister indicated her earnestness by creating a portfolio and taking it over herself. A short-term employment programme was prepared by the Ministry of Planning and Employment with a view to providing jobs straightaway for 105,500 persons. Besides, a national apprenticeship scheme with private sector cooperation and the compulsory retirement of public sector employees over 55 years of age absorbed a consider-able section of the unemployed graduates.

In the long term, the government is busy encouraging the launching of rural-based industrial projects by divisional development councils in the hope that these would arrest the drift of the jobless and the underemployed from the countryside to the towns.

More important, a Five-Year Plan presented by the Prime Minister in November 1971 seeks in various ways to absorb, by the end of the plan period in 1976, 810,000 of the 1,100,000 who will be in need of employment.[7] The remaining 290,000, the planners hope, will obtain employment in special works programmes in the rural, urban and plantation sectors.

The Five-Year Plan is designed to achieve an annual growth rate of 6 per cent, raise domestic savings from the present level of 12.5 per cent of national income to 17 per cent and improve the standard of living of some 40 per cent of the island's population who at present earn incomes of less than Rs. 200 per month. It expects per capita income to rise from Rs. 910 per annum to Rs. 1,150 at the end of the Plan period (at 1970 prices). The Plan provides for an investment of Rs. 14,820 million during its whole term of operation.

The problem of financing the Plan is another question. The private sector is expected to contribute 52 per cent of the envisaged investment. This is sanguine optimism in the context of all that is being done by the Left-oriented Government to control the private sector, if not smother it. In addition, the grave short-age of foreign exchange has resulted in many private sector projects having to close down or reduce production.

The same applies with respect to foreign investment. The Plan sets out in detail the fields in which foreign capital is welcome – tourism, specified manu-factures and technical skills not locally available. Yet measures taken by the Government to control or curb the activities of existing British and U.S. concerns cannot but discourage prospective foreign investors.

The Plan has hardly been able to get off the ground owing to the growing financial crises. Three austerity budgets to date (1973) have been presented by the Minister of Finance, and the evidence suggests that there are not even sufficient resources available to bridge the deficits. As in the past, a sizeable section of expenditure is on the welfare services. And the usual sources of foreign aid have been reduced.

The private sector and the better-off layers of Ceylonese society have had burdens piled on them with hardly any incentives provided to encourage them to greater effort. Together they comprise not more than some 50,000 individuals and are not worth flogging. But the Government gains some benefit from the fact that the exercise gives much satisfaction to the poorer sections of the community.

The Business Undertakings (Acquisition) Act (1972) empowers the state to take over any business concern employing more than 100 persons, if it is in the public interest. The state has acquired power to purchase with compensation shares in plantation companies, to nationalise or acquire not less than 51 per cent of any trade or industry where necessary and to issue directives or appoint directors to the boards of private and public companies. A ceiling of 12 per cent on company dividends for the year has been imposed, as well as a ceiling of Rs. 2,000 per month on individual incomes exclusive of taxes, insurance premia, loan repayments, etc. In addition, a compulsory savings scheme for income earners above a certain limit has made matters more difficult for those in the middle and upper income brackets.

Above all, a limit on landholdings of 50 acres per adult member in a family under the Land Reform Act of 1972, and a restriction on the number of houses a family can own under legislation enacted in the same year, have left the possessing class dispirited and entrepreneurially-speaking listless.

However, the Land Reform Act is an important piece of radical legislation which was long overdue, especially in the context of land reform measures having been in effect for many years in states so disparate as Taiwan, Egypt, the Philippines, Korea and some of the units of the Indian federation. The Act will provide relief to the landless in that an excess of 400,000 acres owned by 5,500 landowners who owned between them 1.2 million acres is now available for distribution by a Land Reform Commission. Just as important is the Agricultural Productivity Act of the same year. Broadly this legislation requires defined standards of production in respect of lands held, with the threat of confiscation if owners do not conform.

The general dissatisfaction bred by these changes and the increasing burdens imposed have resulted in numbers of the owning, professional and administrative classes leaving the island for better situations. The Government has adopted measures to discourage this brain drain, though not with much success. Had the changes been accompanied by a firm and resolute drive towards economic recovery, confidence might have been restored. But the reverse is more true. Growth is imperceptible, verging on stagnancy.

Domestic instability

The conviction that the UF Government cannot provide solutions to the pressing problems of the day, and that it is encroaching on democratic freedoms in its pursuit of 'socialism', has resulted in the undermining and even destruction of confidence in the parliamentary system itself – among the jobless youth, the major minority grouping (the Tamils) and the established sections of Ceylonese society.

Some 52 per cent of Ceylon's population is in the age category below 19 and 40 per cent is under 14. Sixty-eight per cent of the total unemployed in 1968 belonged to the age group 15–29.[8] They numbered 1.69 million in 1968. Over 75 per cent of unemployment is in the countryside.

The enfranchised 18-year-olds among this youth population played a major role in the UF's landslide victory. Their expectations sky-rocketed and they hoped that the wave of a magic wand would produce for them the jobs they were hungering for. But this did not happen.

It is to these young people in the depths of despair that the PLF addressed its message. This ultra-Marxist organisation, subscribing to a hotchpotch of Che Guevarist and Maoist doctrines, had functioned under cover from late 1964 and through the term of office of the 'National Government'. It surfaced after the advent of the UF Government.

The PLF campaigned far and wide in the country during July 1970 through to March 1971. Its leaders inveighed against the traditional Marxists and accused them of betraying the cause. They confined their appeal only to the Sinhalese Buddhist populace. In particular, the PLF leadership was angered by the UF Government's failure to carry out the nationalisation programme they were pledged to. The LSSP Minister of Finance, for instance, had stated in the House in December 1971 that he could not nationalise the foreign-owned banks in the country because a sum of Rs. 700–800 million in foreign currency was owing to them.[9] Rohana Wijeweera, the PLF's chief, ridiculed in his public oratory a Trotskyist Minister of Finance seeking to inaugurate 'socialism through the World Bank and the International Monetary Fund'.

The PLF's programme was epitomised in what is called *The Five Lectures*.[10] These dealt with Indian expansionism, the island's perilous economic straits, an economic analysis which alleges that 80 to 90 per cent or more of the people have not stood to gain anything since independence, the failure of the island's traditional Left-wing leadership, and how to capture power in 24 hours.

The PLF organised a *blitzkrieg*-style insurrection in the first week of April 1971. Their regulars were 'very highly disciplined' and 'well-educated' young people, and about 75 per cent of them were in the age group 18–20.[11] A large number of girls in the same age category were also involved in the insurrection. It is believed that secondary school teachers and minor employees in government service functioned as catalysts, if not actually participating in the insurrection itself.

The PLF planned to kidnap the Prime Minister and to seize Colombo on

13 April, the day of the Sinhalese new year. They launched their attacks in the last days of March and first week of April and gained temporary control of many parts of the country, destroying police stations and other governmental buildings in the process. It was some weeks before the Ceylonese army was able to restore order. Government forces in the first week were unable to overpower the insurgents, owing to lack of adequate supplies.

Some 16,000 insurgents were captured or had surrendered by June (1971) and estimates of those killed vary between 2,000 and 5,000. Of those in captivity, some 13,000 have been released and in mid-1972 there were 3,000 still in custody. Forty-one are being charged before a special tribunal, the Criminal Justices Commission, brought into existence by legislation enacted in 1972.

The rebels caused considerable damage to communications and property. The Minister of Finance estimated the losses to be in the region of Rs. 300 million.[12] The Minister complained with some justification that the trail of disaster left behind by the PLF had put back the clock of development and retarded economic progress for a long time to come.

The insurrection created a sense of urgency in the ranks of the UF leadership about the need for radical socialist measures to pacify discontent. Legislation dealing with land reforms, already referred to, was enacted. In November 1971 the Prime Minister presented the *Five-Year Plan 1972–6* and her Government's proposals to alleviate social distress under what came to be called the 'package deal'. At the same time, the UF Government took the opportunity to restructure the country's higher educational system. Many of the organisers of the PLF movement were frustrated university students in the liberal arts and humanities as well as jobless graduates. There was no social utility, the Government felt, in the state-financed universities producing a surplus of graduates in these fields of learning. The Government therefore decided to go back on the pledges it had given the academic staff and student population of the four universities and the Institute of Higher Technology to liberalise the excessively rigid administrative structure imposed on them by the previous regime under their Higher Education Act of 1966. Instead, an Act much more severe than that of 1966 was passed in 1972. Besides tightening the administration, it also, more importantly, amalgamated all five university institutions into one unified structure. Some of the reforms instituted serve a purpose: for example, the rationalisation of courses and the cutting down on wasteful admissions into the humanities and the liberal arts. It was hoped that these changes would introduce a degree of quiescence in the university. They have, on the contrary, produced further problems and have left the university population seething with discontent.

Trouble is also brewing on another front – the protesting Tamil minority, both Ceylon and Indian. The CWC is against any attempt to forcibly repatriate Indians in Ceylon who opted for Indian citizenship in the hope that, under the terms of the legislation of 1968 enacted by the 'National Government', they would be permitted to carry on in their occupations till they reached the age of retirement. The UF Government has revoked this and seeks to speed up the process of implementing the terms of the Sirima–Shastri Pact of October 1964 as was envisaged by them.

The Ceylon Tamils feel they are being edged out of the public services and the university institutions, and are being denied any significant place in that part of the economic sector which is falling increasingly under governmental control. More importantly, they are resentful of the new Republican constitution, which they look on as an imposition and under which they feel they have been relegated to the status of second-class citizens. Though some place has been given to the Tamil language under the constitution (see below for the details), the concessions made, significant as they definitely are, have come fifteen years too late. The Tamils by and large have rejected the Republican constitution.

The end result has been that all Tamil political groupings save those which are Left-oriented have closed their ranks. On 14 May 1972 these organisations – the FP, TC, CWC, ATM among others – merged into the TUF under the leadership of the FP head, S. J. V. Chelvanayakam, to assert 'the freedom, dignity and rights of the Tamil people'.[13] The Front launched a protest campaign in October 1972, marked by Chelvanayakam's resignation of his parliamentary seat. The Front also established a school in March 1973 in a town in the Jaffna Peninsula in violation of the state's educational code.

More disturbing is the fact of an insurrectionary organisation of Tamil youths taking root in the Tamil areas of north Ceylon. As if to keep pace with them, the TUF momentously resolved on 17 May to go ahead with drafting a constitution for a separate state.[14] The TUF takes its cue from Bangladesh and there is the unexpressed hope that India will come to their assistance. The question naturally arises whether Ceylon is in the first stages of nation-breaking.

Lastly, the established sectors in society, inclusive of their principal political instrument, the UNP, have begun to grow increasingly apprehensive about the ability of Parliament to safeguard what they regard are the essential freedoms of a democratic society. The UNP expressed strong opposition to some of the important clauses of the Press Councils Act of 1973 as being restrictive of the freedom of the press. The passing of the Associated Newspapers of Ceylon Limited (Special Provisions) Act by the National State Assembly in May 1973 made it even more fearful that the accepted freedoms are vanishing. The Act in question seeks to disperse, under governmental supervision, ownership of the Lake House Group of newspapers. The UNP's position was that the UF received no mandate for this nor had it canvassed the proposition during the general election campaign.

The party's President, J. R. Jayawardene, declared in a press release in May 1973 that 'if we think that attempts are being made to do away with the liberties of the people, it is our duty to alert them and with their help take steps to prevent these attempts from succeeding'.[15]He called for a boycott of Lake House newspapers when they pass under state control and added quite significantly that his party would launch a non-violent campaign to persuade the Government to change its course of action.

The point in the activities of youth insurrectionists, Tamil parties and the UNP is that there is a growing erosion of faith in Parliament being a problem-solver. There is an increasing tendency to fall back on extra-parliamentary modes of protest and pressure in the belief that these could bring in speedier returns than mere debate in the National State Assembly. The question again arises as to whether we are witnessing the beginning of the end of Parliament as it used to be traditionally.

Constitutional changes

The objectives of a socialist and participatory democracy have been enshrined in the constitutional and administrative changes effected.[16] The SLFP's Left-wing partners sought to correct the existing imbalances in parliamentary representation by advocating 'a free and secret exercise of an equal, direct and universal suffrage on a territorial basis',[17] but there was resistance from those quarters in the SLFP which benefited from the system in operation and it there-fore had to be abandoned. They were also foiled by the vigilant SLFP Minister of Public Administration in their attempt to utilise the paraphernalia of par-ticipatory democracy – people's committees, workers' councils and advisory committees and divisional development councils – as the instruments of mass agitation.

A Constituent Assembly was convened by the Prime Minister in July 1970 and it completed its endeavours in May 1972. On 22 May, the new Republican Constitution was proclaimed. The UNP refused to accept the constitution. Dudley Senanayake stated in the Constituent Assembly on the day the vote was taken that the people had not been given an adequate opportunity to express their views, there were many defects and omissions in the constitution and it contained sections which eroded the liberties of a democratic society.[18]

The FP withdrew from the assembly at an early stage – in June 1971 – when it failed to secure its demands on language, citizenship and regional autonomy or even a compromise solution to these.

Despite all the assertions that the new system marked a clear break with the past and is a home-made product, the constitution incorporates much of what was in its discarded predecessor. It provides for the Cabinet system and, as already stated, retains the old scheme of parliamentary representation. The legislation of 1948 and 1949 excluding Indians from citizenship and the fran-chise is also retained. There are, however, other features in the new constitution which provide evidence of the UF Government's anxiety to utilise it as an instrument of legitimacy to get through as much as possible of the radical social and economic changes it contemplates.

Thus the unicameral National State Assembly is 'the supreme instrument of state power' and all impediments to the exercise of legislative authority by the UF Government have been removed. In fact, even before the Assembly came into being, the UF Government, chafing at the obstructionist tactics of the

UNP majority in the second chamber, the Senate, had the latter abolished under the existing procedure for constitutional amendment on 28 September 1971.

Further, the ordinary courts are excluded from pronouncing on the constitutional validity of legislation. Instead, a special constitutional court comprising five judges is vested with the power of declaring within a specific time limit whether a law contravenes the constitution or not, in the event of it being so challenged.[19] Three members of the court, selected by the drawing of lots, hear each issue that is referred to it. The Assembly, however, has the power to override an adverse opinion by the use of the constitutional amending procedure.

Finally, the public services are vested now in the control of the Cabinet of ministers, not as previously in an independent public services commission. This implies that the Government is assured that it will get the state employees it needs, especially at the middle and higher grades, to implement the policies that it seeks to. There is, in this provision, scope for any Government so inclined to indulge in jobbery, nepotism and political favouritism – in effect for a limited kind of spoils system to be brought into operation.

When the UF Government took office, significant changes were effected in the higher sectors of the administration. Established administrators were ignored for outsiders and in other cases junior men were considered more reliable. But the objective was not to provide rewards for political and other services but a desire to get officials whom ministers could depend on for advice and effective implementation of radical measures.

Further, in order to secure the cooperation of the lower rungs of the administration, legislation was enacted in October 1971 granting political rights to certain categories of Government and state corporation employees, inclusive of the right to seek election to Parliament and to local bodies. More importantly, workers' councils and advisory committees comprising the lower rungs in Government offices were established. The former were elected by employees in state enterprises and are intended to associate them in the management of these enterprises, but only in an advisory capacity. The latter function in Government offices 'to combat bureaucracy, inefficiency, corruption, sabotage and waste'.[20] They are permitted only to make representations to the authorities concerned. Administrators have complained that some committees have tried to usurp powers that do not properly come within their province.

The constitution contains a statement on the Principles of State Policy (Sections 16 and 17). Though these are not enforceable in any court of law, Section 18(2) of the constitution stipulates that the exercise and operation of fundamental rights and freedoms provided for in Section 18(1) shall, among other things, be subject to any measures the state may take to give effect to the aims and objectives detailed in the Principles of State Policy. These Principles leave no room for doubt that the UF Government is determined to take the country in the direction of a Left-oriented socialist democracy. The state is required to provide for full employment, equitable distribution of the social product, development of collective forms of property, elimination of economic and social privilege, social welfare and the maximum participation of the people in government.

The rights of citizens and groups are provided for in Section 18(1). But they are not absolute and cannot stand in the way of the UF Government's progress towards a socialist democracy. Accordingly subsection 2 of this Section states that all rights are subject to restrictions that may be placed in the interests of, among other things, national economy, which could mean implementation of policies that work toward a socialistic set-up. As well there is Section 18(2), to which we have referred in the previous paragraph.

The framers also provided their own solution to the conflicting claims of the feuding groups in Ceylon's plural society. Buddhism is given 'the foremost place' (Section 6) and it therefore becomes the duty of the state 'to protect and foster' it, while assuring to all other religions freedom of worship and the right to propagate their faiths (Section 18(1) (d)).

Section 7 declares Sinhala to be the official language but the succeeding sections make detailed provisions for the use of the Tamil language for administrative and judicial purposes. The proviso to Section 11(1) declared that the National State Assembly may by or under its law provide for the use of a language other than the Sinhalese language in courts and other institutions exercising original jurisdiction in the Tamil-speaking Northern and Eastern provinces. Legislation was enacted in 1973 for the use of Tamil in the provinces referred to.

The instruments of participatory democracy are, besides the workers' councils and advisory committees mentioned already, people's committees and divisional development councils. People's committees are, as the Prime Minister stated when they came into operation, institutions 'where people at grass roots level are brought into participation with the administrative machinery in an attempt to bring about better understanding between the people and the administration'.[21] Such committees have been established for each ward in a local authority. Its members are appointed by the Minister of Public Administration from panels of names submitted by local organisations. Members of Parliament are also consulted. The chairmen of these committees are appointed by the Minister who will also have the power to remove them as well as other committee members without cause assigned. These committees invite attention to local needs, suggest remedial measures and assist local villagers to make representations on individual or group grievances. They have the power to report public officers, write to Government departments which are obliged to reply to them, get copies of letters not considered confidential from state and state-assisted establishments and institute legal action against persons in certain kinds of cases. There have been some abuses in the functioning of these committees but they did not turn out to be the instruments of persecution and tyranny that the UNP alleged they would become in the heat of the election campaign. Nor have the SLFP's Left-wing partners succeeded to date in manipulating them.

Divisional development councils are indirectly constituted in the rural areas and include members of local bodies and officials of the central Government functioning in the area. They plan and implement projects which draw on local raw materials and are supervised and assisted by the Ministry of Planning. They are intended to provide employment to the people of the area. Some of these councils have been very successful in carrying out useful development programmes.

These popular institutions have worked reasonably well since their coming into being. They have added to the growing politicisation of the masses. But it could be argued that an excess of political activity could result therefrom and consequently with the exception of the divisional development councils the others could hamper the efficiency of the administrative apparatus.

The party situation

The UF

Relations between the SLFP and the two Marxist parties have not always been at their best but the disagreements were not serious enough to cause a permanent rift. The LSSP front bench proved willing to resolve any differences with its partners at the summit level, though their rank and file continue to be restive. The CP however remains a problem.

Contrary to expectations, the Marxists to date have not caused much concern to the SLFP Right wing. The LSSP especially has been careful not to push too hard policies which might be interpreted as being more Left-oriented. But the party hopes that the objective situation will change, at which time its hour will arrive.

LSSP and CP strategy

Though the LSSP and CP have decided to tread a Left-of-centre democratic socialist path, it cannot be said with certainty that they have dumped their Marxist goals. There is a certain ambivalence in the pronouncements of their leadership which appear to indicate that they see in the Leftward trend in the SLFP an opportunity for them in their striving towards a Marxian socialist society. Besides, both parties, even after the formation of the UF Government in May 1970, have reiterated their Marxist objectives. Their trade unions have been even more strident in the proclamation of these goals.

The LSSP leader, Dr N. M. Perera, has stated that 'with calculation and deliberation' they have 'succeeded in making solid progress without any major setback' in their 'steady advance'. But he cautioned that 'socialism is a hard road of social re-organisation to be patiently built up stone by stone in accordance with the level of consciousness of the masses'.[22] The party's deputy leader, Dr Colvin R. de Silva, warned that 'the pressure of circumambient imperialism in Ceylon is powerful and even heightened'.[23] He added that 'the dominant issue in contemporary Ceylon is the overthrow of capitalism'. Quite rightly he argued that his party 'is now on a new track and is today the soul of the UF which rules Ceylon'. V. Karalasingham, a leading theorist in the party, emphasised that the Common Programme is 'not so much a milestone as a spring board . . . not so much a stage in a journey but is a spring board from which the journey itself will really commence'.[24]

Both Left parties, besides, are anxious to keep constantly in view their ultimate aims. In this matter, however, the CP is at variance with the LSSP in urging quicker action in the implementation of the socialist aspects of the Common Programme and openly critical of the economic policies of the LSSP Minister of Finance (Dr N. M. Perera). In its statement of 17 September 1970 after its first post-election plenary session, the CP stressed that 'in seeking to overcome the present financial crisis the country is faced with, emphasis should be laid, not so much on sacrifices by the working people or the pursuit of loans from the West, as getting into State hands the financial resources of foreign banks, industries and plantations'.[25]

The Minister of Finance had already stated that it was not the Government's policy to nationalise the plantations and that he was not in a position to go ahead with the UF's pledge to take over the foreign banks, in view of the country's critical financial situation.[26]

Further, the LSSP's central committee, which met in late August 1971 to consider the crisis resulting from the PLF insurrection (of April 1971), suggested measures which were somewhat different from those advocated by the CP.[27] Its emphasis was on the need to create mass consciousness to 'wean the public away from welfarism and direct its attention towards real socialist measures'. It urged speed in the implementation of 'an anti-capitalist programme of work that will effect the necessary basic changes'. But instead of the nationalisation of foreign banks, it suggested the setting up of an export–import bank in order 'to undermine their power'. In place of the nationalisation of foreign-owned plantations, it proposed compulsory registration in Ceylon of all sterling companies, the appointment of Government directors to the boards of any foreign or local company, 'liquidation of the control exercised by capitalist companies and capitalists in the plantations sector', acquisition by Government of uneconomically run estates and their distribution among those willing to cultivate, and even the acquisition of limited extents of the better plantations in areas where uneconomic estates are not available for distribution, and the prohibition of land ownership in Ceylon by non-citizens. It also urged a ceiling on incomes, nationalisation of the main industries, the main trade establishments and the Lake House press, the ending of rural indebtedness and the effective implementation of the Paddy Lands Act. It further advocated the reform and democratisation of the administrative system and the adoption and implementation of a charter of workers' rights. But the party stressed that these are only 'the starting points to take the Government forward'. However, at its Congress in November 1972, there were indications of increasing dissatisfaction in the party's rank and file with the progress towards 'socialism'. An attempt was made to challenge the present leadership but the crisis was eventually overcome.

The LSSP, being the stronger of the traditional Left parties, stands for a gradual transition, on the basis that 'instant socialism' is not possible. As Dr N. M. Perera remarked, the 'whole question had to be gauged in accordance with the feelings of the people' who he added 'wanted changes within the framework of the law'.[28] The Government was therefore, he said, obliged to work within that framework.

The CP, on the other hand, is not exactly at the centre of power as the LSSP and is, therefore, less prudent in its advocacy of swift change which the LSSP leadership feels could result in disaster. Its daily, *Aththa*, has constantly criticised the 'wrong policies of the Government'.

These statements and pronouncements of both Left parties make it obvious that if the situation proves untenable for them within the UF, they would revert to their Marxist positions. The dilemma that the Left faces in Ceylon is whether to compromise with its declared Marxist objectives in order to continue remaining as partners with the SLFP in the UF administration, or leave the latter when their position is no longer tenable. This could happen if the Right wing in the SLFP gains ascendancy. The general-secretary of the LSSP, Leslie Goonewardena, was well aware of such a possibility when he wrote 'while it is necessary in Ceylon to utilise one hundred per cent Parliament and a Government set up within Parliament for the journey towards Socialism, in the final analysis, the LSSP reposes its trust only in the masses'.[29]

He left the dilemma unresolved when he also wrote in the same contribution: 'On the question how far the journey towards Socialism can be made through Parliament and the parliamentary system, the LSSP has not made any final judgement. Even today it does not make any final judgement. The answer to this question does not lie in our hands but in the hands of our enemies.'

The Left obviously gambles on the fact that once the changes they have proposed get under way, a certain momentum would develop which would involve the masses and make them take the initiative in pushing the UF Government further towards the Left. A revolutionary situation could then arise, they hope, which would ensure the inauguration of the Marxist state.

There are, however, many variable factors to contend with in this simple theorising. As Leslie Goonewardena himself implied, there is the possibility of a total coalescence of the traditional and conservative elements in Ceylonese society which could mobilise themselves to resist a definite trend towards Marxism. More pertinent is the balance-of-payments crisis and the worsening domestic economic situation. This would necessitate severe cuts in the welfare services which could provoke mass resentment.

Further, the relations between the two Left parties in the UF are far from satisfactory. There is sharp rivalry between them in the trade union sector. Besides, there are differences of opinion between them on the attitude to be adopted towards the Soviet Union. For instance, in August 1968 (when in Opposition) the LSSP along with the SLFP in a strongly worded statement criticised the

Soviet Union's invasion of Czechoslovakia. The CP in a separate statement provided an apologia. In March 1971 the LSSP issued a press statement condemning the Prague trials. Recalling its earlier condemnation of the Soviet invasion, the LSSP remarked 'as anticipated then, the Soviet invasion of Czechoslovakia in August (1968) solved no political problems, it only aggravated them. Conqueror and conquered are unreconciled.'[30]

The growing differences between the CP, on the one hand, and the SLFP and LSSP, on the other, came to a head in April–May 1972 when three CP members of Parliament, including the President of the party, Dr S. A. Wickremasinghe, declined to cast their votes in favour of the controversial Criminal Justice Commissions Bill. The M.P.s in question were asked for their explanations, and as these were found unsatisfactory they were expelled from the Government Parliamentary Group. The LSSP supported the expulsions. They were re-admitted when the eighth Congress of the CP in August 1972 adopted a resolution backing the UF.

Differences of opinion as to the attitude that should be adopted to the UF Government have arisen between the Keuneman (Keuneman is general-secretary of the party and a minister in the UF Cabinet) and Wickremasinghe wings of the party. The Keuneman wing favours the CP remaining in the UF Government. The differences have still to be resolved. But in the meantime, the editorial staff of the CP's vitriolic daily *Aththa* was replaced with more amenable editors. For several months the earlier staff had been making ferocious attacks against members of the Government, particularly against the LSSP ministers, and these had obviously riled both the SLFP and the LSSP.

The revolutionary Marxist parties

With the PLF proscribed and the death of the MEP leader, Philip Gunawardena, in March 1973, the only revolutionary group which is active is the CP (Peking). The LSSP (R) confines itself to speech-making and press releases.

After the UNP defeat, Philip Gunawardena had much to explain. He claimed that his party 'had had faith in Dudley Senanayake alone as a leader of integrity' and that by his acceptance of a Cabinet post in the 'National Government' he had 'saved the corporations and industries from the capitalists'.[31]

The MEP leader stated that in the current situation his party would function as a separate group. He condemned the UNP as a party in the grip of 'capitalists and monopolists', while he characterised his erstwhile friends in the LSSP as 'the saviours of both the local and foreign capitalist classes'.[32] He added that the fact that the LSSP and CP leaders had joined hands with the SLFP did not mean that the latter 'had turned truly socialist overnight'. On the other hand, he insisted that the SLFP was still 'a *radala* (feudalist) capitalist party'. He declared his party's support for the aims and ideals of the PLF, emphasising that he and his party had never placed any reliance on the parliamentary system.[33]

In the pamphlet *The Present Political Situation* that he presented to his party in January 1971, Philip Gunawardena used the metaphor of the chicken and the egg to illustrate his condemnation of 'the system of electing governments by the ballot', viz. 'the chicken in the egg must use its beak and break the egg shell a bit before it can come out. Otherwise it would die inside the shell. In the same way, it is difficult to build a socialist base without a revolution.' During most of 1970 to 1972, the MEP remained inactive and, with Gunawardena's death in March 1973, it is doubtful whether the MEP will be able to function any longer as a viable political entity.

The CP (Peking) remains very much active on the political and trade union fronts. It has been critical of the PLF's tactics. Its leader, N. Sanmugathasan, in a letter to the *Ceylon Daily Mirror* on 1 May 1970, insisted that his party 'is guided by the philosophy of Marxism–Leninism–Mao Tse-tung Thought' and 'as such, ideologically we have no truck with the so-called Guevara line' which he condemned as 'nothing but petit-bourgeois romanticism'. In August 1970 the party issued a pamphlet on the PLF in which the latter's leader, Rohana Wijeweera, was attacked as one who had 'been trained by Soviet revisionists in Moscow's Lumumba University and sent here to sabotage the Marxist–Leninist movement from within'.[34] In several other statements, the party condemned the PLF for its reluctance to place its confidence in the masses. Yet, despite this open and unmistakable evidence of the party's disavowal of the PLF, Sanmugathasan was taken into preventive detention by the UF Government shortly after the outbreak of the PLF insurrection in April 1971 as 'a security risk' and released several months later, in March 1972.

The party has in its public pronouncements sharply denounced the foreign policies of the Soviet Union and the United States. Its central committee condemned in August 1970 the American peace plan for the Middle East as a 'sell out' by the Soviets, and stated that the peoples of the world 'just as they have learned to identify U.S. imperialism as enemy No. 1 ... must also learn to identify Soviet social-imperialism as the greatest betrayers of the working class and of the national liberation movements all over the world'.[35] In February 1971 Sanmugathasan on behalf of his party issued a press statement attacking 'the further escalation of the Indo-China war into Laos by U.S. imperialism', adding that they 'deplore the fact that the (UF) Government of Ceylon has not yet thought it fit to condemn this brazen act of aggression'.[36]

Sanmugathasan and his party have been consistent in their denunciations of the parliamentary system as a 'fraud' and a 'game of musical chairs' which they insist can never solve the fundamental problems of the people.

The UNP

After the UNP's rout, Senanayake's dejection resulted in the leadership of the Opposition devolving on J. R. Jayawardene. The ex-Prime Minister, however, returned to the fray after a while; he was still the President of the party. He had a special committee of twenty members of the party's working committee appointed to revamp policies with a view to giving it a new image. Nothing tangible came of its endeavours.

Soon, however, the differences between Senanayake and Jayawardene, which up to the time of the general election had been contained, came into the open. They quarrelled over the tactics the party should adopt in the fast-changing political situation.

Jayawardene took the position that the party had no future. He set out his reasons for this conclusion in a confidential mimeographed memorandum entitled *The UNP in Opposition, 1970* which he had circulated among members of the party's working committee in February 1971. The substance of his thesis was that the UNP is considered by the majority of voters 'to represent the "haves", the affluent and the employer', whereas its opponents, the SLFP and its Marxist allies, are accepted as the representatives of 'the "have-nots", the needy and the employed'. He bemoaned the fact that 'a peasant or worker put forward as a candidate by the party loses to a candidate put forward by its opponents who owns vast extents of land, wealth, or one who belongs to the *radala* clan; on the contrary, if the latter type is put forward by the party such a candidate loses.

In Jayawardene's view, a country such as Ceylon, going through the crisis of balance-of-payments deficits, economic stagnancy, etc., could not afford the luxury of an Opposition. He therefore advocated support for any measures to solve these difficulties even though they may not be popular. In addition, he also advocated cooperation with the Government in all the socialist measures it would take within the context of a democratic framework, while insisting that any measures which 'violate the democratic freedoms' should be opposed.

With much reason Jayawardene criticised the attitude his party had taken during its years in the Opposition from 1956 to 1965, an attitude which he himself was also instrumental in formulating, when he asked: 'Are we to criticise all Government proposals and also Government members, raising issues even of a personal nature, seeking to poison public opinion against the Government individually and collectively, as we did from 1956 to 1965, with the results that we have seen?' Jayawardene developed this theme further after the ultra-left PLF insurrection of March–April 1971. He urged that in a national crisis of such proportions the democratic forces in the country should close their ranks and join in the formation of a national Government.[37]

Actually many more motives than those proclaimed could be seen in Jayawardene's manoeuvres. It was a way of neutralising Dudley Senanayake if the exercise succeeded. It would effectively check the growing ascendancy of the Left in Mrs Bandaranaike's UF Government, if the UNP entered the Cabinet. It would also provide an opportunity for the Right-wing elements in the SLFP to coalesce against the growing Left.

The majority in the UNP was not in favour of Jayawardene's proposed line of action. The UNP's working committee met on 18 December 1971 and adopted a resolution moved by Senanayake himself by an overwhelming majority to oppose the UF Government 'unequivocally'.[38] Senanayake indicated that his resolution did not mean that the party should oppose every measure of the Government. But its text indicated a sharp condemnation of the Government's measures to reduce the welfare services, which Jayawardene urged, in his confidential memorandum, should be supported.

Senanayake drew a distinction between the 'democratic socialism' of the UNP with its concepts of a mixed economy, controlled private enterprise, and decentralisation of power, and the UF's objective of a 'socialist democracy' which he insisted was a step in the direction of a totalitarian system. Also, in his view, for the parliamentary system to continue to function, it was necessary for a democratic Opposition to be active in keeping the Government on its toes.[39]

Jayawardene's reaction to the UNP working committee's rejection of his proposal for cooperation with the UF Government in implementing its socialist measures was that possibly 'some of them do not wish their privileged position to be changed and are opposed to the new society which the Government seeks to usher'.[40] He added that 'members of the UNP parliamentary group do not share that view'.

Jayawardene's public pronouncements caused disquiet in his party and, during early 1972, a strong section in the UNP initiated steps to have him ousted. A disciplinary committee investigated his conduct but, before any further action could be taken, Jayawardene succeeded in obtaining an order from the Supreme Court restraining his party from proceeding against him.

Shortly thereafter other responsible elements in the party not directly involved in these factional squabbles succeeded in effecting a reconciliation between the two leaders. When the Opposition met for the first time before the first meeting of the National State Assembly under the new constitution, Senanayake provided evidence of the closing in of their ranks when he proposed Jayawardene's name for the Leadership of the Opposition – and this was unanimously accepted by the UNP parliamentary group.

In late 1972, the UNP revised its constitution with a view to reactivating its branch organisations in the various electorates. There was opposition to the revision from a minority section in the party led by Senanayake's close associate, R. Premadasa. Senanayake declined to countenance Premadasa's attempts to baulk the move to revise the party constitution and a rift began to develop between Premadasa's supporters and the party high command. A number of organisations called 'citizens' fronts' began to emerge in various parts of the country, particularly in Premadasa's own electorate in Colombo Central. Premadasa and his supporters addressed meetings under the auspices of these fronts at which they made appeals for a reformed and socialistic UNP. These indeed proved embarrassing to the party leadership.

In April 1973 the party suffered a serious blow when Dudley Senanayake succumbed to a heart ailment. Senanayake died at a time when the electors had begun seriously to turn to him. His charisma had revived and he was gaining increasing popularity as well as success upon success in his campaigns against the UF throughout the country. His death has deprived the UNP of a charismatic leader with a mass appeal. His funeral, attended by nearly two million persons, provided surprising evidence of the immense affection he commanded in the hearts of even people who had rejected his party in 1970.

Shortly after, the UNP met and elected Jayawardene as its new President. At the age of 67, it is open to question whether the new President will be able to get across to the youth in the country. But there is enough evidence that Jayawardene has a tremendous bank of electoral goodwill bequeathed by his late predecessor which, if he wisely exploits it, can bring his party back to the seats of power.

The Tamil parties

As stated earlier, the major Tamil political groupings, except for those with Left-wing affiliations, have united in a TUF under the leadership of S. J. V. Chel-vanayakam. They have reached a stage in their campaign when they have accepted a common national flag, that of the rising sun, and have declared their intention of agitating for a separate Tamil state. The situation is full of dangers, especially in view of the fact that there are Tamil communities in the Sinhalese areas which will be exposed to communal violence should the TUF decide to launch a campaign to achieve its objective.

On the other hand, the TC parliamentary group, comprising two Members of Parliament have entered the Government Parliamentary Group. They have, however, been repudiated by their own party. The SLFP for its part has opened a number of branches in the Jaffna Peninsula but these do not appear to have made much headway.

Conclusion

It is less than fortunate that in near-stagnant societies with contracting resources, ethnic and religious cleavages, primitive birth rates and modern death rates, in sum, exploding populations, the mechanisms of democracy and its dynamics, such as political parties and political leadership, and the massive public education they provide at general elections, and at intervals between elections, engender instability rather than political order and political stabilisation. General elections in India, Ceylon and Malaysia produce Governments with clear majorities but the experience has been that instability increases with every succeeding election because of the inability of the Governments returned to respond adequately to popular demand.

The political awareness that results from the campaigns of political parties produces rising expectations. Economic factors – population, slow growth, balance-of-payments crises – cannot keep pace with rising demands for social amelioration, employment opportunities, etc. The failure of parties elected to office to satisfy such expectations, which they themselves have stimulated in the heat of political rivalries, results in one of two situations – displacement or violence, sometimes both, but more dangerously a growing realisation that the system itself will not be able to deliver the goods. In such an event, the man on horseback or a political party pledged to end the system becomes the saviour. Pakistan under Field Marshal Ayub Khan's basic democracies, General Ne Win's Burmese isolationist socialism, Soekarno's guided democracy and his successor's (General Suharto) military–civil administration in Indonesia, are examples of some of the new states of south and southeast Asia resorting to the latter remedy.

Ceylon, and to a limited extent India, have preferred to displace their ruling dominant parties, which at first provided their societies for a reasonable period of time with stable government, with other parties just as enduring. Malaysia continues to remain at the one-party-dominance level that Ceylon and India were in for some time after independence.

The post-independence Congress, basking in the shade of Nehru's tremendous charisma till his death in 1965 and acting as a 'dynamic core' under which 'several parties of pressure operate upon a single party of consensus', provided a measure of democratic stability.[41] On the other hand, Ceylon's UNP from 1947 to 1956 and Malaysia's Alliance Party since 1957 provide examples of dominant parties failing to effect the consensus that could accommodate dissent and often opposing demands. Consequently, the UNP collapsed in 1956 and the Alliance has begun to show signs of disintegration with the general election of 1969. The Indian Congress's progress after Nehru was similar to that of Malaysia's Alliance. It received a rude setback at the general election of 1967. However, with Indira Gandhi now playing a role similar to the Bandaranaikes in Ceylon, Congress has acquired a new lease.

Displacement occurs in two ways. A breakaway group from the dominant party provides a focus for a constellation of radical elements in the body politic. With a skilful leader and the proper mixture of nationalism, social conscience and an attractive economic programme, it achieves power. The MEP in 1956, the SLFP in July 1960 and the UF in 1970 achieved this feat. In the process, the displaced party reforms itself in various ways, stealing some of the policies of the victor. The UNP did this, though to a very limited extent, and was restored to power in 1965.

The other alternative is when the dominant party expels the backwoodsmen and dead wood from its ranks and emerges with a refurbished image. Mrs Indira Gandhi accomplished this task with her Congress-R and emerged triumphant at the general election of 1971. The Malaysian Alliance will have to follow a similar path or abandon the country to military–civil rule as in Indonesia. The alternative could also be an unstable coalition of unruly and disparate political elements knitted together, perhaps under the leadership of the obscurantist Pan-Malayan Islamic Party, for the sole purpose of ousting the Alliance.

Violence in these societies has become part of their political way of life, but fortunately contained so as to inhibit Congolese- or Biafran-type situations. Their institutional framework provides the necessary instruments of control such as the emergency powers vested in the federal centre under the Indian and Malaysian constitutions or the Public Security Act which is now part of Ceylon's Republican constitution. Thus widespread communal disturbances in Ceylon (1958) and Malaya (1969), and language and Hindu–Muslim rioting in India were not permitted to brim over. And at the political level, the PLF insurrection in Ceylon, communist guerrillas in Malaya and the Naxalites in India were controlled.

Further, the English-educated political elites in these three countries are a stabilising factor. Despite their political differences and religious and ethnic rivalries, their common Western outlook and medium of communication serve to help bridge the gap and reconcile opposing viewpoints. The question is whether political synthesis and national integration can be effected before leadership devolves to those educated in the national languages of these countries. And there is already evidence of a widening gap – between Hindi- and non-Hindi-speakers, Sinhalese and Tamils, Malays and Chinese. The saving feature in this babel of tongues is that political leaders educated in their national languages have had transmitted to them the ideas and values of a modern democratic society from teachers, translated books and politicians. It is also possible that English may continue as a common medium or that, alternatively, interpreters will help in the task of bridging the communication gap.

The question arises whether democracy will continue to survive in the three countries that have nurtured it for so long. An answer is to be found in the various measures that India and Ceylon are taking to limit their population consistent with planned efforts to promote economic growth of some kind. Malaysia does not have this problem. She maintains an optimum population. And the new units of Sarawak and Sabah provide opportunities for sustaining a moderately growing Malaysian economy.

But more significant is the fact of big-power interest in the future of these three countries. This is evidenced by the fairly large amounts of foreign aid that are being provided to sustain their Governments, if not the democratic systems that underpin these Governments. In this way both Western and Communist states, ironical though it is in the case of the latter, have evinced a desire to keep these Asian systems viable. Soviet and U.S. aid to India, the Aid Ceylon Consortium of Western states, coupled with munificent Chinese financial and project aid to the Bandaranaike Governments, and U.S. and British investments in Malaysia, may in the long run help to maintain these emergent states until they are able to become viable entities in themselves.

Appendix 1. Selected newspaper items during the election campaign

Date (1970)	Title of editorial	Brief description of subject matter
3 March	'A New Calculus of Development'	Qualified Praise for the Government's Mahaveli Project
25 March	'A Pledge Fulfilled'	Praise for Senanayake's 5-year record
29 March	'Record of Peace and Harmony'	Eulogy of Senanayake's success in forging national unity
23 April	'From Production to Profit'	Praise for Government's industrial policies
24 April	'A Democratic and Peaceful Election'	Need for law and order stressed, with a swipe at Marxist dictatorship
26 April	'A Clear Prelude to Dictatorship'	Condemnation of Marxist tactics and Marxist dictatorship
27 April	'People's Committees'	Dangers of dictatorship through people's committees and of Marxist infiltration stressed
29 April	'For Youth: Promise of a Better Future'	Praise for Government's national youth service scheme
30 April	'Imprisoning the People's Mind'	Attack on UF's alleged plan to seize the press
1 May	'Threat of Tyranny in Disguise'	Dangers of Marxists using workers to ride to power
2 May	'The Choice Before the Young'	Liberal democracy, or forcible call-up of youth to form bootlicking platoons
4 May	'Timely Warning'	Danger of Marxists using people's committees for their own ends
9 May	'Racist Slogans'	Attack on anti-Tamil slogans of the UF, in particular of the Marxists
10 May	'Red Absolutism'	Parliament threatened through people's committees by Marxists
11 May	'Strange Shibboleths'	Attack on Felix Dias Bandaranaike's anti-Tamil pronouncements
14 May	'Scare-Mongering'	Attack on UF's charge that there was a danger of chaos being created to upset elections
15 May	'Rule by Committee'	People's committees are the instruments of Marxists
18 May	'On the Right Road'	Praise for the Government's economic policies
19 May	'Creed of Non-Violence'	Indirect attack on Marxist belief in violence
22 May	'The Best Test of a People's Freedom'	Danger of the right to use the vote to oust a Government being lost under a UF Government stressed
23 May	'Lie to Liberalism'	Attack on UF policies of socialism

Date	Title of editorial	Brief description of subject matter
24 May	'Make no Mistake'	Dangers to democracy and Buddhism under Marxism
25 May	'Political Tyranny'	Praise for Government's record of economic success, and dangers of UF totalitarianism stressed
26 May	'A Clear Choice'	Choose the UNP as against the UF
27 May	'Their Canard Nailed'	Condemnation of UF, the newspapers of the Independent Newspapers of Ceylon Limited and the *Sirilaka* (SLFP) for publication of an allegedly false report to the effect that the Head of the main Buddhist sect in Ceylon had expressed his support for the UF, on 26 May

II. *Ceylon Daily News*

Date	Title of article	Brief description of subject matter
2 March	'Protecting Democratic Rights', point of view *by an SLFP voter*	Innocuous – an argument for strengthening the party system
21 March	'Farsighted, Shrewd Statesman'	An appreciation of D. S. Senanayake on the anniversary of his death
23 March	'Acid Test for Realism', point of view *by Susil Moonesinghe*	Attack on UNP regime by an SLFP stalwart
24 March	'Window on India: Marxists Show their Fangs', *by our New Delhi correspondent*	Obvious conclusions to be drawn by those who ally with Marxist parties
25 March	'Good Communists don't Eat Babies', *by Tori de Souza*	Attack on Ceylonese Marxists
25 March	'Ilangaratne Sums up Opposition Role', *by Joe Segera*	Praise for the constitutional methods and democratic behaviour of the Opposition by T.B. Ilangaratne, an SLFP leader
25 March	'Opposition in Parliament', *by Joe Segera*	Favourable comments on the Opposition by a Lake House journalist
26 March	'Dudley's Image Riles the Left', *by Ringsider*	Attack on Ceylonese Marxists
4 April	'Left and Right or Vice Versa', point of view *by M. S. Themis*	Attack on Ceylonese Marxists by a UNP candidate for Parliament
10 April	'When Right becomes Left', point of view *by M. S. Themis*	Repeat of what was stated by the same writer on 4 April – perhaps for greater emphasis
17 April	'A Point of View', *by E. Samarasekera (in the form of a long letter to the Editor)*	A defence of Bandaranaike policies and a searing attack on the UNP and its leader

Date	Title of article	Brief description of subject matter
17 April	(i) 'Mrs Bandaranaike is 54 today. – Ten Active Years', *by Maithripala Senanayake* (ii) 'A Fascinating Enigma' *by a staff writer*	Both are encomiums but the second is interspersed with attacks on the Marxists
20 April	'When Right is Wrong', point of view *by Dhanapala Weerasekera*	A reply to M. S. Themis by an LSSP parliamentary candidate
20 April	'The Choice before the People' *by Pericles*	Mrs Bandaranaike has joined Leftists. The choice is between Marxists and democrats
20 April	'A Controlled and Conducted Press', *by V. Kabra (Director, I.C.F.T.U. Asian Trade Union College)*	A description of communist methods of press control
23 April	'Blowing up Parliament'	Quotations on parliamentarianism collected from the Theses and Statutes of the Third Communist International
25 April	'Breaking the Constitution from Within', *by Achariya J. B. Kripalani*	Exposure of communist tactics in India – lessons obvious for Ceylon
26 April	'Left Unity', *by Pradip Bose*	Exposure of communist tactics in India
27 April	'Communism through Democracy', *by Pericles*	Criticism of Mrs Bandaranaike's alliance with the CP and LSSP
27 April	'Leftists plan their Future', *by Ringsider*	Plans of Left parties regarding manning the public services in the event of a UF victory
27 April	'Lenin the Revolutionary', point of view *by N. Sanmugathasan*	Mao Tse-tung is the Lenin of today, by the Peking-wing CP leader
30 April	'Eradicating Religion', *by V. Keybis (Ukraine 'Pravda')*	Methods employed in U.S.S.R. to fight religion
1 May	'How the Worker has Benefited', *by M. H. Mohamed, Minister of Labour*	List of benefits conferred on worker by the UNP Government
1 May	'After Forty Years of this Farce', *by Tori de Souza*	Attack on Ceylonese Marxists
2 May	'Buddhism: A Communist View'	Criticism of Buddhism's efforts to pacify the suppressed – quotations from the Russian publication *Buddhism* by A. N. Kochetov
3 May	'And Now Rice'	Sections of Felix Dias Bandaranaike's budget speech of July 1962 proposing a cut in the rice subsidy

Date	Title of article	Brief description of subject matter
3 May	'Who are the People' [Note: The *Silumina* of 21 April commenced a similar series entitled: 'The People's Committees of the Marxists: What a Trap?']	People's committees are a communist device
4 May	'Decline of Bandaranaike Socialism', *by Pericles*	The Marxists have infiltrated the SLFP after the death of S.W.R.D. Bandaranaike
4 May	'The Face behind the Mask', *by Clare*	Attack on Ceylonese Marxists
6 May	'No Truck with the Marxists' (the title misleads – there was a reference to Marxists who were opposing him at the time, but there were references to many other matters as well.)	Speech of S.W.R.D. Bandaranaike to the Kurunegala Sessions of the SLFP in 1959 – his last policy statement a few months before his assassination
6 May	'How We Suffered', point of view *by Paul*	A description of the hardships that Roman Catholics underwent under the two Bandaranaike regimes
9 May	'Who are the Naxalites? Sinister and Strong'	Lessons for Ceylon are obvious
10 May	'Socialism and Revolution', point of view *by P. Vimalachanthiran*	General criticism of Marxist practices – an academic exposition – but the title is misleading
10 May	'Beyond Masaryk's Murder', *by a Special Correspondent*	A discussion of the evidence on Masaryk's suicide
11 May	'People's Committees – To Hell with M.P.s', point of view *by Vigilante*	Attack on people's committees. Note: the *Dinamina* of 14 May began a series on People's Committees. The first of these was called: 'To gain personal power do not insult the memory of the late S.W.R.D. Bandaranaike'. It was an analysis and criticism of Mrs Bandaranaike's statement on people's committees
12 May	'The Great Betrayal'	Mrs Bandaranaike's alliance with the Marxists
14 May	'Why I Quit', *an interview with D. S. Goonesekera*	A former SLFP minister in S.W.R.D. Bandaranaike's Cabinet criticises present trends in the SLFP
15 May	'The Coalition's New Language Policy – Will Tamils be Deceived?', point of view *by Yalpadi*	Exposure of anti-Tamil campaign of the UF
15 May	'Trade Fiasco', *by Dan*	A criticism of UF's plan to nationalise import trade and trade in essential commodities

Date	Title of article	Brief description of subject matter
18 May	(i) 'Muslims, the UNP and the Coalition', *an appeal by Dr M. C. M. Kaleel*	Why Muslims should not vote for the UF
	(ii) 'Islam can have no Truck with Marxism'	An account of the persecution of Muslims in the Soviet Union and China
19 May	'Road to People's Democracy', *by Pericles*	Marxists are infiltrating the SLFP
22 May	'Our Religion Derided', *by the Venerable Meetiyagoda Gunaratne (general-secretary, Maha Sangha Peramuna)*	Excerpts from *The Great Soviet Encyclopaedia* on Buddhism by a prominent UNP Buddhist monk
22 May	'Villagers are Not so Innocent', point of view *by Rhoda Miller de Silva*	The first half of this article speaks up for the staff and students of the universities in their campaign against the Minister of Education
23 May*	'Lest we Forget', point of view *by Anthony*	Will the Tamils be taken for a ride by the UF?
23 May	'Who's Fooling Whom?', *by the Hammer*	Attack on Ceylon's Marxist leaders. Under the UNP however there will be freedom to criticise their (the UNP) leadership
24 May	'Getting the Record Straight', *by Siyadoris*	An account of the queues and scarcities under Mrs Bandaranaike's Government of 1960–4
24 May	'Rice, Economics and Politics–A Realistic Look at the Options', *by Patriot*	Need for utilising expenditure for investment to provide employment for the younger generation instead of spending it on subsidies
25 May	'Communist Terror in Calcutta', *by Pran Chopra*	The lessons for Ceylon are obvious
26 May	'If the Marxists Come to Power', *by J. R. Jayawardene*	It will be the end of democracy. 'Let the people not be misled.'

III. *The Ceylon Observer (CO) and The Ceylon Observer Magazine Edition (COME)*

Date	Title of article	Brief description of subject matter
6 April (*COME*)	'Man who won the Crown–Four Times', *by H. L. D. Mahindapala.*	A panegyric on the Senanayakes, particularly on Dudley Senanayake. (This was continued as a series in the succeeding editions of the *COME*.)
28 April (*COME*)	'Pennies for the Poor Guys' *by Denzil Peiris* (Editor)	Attack on the UF's Rupee Fund and details of the wealthy men in the UF.

Date	Title of article	Brief description of subject matter
28 April *(COME)*	'Comment–How Do You Give It'. (Note: the *Dinamina* of 1 May carried a similar feature with the heading 'The Country will be Ruined again if Two Measures of Rice are Given'.)	A detailed statistical analysis of the adverse implications for the Ceylon economy that would result from the UF's pledge to restore the cut in the rice subsidy
2 May *(CO)*	'The Coalition Manifesto –And the Threat to Democracy in Ceylon', *by Stanley Mendis (a former member of the LSSP)*	A critique of some of the items in the Common Programme of the UF
5 May *(COME)*	'Parliament as the Marxists See it–Murder, Gruesome Murder–West Bengal in the Terror', *by Denzil Peiris* (Note: the *Silumina* of 28 April carried the same article but with the following headlines and subheadings to make the whole description revolting to the mind: 'Destruction of a nation because of Marxists: Buses burned with people inside: Cold blooded murder with the throwing of acid: The food and land of people seized and houses destroyed: Unless you bribe, your life and property are in danger.')	An account of the violence and chaos caused by Indian Marxists
5 May *(COME)*	'Slogans that Hide the Facts–Where are the Have-Nots', *by Denzil Peiris*	The Marxisis are wealthy, the SLFP has feudalists and wealth in its ranks; the UNP's membership on the other hand has been dramatically modified–with many poor men in its ranks
6 May *(CO)*	'The Government and the Worker'	Government servants, workers in the private sector and even non-wage earners in rural areas have benefited from UNP's rule, 1965–70
7 May *(CO)*	'Science Reaches the Rural Child'	Improvement in scientific education during UNP's rule, 1965–70

Date	Title of article	Brief description of subject matter
8 May (*CO*)	'Our Junior Universities. A New Feature of Ceylon's Educational Set-up'	Good record of the Ministry of Education during 1965–70
17 May (*CO*)	'Who Has the Haves?', *by Susil Moonesinghe* (*SLFP stalwart*)	Enumeration of the wealthy men among the UNP parliamentary candidates
17 May (*CO*)	'A Hypocritical Claim', *a reply to the above by Denzil Peiris*	Provides a list of the wealthy men among the UF's parliamentary candidates
20 May (*COME*)	'Forward to Socialism with the Feudalists–The Radala Revolution', *by Buddhika Kurukularatne*	'Exposure' of the feudal inter-relationships among the parliamentary candidates of the SLFP
20 May (*COME*)	'How United is the Front?' *by H. L. D. Mahindapala*	The UF has many internal differences
20 May (*COME*)	'The Policies of Mr Bandaranaike', *by M. P. de Zoysa (former SLFP stalwart)*	They are no longer the same under Mrs Bandaranaike
20 May (*COME*)	'The Lament of a Left Leader–The Seeds of Chaos', *by Denzil Peiris*	Attack on CP candidate, Pieter Keuneman and criticism of UF policies
22 May (*COME*)	'Real Wages have Risen Sharply', *by S. Rabind-ranath*	Economic progress under UNP rule, 1965–70, has been phenomenal and workers have benefited
25 May (*CO*)	'Listening to the Voice of the Worker'	Dudley Senanayake as Prime Minister consulted with trade unions and was sympathetic to their problems

Appendix 2. Note on rural and urban constituencies

Our division of the 145 electoral districts of the island into (1) Rural and (2) Urban and Quasi-urban is not perfect, but it is the best that we could do under the circumstances to enable us to examine the performances of the various political parties in these respective sectors.

Our division was based on the broad theoretical propositions and other material contained in Ashish Bose's chapter, 'The Urbanisation Process in South and Southeast Asia', and Gerald M. Desmond's chapter, 'The Impact of National and Regional Development Policies on Urbanization', in *Urbanisation and National Development*, Vol. 1, South and Southeast Asia Urban Affairs Annuals (California: Sage Publications Inc., 1971). We also obtained useful information for this purpose from the United Nations, *Growth of World's Population, 1900–2000*, and the United Nations Demographic Year Books of recent years.

Based on the material contained in these references, we used the criterion of agglomerated population clusters of 20,000 and over in large town council and urban council areas and municipalities in electoral districts to decide whether to characterise the districts as (1) Rural or (2) Urban or Quasi-urban. We were aided in this by the valuable data available in the *Report of the Delimitation Commission, Sessional Paper XV–1959* relating to the boundaries hemming electoral districts, and the village committees, town councils, urban councils and municipalities within each such electoral district. The population figures available at the time in the Ceylon Census (1963) returns also helped us to arrive at our findings. On this basis, we placed 117 electoral seats in the category of 'Rural' and 34 in the category of 'Urban' or 'Quasi-urban', inclusive of multi-member seats.

The only exception to our classification is Pottuvil constituency. The Sammanturai Town Council area has a population cluster of over 26,000. On the basis of our categorisation, Pottuvil constituency should be quasi-urban, especially as this cluster is more than half the population of the constituency. But this constituency has also a large forest belt and vast acreages of paddy. Both these factors tend to dilute the quasi-urban character of the Sammanturai area. For these reasons, we determined that Pottuvil constituency should be placed in the 'Rural' category.

We also took into consideration the fact that, during the last ten years or so, there has been a considerable overflow of urban workers of both the white-collar and blue-collar categories from Colombo City and the Greater Colombo area to the rural suburbs – to constituencies such as Kelaniya, Mahara, Gampaha, Jaela, Kesbewa, and Homagama. We also noted that a constituency such as Kottawa and Kelaniya had a number of industrial ventures. But on balance, after examining the social and economic geography of these constituencies, we decided that they were more rural than urban or quasi-urban. The following table is therefore our final classification of constituencies as 'Urban' or 'Quasi-urban'. All others are 'Rural'.

Table 2.1 *Urban and Quasi-urban constituencies*

Urban		Quasi-urban
	Western province	
Colombo North		Wattala
Colombo South (2 Seats)		Kolonnawa
Colombo Central (3 Seats)		Panadura
Borella		Kalutara
Negombo		Beruwala
Kotte		
Dehiwala – Mt Lavinia		
Moratuwa		
	Southern province	
Galle		Balapitiya
		Matara
	Sabaragamuwa province	
		Ratnapura
	Central province	
Kandy		Matale
Senkadagala		Nuwara Eliya
	Uva province	
		Badulla
	North Central province	
		Anuradhapura
	North Western province	
		Puttalam
		Chilaw
		Kurunegala
	Eastern province	
		Trincomalee
		Batticaloa (2 Seats)
	Northern province	
Jaffna		Nallur

Appendix 3. Constituencies in which the proportion of Christian voters exceeds 7 per cent of the total electoral strength.
Based on figures from the *Report of the Delimitation Commission, Sessional Paper XV–1959* (Colombo: Government Press, September 1959) and the latest Ceylon census returns (1972).

In the Sinhalese areas

Constituency	Christians	Buddhists	Others
Avissawella	9.0	82.5	8.5
Beruwala	13.5	64.2	22.3
Bingiriya	13.5	81.7	4.8
Borella	19.7	60.1	20.2
Chilaw	35.3	47.6	17.1
Colombo Central (3 members)	14.2	32.0	53.8
Colombo North (Roman Catholic)	46.9	28.2	24.9
Colombo South (2 members)	23.4	48.5	28.1
Divulapitiya	15.5	83.3	1.2
Gampaha	14.3	84.7	1.0
Jaela (Roman Catholic)	62.3	34.3	3.4
Kalutara	9.3	82.6	8.1
Kandy	12.3	57.3	31.4
Katana (Roman Catholic)	49.5	48.2	2.3
Katugampola	7.4	88.3	4.3
Kelaniya	14.6	78.1	7.3
Kolonnawa	8.3	82.6	9.1
Kotte	12.6	80.7	6.7
Kurunegala	7.6	80.1	12.3
Mahara	11.8	83.6	4.6
Maskeliya	7.0	18.0	75.0 (mostly disfranchised Indian Tamils)
Minuwangoda	7.6	89.9	2.5
Moratuwa	37.0	59.0	4.0
Nattandiya (Roman Catholic)	47.4	45.5	7.1
Negombo (Roman Catholic)	74.3	11.8	13.9
Nuwara Eliya	8.0	14.0	78.0 (mostly disfranchised Indian Tamils)
Panadura	7.1	82.4	10.5
Puttalam	38.7	8.9	52.4 (41.0 are Ceylon Moors)
Senkadagala	12.3	64.6	23.1
Wattala (Roman Catholic)	49.1	41.2	9.7

Constituency	Christians	Buddhists	Others
Wennappuwa (Roman Catholic)	64.0	33.1	2.9

In the Tamil-speaking Northern and Eastern provinces

Constituency	Christians	Hindus	Others
Batticaloa (2 members)	12.3	47.4	40.3 (mostly Muslims)
Jaffna	40.4	44.0	16.0
Kankesanturai	15.7	83.2	1.1
Kayts	20.3	78.8	0.9
Kilinochchi	13.0	80.3	6.7
Mannar (Roman Catholic)	40.0	26.0	34.0 (mostly Muslims)
Point Pedro	9.4	90.0	0.6
Trincomalee	17.4	46.5	36.1
Uduvil	9.8	89.4	0.8
Vavuniya	13.0	62.0	25.0 (mostly Buddhists and Muslims)

Note: It was not possible to obtain an exact breakdown of Muslims as between Ceylon Muslims, and Indian Muslims who may or may not be disfranchised. We have therefore placed them in the category of 'Others'.

Notes

Notes to chapter 1

1. For some good literature in regard to party development in relation to elections, among other things, in the three countries, see C. A. Woodward, *The Growth of a Party System in Ceylon* (Providence: Brown University Press, 1969); Myron Weiner, *Party Politics in India: The Development of a Multi-Party System* (Princeton: Princeton University Press, 1957) and *Party Building in a New Nation: The Indian National Congress* (Chicago: University of Chicago Press, 1967); F. G. Bailey, *Politics and Social Change: Orissa in 1959* (Berkeley: University of California Press, 1963); Paul R. Brass, *Factional Politics in an Indian State: The Congress Party in Uttar Pradesh* (Berkeley and Los Angeles: University of California Press, 1965); Angela S. Burger, *Opposition in a Dominant-Party System: A Study of the Jan Sangh, the Praja Socialist Party and the Socialist Party in Uttar Pradesh, India* (Berkeley and Los Angeles: University of California Press, 1969); K. J. Ratnam, *Communalism and the Political Process in Malaya* (Kuala Lumpur: University of Malaya Press, 1965); K. J. Ratnam and R. S. Milne, *The Malayan Parliamentary Election of 1964* (Singapore: University of Malaya Press, 1967); and Gordon P. Means, *Malaysian Politics* (London: University of London, 1970), especially chapters 10 and 11. For analyses of recent general elections in these three states, see A. Jeyaratnam Wilson, 'Ceylon: A New Government Takes Office', *Asian Survey*, Vol. xi, No. 2 (February 1971), pp. 177–84; W. H. Morris-Jones, 'India Elects for Change and Stability', *Asian Survey*, Vol. xi, No. 8 (August 1971), pp. 719–41; Lloyd I. Rudolph, 'Continuities and Change in Electoral Behaviour: The 1971 Parliamentary Election in India', *Asian Survey*, Vol. xi, No. 12 (December 1971), pp. 1119–32; and K. J. Ratnam and R. S. Milne, 'The 1969 Parliamentary Election in West Malaysia', *Pacific Affairs*, Vol. 43, No. 2 (Summer 1970).
2. Maurice Duverger argues that a correlation can be seen between the single-member constituency with its first-past-the-post result and the two-party system. See his *Political Parties–their Organisation and Activity in the Modern State*, trans. Barbara and Robert North (London: Methuen, 1954), p. 239.
3. Note the Thirteenth Schedule, Section 2(c), Part 1 in the Malayan constitution states *inter alia* that 'having regard to the greater difficulty of reaching electors in the country districts and the other disadvantages facing rural constituencies, a measure of weightage for area ought to be given to such constituencies, to the extent that in some cases a rural constituency may contain as little as one half of the electors of any urban constituency.' For further details, see *Malayan Constitutional Documents* (2nd ed.; Kuala Lumpur, 1962), Vol. 1, pp. 170–2. Provisions of a related nature are to be found in the Ceylon constitution. Refer to chapter 3 within.
4. See R. S. Milne, *Government and Politics in Malaysia* (Boston: Houghton-Mifflin, 1967), ch. 6, and Means, pp. 225–32.
5. For the official document explaining the circumstances of the riots and the reasons for the suspension of the parliamentary processes, see The National Operations Council, *The May 13 Tragedy: A Report* (Kuala Lumpur, 1969).
6. Miss J. L. Goldman has been making a comparative study of elections in Malaya and other new states at the Institute of Commonwealth Studies, University of London.

Notes to chapter 2

1. The latest census figures (1971) indicated there were 5,445,706 Low Country Sinhalese (42.8 per cent of the population); 3,700,973 Kandyan Sinhalese (29.1 per cent); 1,415,567 Ceylon Tamils (11.1 per cent); 1,195,368 Indian Tamils (9.4 per cent); 824,291 Ceylon Moors (6.4 per cent); 29,416 Indian Moors (0.2 per cent); 44,250 Burghers (0.3 per cent); 41,615 Malays (0.3 per cent) and 13,957 Britishers and other foreigners (0.1 per cent).

    The figures on religions show that there were 8,567,570 Sinhalese Buddhists (67.4 per cent); 2,239,310 Ceylon and Indian Tamil Hindus (17.6 per cent); 909,941 Muslims comprising Ceylon Moors, Indian Moors and Malays (7.1 per cent); 883,111 Roman Catholics from among Sinhalese, Tamils, Burghers and foreigners (6.9 per cent) and 103, 576 Christians from other denominations from among the same ethnic groups as the Roman Catholics (0.8 per cent).

    Figures for caste are not available.
2. James D'Alwis, *The Sidat Sangarawa–A Grammar of the Sinhalese Language* (Colombo: Government Press, 1852), pp. 133–4.
3. See Robert N. Kearney, *Communalism and Language in the Politics of Ceylon* (Durham, North Carolina: Duke University Press, 1967), especially ch. 2, 'Sinhalese National Resurgence', pp. 41–51.
4. See Ananda Guruge, ed., *Anagarika Dharmapala: Return to Righteousness* (Colombo: Government Press, 1965).
5. His best-known work was *Medieval Sinhalese Art* (Broad Campden: Essex House Press, 1908), a second edition of which was published in 1956 by Pantheon Books, New York.
6. See Ananda Guruge, p. LXVII.
7. *Ibid.* pp. LXXIX–LXXX.
8. *Ibid.* p. LXVIII, quoted by Guruge from a police report of a meeting addressed by the Anagarika on 16 June 1922. See also p. LXVII.
9. Published by Dharmavijaya Press, Balangoda, Ceylon, 1956.
10. Their number was estimated at 60,000.
11. See Central Bank of Ceylon, *Survey of Ceylon's Consumer Finances 1963* (Colombo, 1964), tab. II, p. 22.
12. For further information, see V. K. Jayawardene, *The Rise of the Labour Movement in Ceylon* (Durham, North Carolina: Duke University Press, 1972). Also R. N. Kearney, *Trade Unions and Politics in Ceylon* (Berkeley: University of California Press, 1971); G. J. Lerski, *Origins of Trotskyism in Ceylon* (Stanford, Hoover Institution of War, Revolution and Peace: Stanford University Press, 1968).
13. *Survey of Ceylon's Consumer Finances 1963*, p. 97.
14. Government of Ceylon, Department of Census and Statistics, *Ceylon Census of Agriculture 1962*, Vol. 1 (Colombo: Government Press, 1965), p. 29.
15. See M. U. A. Tennakoon, 'A Note on some Social and Economic Problems of Subsistence Farming in Rural Settlements of the Dry Zone of Ceylon', *Staff Studies*, Central Bank of Ceylon, Vol. 2, No. 1 (April 1972), pp. 1–55 and p. 6.
16. See *Report of the Land Utilization Committee* (Colombo: Government Press, 1968).
17. *Ibid.*
18. Central Bank of Ceylon, *Socio-Economic Survey of 1969/70*, First Round (Colombo, 1970).
19. See the Report of an Inter-Agency Team organised by the International Labour Office, *Matching Employment Opportunities and Expectations* (Geneva: I.L.O., 1971), pp. 25–6.
20. From *Report of the Official Committee on Mobilisation of Surplus Manpower for*

Development, a confidential document addressed to the Prime Minister, n.d.–probable date mid-1968, Ministry of Planning and Economic Affairs. See also The Institute of Development Studies Conference, *Process of Development Planning in Ceylon 12–14 September, 1969* and R. K. Srivastava, S. Selvaratnam and A.T.P.L. Abeykoon, *Ceylon: Labour Force Projections 1968–1978* (Colombo: Ministry of Planning and Economic Affairs, October 1968).

21. *Socio-Economic Survey of 1969/70,* First and Second Rounds.
22. *Parliamentary Debates* (House of Representatives), Vol. 5, cols. 3065–66.
23. Such fears have been particularly aggravated by the writings of Indian scholars such as K. M. Panikkar. See his *The Strategic Problems of the Indian Ocean* (New Delhi: Indian Institute of International Affairs, 1944).
24. *Parliamentary Debates* (House of Representatives), Vol. 3, cols. 784–5.
25. *Ceylon Daily News,* 12 June 1950.
26. For further information, see A. Jeyaratnam Wilson's article 'The Tamil Federal Party in Ceylon Politics', *Journal of Commonwealth Political Studies,* Vol. 4, No. 2 (July 1966), pp. 117–37.
27. *Parliamentary Debates* (House of Representatives), Vol. 1, cols. 383–4.
28. *Ibid.* cols. 1352–3.
29. *Ceylon Observer,* 3 March 1951.
30. For the details, see A. Jeyaratnam Wilson's article 'The Tamil Federal Party in Ceylon Politics'.
31. For an authentic account, see T. Vittachi, *Emergency '58: The Story of the Ceylon Race Riots* (London: André Deutsch, 1958).

Notes to chapter 3

1. Information based on interviews with FP leaders.
2. Interviews with CWC leaders.
3. *Journal of the Parliaments of the Commonwealth,* Vol. XLVI, 1965, p. 367.
4. *Ibid.*
5. All this information has been abstracted from Central Bank of Ceylon, *Annual Report for the Year 1969.*
6. *Ibid.*
7. See Ceylon, Ministry of Planning and Economic Affairs, External Resources Division, *Foreign Aid* (Ceylon: Government Press, 1969) and *Budget Speech 1970–1971* by the Hon. Dr N.M. Perera, M.P., Minister of Finance (Colombo: Government Press, n.d.), p. 11.
8. *Ibid.*
9. See the *Budget Speech 1970–1971,* pp. 7–10.
10. One measure is the equivalent of two pounds. 1 Cdn. or U.S. dollar exchanges at 5.95 Ceylon rupees. 100 cents make a Ceylon rupee.
11. Central Bank of Ceylon, *Annual Report for the Year 1969.*
12. See the useful pamphlet setting out the *raison d'être* for these institutions and details about them in Government of Ceylon, *Proposals for the Establishment of District Councils under the Direction and Control of the Central Government* (Colombo: Government Press, 3 June 1968).
13. Interview with S.J.V. Chelvanayakam, the FP leader.
14. The issue on which the FP Minister of Local Government, Senator M. Tiruchelvam, chose to resign was the decision of the Prime Minister to scrap the committee that the Minister had appointed to examine the possibilities of declaring the Koneswaram Temple and its precincts (of significance to the Tamil Hindus), in the strategic and

politically sensitive town of Trincomalee in east Ceylon, a sacred area. Actually this was simply the last straw. More importantly, the FP realised that it would be political folly for them to continue any further in a Government which had already let them down on a number of other more important issues, such as the District Councils Bill and their demand for a Tamil-medium university in Trincomalee.

Notes to chapter 4

1. See, for example, Memorandum of Mr (later Sir) James Peiris to the Under-Secretary of State, dated 19 December 1908, in *Papers Relating to the Constitutional History of Ceylon, 1908–1924*, p. 3.
2. For further details, see A. Jeyaratnam Wilson, 'The Crewe–McCallum Reforms, 1912–1921', *The Ceylon Journal of Historical and Social Studies*, Vol. II, No. 1 (January 1959), pp. 73–95.
3. For further information, see A. Jeyaratnam Wilson, 'The Finance Committee under the Manning Constitution of 1924', *University of Ceylon Review*, Vol. XVIII, Nos. 3 and 4 (July and October 1960), pp. 223–55.
4. See Despatch of 1 March 1922 by Governor Sir William Manning to the Secretary of State, in *Command*, 1809, p. 6.
5. See *Command*, 3131 (Donoughmore Commission Report), pp. 90–1.
6. See *Sessional Paper XI* of 1930. Also *Sessional Paper XVII* of 1935.
7. See paragraphs 5–9 of *Sessional Paper XIV* of 1944.
8. See *Command*, 6677 (Soulbury Commission Report), paragraphs 265–78.
9. *Sessional Paper XIV*, paragraph 5.
10. *Ibid.* paragraph 6.
11. *Ibid.*
12. *Ibid.* paragraph 7.
13. *Ibid.*
14. *Command*, 6677, paragraph 274. Owing to differences between the Board of Ministers and His Majesty's Government over the propriety of appointing the Soulbury Commission, the ministers decided to boycott the Commission.
15. *Ibid.* paragraph 278.
16. Jennings, *The Constitution of Ceylon* (Bombay: Oxford University Press, 1953, 3rd ed.), pp. 213–14.
17. *Report of the First Delimitation Commission, Sessional Paper XIII of 1946* (Colombo: Government Press, 1946).
18. For a criticism of the legislation, see the late I.D.S. Weerawardena, 'The Minorities and the Citizenship Act', *The Ceylon Historical Journal*, Vol. 1, No. 3 (January 1952), pp. 242–50, and for the consequences it had on the position of the minorities, see A. Jeyaratnam Wilson, 'Minority Safeguards in the Ceylon Constitution', *The Ceylon Journal of Historical and Social Studies*, Vol. I, No. 1 (January 1958), pp. 73–95.
19. *Report of the Delimitation Commission, Sessional Paper XV* (Colombo: Government Press, 1959), paragraph 23.
20. *Ibid.* paragraph 24.
21. See *Command*, 6677, paragraph 191.
22. *Ibid.* paragraph 194.
23. *Ibid.* paragraph 247.
24. *Ibid.* paragraph 248.
25. See his article, 'The General Elections in Ceylon, 1952', 'Special Supplement' in *The Ceylon Historical Journal*, Vol. 2, Nos. 1 and 2 (July and October 1952), p. 144.

26. 'Additional Notes on the General Election of 1952', *The Ceylon Historical Journal* Vol. 2, Nos. 3 and 4 (January and April 1953), p. 204.
27. *Ceylon Daily News*, 10 March 1956.
28. *Report on the Sixth Parliamentary General Election of Ceylon – Sessional Paper XX – 1966* (Colombo: Government Press, 1966), p. 10.
29. The Ceylon Constitution and Parliamentary Elections (Amendment) Act No. 8 of 1964. The Commissioner is appointed by the Governor-General on the advice of the Prime Minister. He is answerable only to Parliament and cannot be removed from office except through a prayer addressed to the Governor-General by both Houses of Parliament. His position is entrenched to the extent that it cannot be altered except by constitutional amendment.
30. This includes the voters in Welimada electoral district, which returned a member uncontested.
31. Inclusive of the two-member electoral district of Colombo South which returned both its members uncontested.
32. *Report on the Seventh Parliamentary General Election in Ceylon 27 May 1970 – Sessional Paper VII – 1971* (Colombo: Government Press, 1971), p. 11.
33. The Ceylon Parliamentary Elections (Amendment) Act No. 11 of 1959.
34. *Report on the Seventh Parliamentary General Election in Ceylon*, p. 9.

Notes to chapter 5

1. *Daily Mirror*, 28 December 1969.
2. *Ceylon Daily News*, 2 April 1970.
3. *Ibid.*
4. *Ceylon Daily News*, 24 April 1970.
5. J.R. Jayawardene in *Ceylon Daily News*, 9 May 1970.
6. Central schools are the institutes of higher secondary education established by the state after the introduction in 1945 of the scheme which enabled children to have free education from kindergarten through to university. See the report of Nimal Karunatilleke's speech in *Ceylon Daily News*, 12 May 1970. Note, the reference to 'family trees' was an attack on Mrs Bandaranaike's relatives being nominated for some seats.
7. *Sun*, 15 May 1970.

Notes to chapter 6

1. *Sun*, 18 March 1970.
2. See the report of the House of Representatives proceedings, in *Ceylon Daily News*, 13 March 1970.
3. See 'Commentary on the News of the Week' in *Ceylon Daily News*, 14 March 1970.
4. See Mrs Bandaranaike's press release on the Mahaveli loan in *Ceylon Daily News*, 14 March 1970.
5. *Sun*, 18 March 1970.
6. Note, both ministers suffered defeats.
7. See the report of the speech in *Ceylon Daily News*, 16 March 1970.
8. *Ceylon Daily News*, 23 March 1970.
9. *Ibid*. The *dagoba* is a huge dome-shaped Buddhist shrine usually storing a relic of the Buddha or one of his important disciples.
10. *Ceylon Daily News*, 27 March 1970.
11. *Sun*, 18 March 1970.
12. *Ceylon Daily News*, 16 March 1970.

13. *Sun*, 18 March 1970.
14. *Ceylon Daily News*, 18 March 1970.
15. *Ceylon Daily News*, 27 March 1970.
16. *Ceylon Daily News*, 26 March 1970.
17. *Ibid.*
18. *Ceylon Daily News*, 28 March 1970.
19. For the full statement, see *Sun*, 26 March 1970.
20. For further details, see *Ceylon Daily News*, 28 March 1970.
21. Note, foreign exchange entitlement certificates (*feecs*) further devalued the Ceylon rupee for a limited number of transactions.
22. *Ceylon Observer Magazine Edition*, 30 March 1971.
23. See *Sun*, 28 March and 22 May 1970.
24. *Sun*, 3 April 1970.
25. *Sun*, 27 April 1970.
26. *Sun*, 16 April 1970.
27. See *Ceylon Daily News*, 29 April 1970.
28. *Sun*, 9 April 1970.
29. For the details, see *Sun*, 10 April 1970.
30. As stated by Maithripala Senanayake, see *Ceylon Daily News*, 16 April 1970.
31. *Ibid.* Also see *Sun*, 16 April 1970.
32. For the contents of the letter, see *Ceylon Daily News*, 18 April 1970.
33. *Ceylon Daily News*, 20 April 1970.
34. Kandy, the hill capital of Ceylon, houses the Temple of the Sacred Tooth of the Buddha.
35. Prime Minister Senanayake had mentioned this to sources very close to him whom we interviewed, as one of his immediate priorities if returned again.
36. *Sun*, 14 May 1970.
37. See *Ceylon Daily News*, 18 May 1970.
38. *Sun*, 12 May 1970.
39. *Ceylon Daily News*, 12 May 1970.
40. *Ceylon Observer*, 2 May 1970.
41. *Sun*, 24 May 1970.
42. *Ceylon Daily News*, 25 May 1970.
43. *Ceylon Observer Magazine Edition*, 20 May 1970.
44. *Ceylon Observer Magazine Edition*, 13 May 1970.
45. *Ceylon Daily News*, 15 and 16 May 1970.
46. *Ceylon Daily News*, 9 May 1970.
47. *Ceylon Daily News*, 11 May 1970.
48. *Ceylon Daily News*, 22 May 1970.
49. *Ceylon Daily News*, 18 May 1970.
50. For the full contents of the letter, see *Ceylon Daily News*, 18 May 1970. Note, the term United *Left* Front was used for propaganda purposes by the Prime Minister whereas the Front called itself simply the United Front.
51. See *Ceylon Daily News*, 25 May 1970.
52. *Ibid.*
53. See, for example, 'The Eve-of-Election Call to Voters by Religious Heads' in *Daily Mirror*, 26 May 1970. Note, however, that the appeal of the Venerable Maha Nayake Thero of the Malwatte Chapter that was published in this report was his call for the two main 'Sinhalese parties' to get together in the event of an inconclusive result. The Head of the Roman Catholic Church in Ceylon gave no message, but below Cardinal Cooray's photograph was published a rather non-committal statement that had appeared in the editorial columns of the *Catholic Messenger* which was certainly not that

of His Eminence. The message, however, could lend itself to the interpretation of being anti-Marxist.

54. *Sun*, 26 May 1970.
55. See *Ceylon Daily News*, 27 May 1970. Note, the Venerable Maha Nayake Thero in his evidence before the Ceylon Broadcasting Corporation Commission on Sunday 15 November 1970 stated that he was 'forced' to make the statement contradicting his earlier message and that he 'regretted' having to make this contradiction and 'wished it had never happened'. See *The Times of Ceylon*, 16 November 1970.
56. See *Sun* of 15 May 1970 for a fairly detailed report of this meeting which we covered.
57. *Ceylon Daily News*, 2 May 1970.
58. *Ceylon Daily News*, 27 April 1970.
59. See *Ceylon Daily News*, 22 April 1970.
60. *Ceylon Daily News*, 26 April 1970.
61. See *Ceylon Daily News*, 23 April and 22 May 1970, and *Sun*, 19 May.
62. *Sun*, 1 May 1970.
63. *Sun*, 22 May 1970.
64. *Ceylon Daily News*, 25 May 1970.
65. *Sun*, 26 April 1970.
66. *Sun*, 15 May 1970.
67. *Sun*, 22 May 1970.
68. *Ceylon Daily News*, 25 April 1970.
69. *Ceylon Daily News*, 26 April 1970.
70. See *Ceylon Daily News*, 22 May 1970.
71. See *Ceylon Daily News*, 26 May 1970.
72. *Ibid.*
73. Only a summary of the manifesto appeared in the *Ceylon Daily News*, 25 April 1970. The *Sun*, 26 April 1970, however, gave a fuller version.
74. *Ceylon Daily News*, 22 April 1970.
75. For details of the manifesto, see *Ceylon Daily News*, 6 May 1970.
76. *Sun*, 2 May 1970.

Notes to chapter 7

1. *Sun*, 26 March 1970.
2. *Ceylon Daily News*, 2 March 1970.
3. *Ceylon Daily News*, 24 March 1970.
4. *Ceylon Daily News*, 16 March 1970.
5. *Ceylon Daily News*, 23 March 1970.
6. See e.g. *Sun*, 14 and 24 May 1970.
7. *Ceylon Daily News*, 24 May 1970.
8. *Sun*, 11 May 1970.
9. *Ceylon Daily News*, 18 April 1970.
10. *Ceylon Daily News*, 22 May 1970.
11. *Ceylon Daily News*, 27 March 1970.
12. *Ceylon Daily News*, 28 March 1970.
13. *Ceylon Daily News*, 1 and 6 May 1970.
14. *Sun*, 16 May 1970.
15. *Sun*, 18 May 1970.
16. *Sun*, 14 May 1970.
17. *Sun*, 17 May 1970.
18. *Ceylon Daily News*, 16 March 1970.

19. *Ceylon Daily News*, 8 April 1970.
20. *Ceylon Daily News*, 27 March 1970.
21. *Ceylon Observer*, 4 March 1970.
22. *Ceylon Daily News*, 28 May 1970.
23. *Ceylon Observer*, 4, March 1970.
24. *Sun*, 14 May 1970.
25. *Ibid.*
26. *Ceylon Daily News*, 11 May 1970, and *Sun*, 24 May 1970.
27. *Ceylon Daily News*, 11 May 1970.
28. *Sun*, 27 April 1970.
29. *Ceylon Daily News*, 31 March 1970.
30. *Ibid.*
31. *Ceylon Daily News*, 12 May 1970.
32. *Ceylon Observer*, 4 March 1970.
33. *Ceylon Daily News*, 1 May 1970.
34. *Ceylon Daily News*, 8 April 1970.
35. So said T.B. Ilangaratne, as reported in the *Sun*, 23 April 1970.
36. *Sun*, 22 May 1970.
37. *Ceylon Daily News*, 31 March 1970.
38. *Ceylon Daily News*, 2 April 1970.
39. *Ceylon Daily News*, 12 April 1970.
40. *Sun*, 14 May 1970.
41. *Ibid.*
42. *Ceylon Daily News*, 9 April 1970.
43. See *Ceylon Daily News*, 20 April and 12 May 1970.
44. *Ibid.*
45. *Ibid.*
46. *Sun*, 24 May 1970.
47. See e.g. *Sun*, 24 May 1970.
48. See *Ceylon Daily News*, 24 March and 5 April 1970.
49. *Ceylon Daily News*, 25 April 1970.
50. *Ibid.*
51. *Sun*, 25 May 1970.
52. *Sun*, 10 May 1970.
53. The *coup* conspirators were reported to have planned to use 'Shelly Silva' in a big way if their plans succeeded. They admitted however that 'Shelly Silva' was unaware of all that was being planned for him.
54. See *Ceylon Daily News*, 18 March 1970, for a report of the talk.
55. *Ceylon Daily News*, 24 March 1970.
56. These were actually suggested in the national debates that took place on the press.
57. *Ceylon Daily News*, 23 March 1970.
58. Jayaratne's denial that he made such a statement was published later in the *Ceylon Daily News*.
59. See *Ceylon Daily News*, 30 April 1970.
60. For the full analysis, see *Daily Mirror*, 27 April 1970.
61. *Ceylon Daily News*, 1 May 1970. Galle Face green is one of Colombo's biggest fresh air parks.
62. See *Ceylon Daily News* of 10 and 23 May 1970.
63. *Ceylon Daily News*, 4 May 1970.
64. *Ceylon Daily News*, 2 May 1970.
65. See *Ceylon Daily News* of 30 April and 19 May 1970 and *Sun* of 22 May 1970.

66. *Sun*, 19 May 1970.
67. For the full statement see *Sun*, 3 May 1970.
68. *Ceylon Daily News*, 20 April 1970.
69. *Ceylon Daily News*, 26 April 1970.
70. See *Ceylon Daily News*, 26 and 30 April 1970 and *Sun*, 23 April 1970.
71. *Ceylon Daily News*, 22 April 1970.
72. See *Ceylon Daily News*, 20 and 22 April 1970.
73. Such was T.B. Subasinghe's response. See *Ceylon Daily News*, 12 April 1970. Other UF leaders also spoke in the same vein.
74. *Ceylon Daily News*, 3 April 1970.
75. *Ceylon Daily News*, 1 May 1970.
76. Personal information.
77. *Ceylon Daily News*, 19 April 1970.
78. See *Sun*, 7 April 1970. Note Sinna Lebbe was not nominated by the UNP's selection board to contest again the seat which he held.
79. *Ibid.*
80. See *Sun*, 22 May 1970.
81. See *Ceylon Daily News*, 13 April 1970.
82. *Ceylon Daily News*, 19 May 1970.
83. *Ceylon Daily News*, 15 May 1970.
84. Their statements appeared in the *Daily Mirror*, 26 May 1970.
85. *Ceylon Daily News*, 15 May 1970.
86. *Ceylon Daily News*, 22 April 1970.
87. *Ibid.*
88. *Ceylon Daily News*, 4 May 1970.
89. *Ceylon Daily News*, 19 April 1970.

Notes to chapter 8

1. Note, all dates referred to in this chapter are for the year 1970, unless otherwise stated.
2. See *Ceylon Daily News*, 23 and 24 April 1970.
3. *Ceylon Daily News*, 4 April 1970.
4. *Ceylon Daily News*, 8 April 1970.
5. *Ceylon Daily News*, 22 April 1970.
6. The figures are approximations based on reliable information given to us by persons intimately connected with both newspapers.

Notes to chapter 9

1. Made available to the writer.
2. The figure is based on the *Report of the Delimitation Commission, Sessional Paper XV – 1959* (Colombo: Government Press, September 1959) and the Ceylon Census returns (1963).
3. This information was obtained from the *Report of the Official Committee on Mobilisation of Surplus Manpower for Development* (marked 'confidential'), n.d., *circa* December 1967, and R. K. Srivastava, S. Selvaratnam and V. Ambalavanar, *Unemployment in Ceylon – A Possible Line of Action* (Colombo: Department of National Planning, June 1966, unpublished).
4. The figure is obtained on the basis of information contained in the sources mentioned in n. 2.

5. The information is based on the same sources mentioned in n. 2.
6. Our categorisation of constituencies as 'paddy-growing' is based on the decision of the Ministry of Housing and Construction and the Ministry of Agriculture to construct 80 new paddy stores by 31 March 1971 in electorates which are in the major paddy-growing areas of the island.
7. See *Report of the Land Utilization Committee, Sessional Paper XI – 1968* (Colombo: Government Press, June 1968).
8. As reported in the *Ceylon Daily News*, 11 April 1971.
9. From the same source mentioned in n. 7.
10. Based on information referred to in n. 2.
11. On the basis of information supplied to us by party functionaries who were directly involved, and some of the polling agents present at the counts.

Notes to chapter 10

1. See *First Manifesto of the SLFP, 1951* (Kelaniya: Vidyalankara Press, 1951).
2. See the Prime Minister's remarks on the subject in the House of Representatives in *Ceylon Daily News* report of 1 December 1971. Also her statement tabled in the National Assembly on 23 June 1972.
3. As stated by the Prime Minister in the House, see *Ceylon Daily News* report of 1 December 1971.
4. See her statement in the Assembly on 5 September 1972.
5. For the full text of the Prime Minister's speech on this subject at the Conference, see *Ceylon Daily News*, 22 January 1971.
6. For the complete text of the Prime Minister's proposals, see *Ceylon Daily News*, 13 October 1971.
7. See *Five Year Plan, 1972–76* (Colombo: Ministry of Planning and Employment, 1971).
8. See *Human Resource Development and Utilisation: A Note on Technical Assistance, Needs and Possibilities in Ceylon* (Colombo: Ministry of Planning and Economic Affairs, n.d.).
9. See *Ceylon Daily News*, 16 December 1971.
10. For a detailed account of the PLF, its programme and activities see A. Jeyaratnam Wilson, 'Ceylon: The People's Liberation Front and the "Revolution" that Failed', *Pacific Community* (January 1972), pp. 364–77; Politicus, 'The April Revolt in Ceylon', *Asian Survey*, Vol. XII, No. 3 (March 1972), pp. 259–74; S. Arasaratnam, 'The Ceylon Insurrection of April 1971: Some Causes and Consequences', *Pacific Affairs* (Fall 1972), pp. 356–71; and Charles S. Blackton, 'Sri Lanka's Marxists', *Problems of Communism*, Vol. XXII (January–February 1973), pp. 28–43.
11. As stated by the Ceylon Army Commander at a press conference. See report in the *New York Times*, 22 April 1971.
12. *Ceylon Daily News*, 13 September 1971.
13. See text of TUF resolution in *Congress News*, 1 August 1972.
14. See report of the TUF resolution in *Ceylon Daily News*, 19 May 1973.
15. For the full text, see *The Ceylon Observer Magazine Edition*, 20 May 1973.
16. See *The Constitution of Sri Lanka* (Colombo: Government Press, 1972).
17. See the text of the twenty draft resolutions framed by the Trotskyist Minister of Constitutional Affairs in the *Sun*, 4 September 1970.
18. For the full text of the statement, see *Ceylon Daily News*, 22 May 1972.
19. Sections 54–65 detail the constitution and powers of the Court and the procedures it may adopt.
20. As stated in the Common Programme.

21. For the complete text of the Prime Minister's proposals, see *Ceylon Daily News*, 13 October 1971.
22. See N. M. Perera, '35 Years After', *Ceylon Daily News*, 22 December 1970.
23. See interview given by Dr Colvin R. de Silva to the *Ceylon Observer Magazine Edition* entitled '35 Years of the LSSP: Overthrowing Capitalism our New Challenge', in its issue of 20 December 1970.
24. See V. Karalasingham, 'An LSSP Viewpoint: What should be Today's Slogans?', *Ceylon Daily News*, 2 September 1970.
25. See statement issued by the Central Committee of the Ceylon CP in *Ceylon Daily News*, 18 September 1970.
26. See the report of a speech by the Minister of Finance in the Ruwanwella constituency in *Ceylon Daily Mirror*, 12 August 1970.
27. For the full text of the resolution of the Central Committee of the LSSP, see *Ceylon Daily News*, 2 September 1971.
28. See the report of Dr N. M. Perera's press conference on the occasion of the 35th anniversary of the LSSP in *Ceylon Daily News*, 7 December 1970.
29. See Leslie Goonewardene, 'New Outlook of the LSSP', *Ceylon Daily News*, 21 December 1970.
30. For the full text of the LSSP statement, see *Ceylon Daily News*, 8 March 1971.
31. See text of statement issued by Philip Gunawardene in *Ceylon Daily News*, 3 October 1970, and sections of his pamphlet entitled *The Present Political Situation* reproduced in *The Times Weekender*, 11 January 1971.
32. See report of Philip Gunawardene's press conference in *The Times of Ceylon*, 3 October 1970.
33. See sections of his pamphlet *The Present Political Situation* reproduced in *Ceylon Daily News*, 9 January 1971.
34. *Ceylon Observer*, 12 August 1970.
35. *Ceylon Daily News*, 8 August 1970.
36. *Ceylon Daily News*, 18 February 1971.
37. See, for instance, the report of J. R. Jayawardene's speech in the House of Representatives in *Ceylon Daily News*, 4 December 1971.
38. For the full text of the resolution see *Ceylon Daily News*, 20 December 1971.
39. See the report of a press conference given by Dudley Senanayake in *Ceylon Daily News*, 2 March 1971.
40. See the report of press interview by J. R. Jayawardene to the *Ceylon Observer Magazine Edition* in its issue of 23 January 1972.
41. See R. Kothari, *Politics in India* (New Delhi: Orient Longmans, 1970), pp. 152–223.

Bibliographical note

Literature on elections and electioneering in Ceylon is difficult to obtain because of the paucity of persons who have worked on the subject and the general lack of interest both in Ceylon and outside in the study of electoral behaviour in Ceylon. However, there is a fairly wide range of resource material available from which useful data could be processed. These may be classified under the headings given below.

Legislation

The publication, *A Reprint of the Ceylon (Parliamentary Elections) Order in Council, 1946* (Colombo: Government Publications Bureau, April 1970) with all the amendments enacted up to 1970, is the most valuable source of information on the law concerning parliamentary elections. It is useful especially for matters relating to the conduct of elections and the exercise of the franchise.

The law relating to Ceylon citizenship is relevant because only a citizen is eligible to vote. The Ceylon Citizenship Act of 1948 and the Indian and Pakistani (Citizenship) Act of 1949 enunciate the terms on which a person can become a Ceylon citizen. Large numbers of Indians who had earlier exercised the franchise were deprived of it under these acts.

The Indo-Ceylon Agreement (Implementation) Act of 1968 provides information on the terms and conditions under which Indians resident in Ceylon could become citizens of the country. This legislation was enacted under the terms of the Sirima–Shastri Pact of October 1964.

The Ceylon (Constitution) Order in Council 1946 gives the details of the law relating to delimitation commissions and the basis of representation in the House of Representatives.

Pacts and agreements

The Nehru–Kotelawala Pact of 1953 and the Sirima–Shastri Pact of 1964 are useful for studying the question of the franchise of Indians in Ceylon.

Government documents

The *Report of the Special Commission on the Constitution (Donoughmore Report) 1928* (Command 3131) and the *Report of the Commission on Constitutional Reform (Soulbury Report) 1945* (Command 6677) are excellent for background information on the franchise and its consequences, and for views on the problem of voting rights for Indians in Ceylon.

The Reports of the Delimitation Commissions of 1946 and 1959 should have priority in any study of the Ceylonese electoral system. So should the Reports on each of the Parliamentary General Elections of 1947, 1952, 1956, March 1960, July 1960, 1965 and 1970 issued by the Commissioner of Parliamentary Elections. The Reports of the Commissioner from March 1960 onwards are of special value for their information on the general elections and for the Commissioner's excellent comments on the law relating to the conduct of elections and to election practices. These Reports contain a wealth of statistical information. But a word of caution needs to be introduced here. The statistical data are not altogether reliable and need to be checked and re-checked.

Handbooks

The *Ceylon Daily News Parliaments of Ceylon* for 1947, 1956 (none was produced for the 1952 general election), 1960, 1965 and 1970 have the best data on the winning candidates, the manifestos of the main parties and a summary of the progress of the election campaign. The statistics on voting etc. are not entirely accurate and should not be depended upon unless checked against other sources.

Theses

The late I. D. S. Weerawardena's Ph.D. dissertation on the Donoughmore Constitution (University of London, 1951), later published as *Government and Politics in Ceylon 1931–1946* (Colombo: Ceylon Economic Research Association, 1951), has sections on the franchise as it worked during the years 1931 to 1946. The material in V. Kumari Jayawardene's 'The Urban Labour Movement with Reference to Political Factors, 1893–1947' (Ph.D. 1964, University of London) and K. H. Jayasinghe's 'Some Political and Social Consequences of the Extension of the Franchise in Ceylon' (Ph.D. 1965, University of London) is informative.

Books

Some of the chapters (e.g. 'The Franchise and the Constituencies', 'The House of Representatives', etc.) and comments on clauses in the Constitution in Sir Ivor Jennings' *The Constitution of Ceylon* (Bombay: Oxford University Press, 1953, 3rd ed.) provide a legal and sometimes political interpretation on matters relating to the franchise, the delimitation commission, the House of Representatives, etc. W. Howard Wriggins' *Ceylon: The Dilemmas of a New Nation* (Princeton: Princeton University Press, 1960), Marshall R. Singer's *The Emerging Elite: A Study of Political Leadership in Ceylon* (Cambridge, Mass.: Massachusetts Institute of Technology Press, 1964), Robert N. Kearney's *Communalism and Language in the Politics of Ceylon* (Durham, North Carolina: Duke University Press, 1967), George Lerski's *Origins of Trotskyism in Ceylon* (Stanford, Hoover Institution of War, Revolution and Peace: Stanford University Press, 1968) and C. A. Woodward's *The Growth of a Party System in Ceylon* (Providence: Brown University Press, 1969) are some of the best works, by non-Ceylonese, on the social and political processes in Ceylon.

Among Ceylonese authors, the late I. D. S. Weerawardena's *Government and Politics in Ceylon, 1931–1946*, S. Namasivayam's *The Legislatures of Ceylon, 1928–1948* (London: Faber and Faber, 1951) provide insights into the working of representative institutions during the colonial period, in the twentieth century up to 1946.

By far the best study available on a general election in Ceylon is the late I. D. S. Weerawardena's *Ceylon General Election 1956* (Colombo: M. D. Gunasena, 1960). It was designed on the basis of the Nuffield College projects.

On other related matters in this field, S. U. Kodikara's *Indo-Ceylon Relations since Independence* (Colombo: The Ceylon Institute of World Affairs, 1965) is the most complete account available on the Indian question in Ceylon with its related problem of the franchise.

The chapters by Donald E. Smith and A. Jeyaratnam Wilson in Donald E. Smith (ed.), *South Asian Politics and Religion* (Princeton: Princeton University Press, 1966) deal with political developments in Ceylon in the period after 1956.

Denzil Peiris' *1956 and After* (Colombo: Associated Newspapers of Ceylon Limited, March 1958) has useful comments to make on the 1956 general election and after, while Philip Fernando's *Mandate '70* (Colombo, 1970) is a first-hand account of the 1970 general election and a careful analysis of the techniques of electioneering in Ceylon.

Reference should also be made to H. A. I. Goonetileke's standard two-volume work (continuing), *A Bibliography of Ceylon: A systematic guide to the literature on the land, people, history and culture published in Western languages from the sixteenth century to the present day* (Zug: Inter Documentation Company, 1970) and his *The April 1971 Insurrection in Ceylon: A Select Bibliography (July 1973)* (Louvain: Centre de Recherches Socio-Religieuses, University of Louvain, 1973) for useful additional information on the literature of Ceylonese politics.

Articles

Sir Ivor Jennings started off the analysis of general elections in Ceylon with his 'The Ceylon General Election of 1947', *University of Ceylon Review* (July 1948). This was informative and contained shrewd analyses of political trends. The late I. D. S. Weerawardena's 'The General Election in Ceylon, 1952', *The Ceylon Historical Journal* (July and October 1952) was a bigger study containing a more detailed analysis of the election campaign of that year.

Index